INTO ALL THE WORLD
An Orthodox Theology of Mission

St Vladimir's Seminary Press

ORTHODOXY AND MISSIONS SERIES

Number 1

Missiology is one of the newest disciplines now accepted in the academy. This series presents historical and contemporary perspectives on the theology of mission, evangelism, church growth, new church planting, parish revitalization, catechetical material for adult converts, and comparative religion. Challenges and opportunities—both domestic and foreign—in the field of missiology will form the core of this series.

Chad Hatfield
Series Editor

Into All the World

An Orthodox Theology of Mission

EDWARD ROMMEN

ST VLADIMIR'S SEMINARY PRESS
YONKERS, NY 10707
2017

Library of Congress Cataloging-in-Publication Data

Names: Rommen, Edward, 1947– author.
Title: Into all the world : an Orthdox theology of mission / Edward Rommen.
Description: Yonkers, NY : St Vladimir's Seminary Press, 2017. | Series: Orthodoxy
  and Missions series ; number 1 | Includes bibliographical references.
Identifiers: LCCN 2017008571 (print) | LCCN 2017012795 (ebook) | ISBN
  9780881415841 (paper) | ISBN 9780881415858 (electronic)
Subjects: LCSH: Orthodox Eastern Church—Missions. | Missions—Theory.
Classification: LCC BV2123 (ebook) | LCC BV2123 .R66 2017 (print) | DDC
  266/.19—dc23
LC record available at https://lccn.loc.gov/2017008571

ISBN 978–0–88141–584–1 (paper)
ISBN 978–0–88141–585–8 (electronic)

PRINTED IN THE UNITED STATES OF AMERICA

Table of Contents

Abbreviations

ACCS NT   *Ancient Christian Commentary on Scripture: New Testament.* Edited by Thomas C. Oden. 12 vols. (vol. 1 in 2 parts). Downers Grove, IL: IVP Academic, 2000–2007.[1]

ACCS OT   *Ancient Christian Commentary on Scripture: Old Testament.* Edited by Thomas C. Oden. 15 vols. Downers Grove, IL: IVP Academic, 2001–2010.[2]

ACW   Ancient Christian Writers Series. New York, NY / Mahwah, NJ: Paulist Press, 1946–.[3]

ANF   *The Ante-Nicene Fathers.* Edited by Alexander Roberts and James Donaldson. 10 vols. Buffalo, 1885–1896. Reprint, Peabody, MA: Hendrickson, 1994.

FC   The Fathers of the Church: A New Translation (Patristic series). Washington, DC: Catholic University of America Press. 1947–.

IRM   *International Review of Mission*

NPNF[1]   *The Nicene and Post-Nicene Fathers, Series 1.* Edited by Philip Schaff. New York, 1886–1889. 14 vols. Reprint, Peabody, MA: Hendrickson, 1994.

---

[1]Page references for *Ancient Christian Commentary on Scripture* are to the first edition/printing, unless otherwise noted.

[2]The *Ancient Christian Commentary on Scripture* was also concurrently published in part by Fitzroy Dearborn (Chicago, IL), which was acquired in 2002 by Routledge.

[3]The Ancient Christian Writers series was also published by The Newman Press, which was acquired in 1962 by Paulist Press.

NPNF²   *Nicene and Post-Nicene Fathers, Series 2.* Edited by Philip Schaff and Henry Wace. New York, 1890. 14 vols. Reprint, Peabody, MA: Hendrickson, 1994.

Philokalia   *The Philokalia: The Complete Text.* Translated and edited by G.E.H. Palmer, Philip Sherrard, and Kallistos Ware. 4 vols. London: Faber and Faber, 1979–1995.

PG   Patrologia Graeca [= Patrologiae cursus completus: Series graeca]. Edited by J.-P. Migne. 162 vols. Paris, 1857–1866.

Introduction

For the last ten years I have been actively engaged in reevaluating much of the missiological content I presented and published during my teaching tenures at various theological schools in Norway, Germany, and the United States. This review has been occasioned by the rapid changes in the world around us, by my move to the Eastern Orthodox Church, and by the opportunities I now have to teach these subjects at Duke Divinity School. Although much has changed, I am still deeply committed to bringing others to a saving knowledge of Christ. So I began by rethinking my approach to evangelism. The result of that study is the book *Get Real: On Evangelism in the Late Modern World* (William Carey Library, 2010). I then turned my attention to the work that David Hesselgrave and I had done on contextualization, which led to another book, *Come and See: An Orthodox Perspective on Contextualization* (William Carey Library, 2013). Next, I turned to the subject of the Church Growth Movement and wrote *Being the Church: An Orthodox Understanding of Ecclesial Growth* (Wipf and Stock, 2017).

I would now like to re-engage a fourth and perhaps most important area of missions: namely, its theology. This has been my primary area of study and publication, and I would like to make use of both the ancient and the contemporary insights of the Eastern Church in order to re-articulate a theological rationale and framework for the mission of the Church in the world today. I believe that this project is timely and will be useful for three reasons: 1) because of the unique nature of the theological insights offered by Orthodox theology; 2) because of the Eastern Church's rich experience with missionary work in the past; and 3) because an awareness of the Church's missionary responsibility has now been reawakened in the East.

1. On the Nature of Orthodox Theology

The Orthodox understanding of theology is focused on the acquisition or experience of the knowledge of God—that is, knowledge of the person, works, and relationships of the one, triune God. As such, theology involves an organized exposition of Christian doctrine that uses human reason, which after all is a God-given gift not to be neglected. However, in Orthodoxy we expect much more than that from our theology. We seek a vision of and a union with the triune God, involving not just the human rational faculty but rather the whole person, the intuitive spiritual understanding, and the heart. *Theologia* is nothing else than *theoria*, or contemplation, with a view toward that divine vision. It presupposes faith and a living communion with God, and it is integrally bound up with prayer. Evagrius of Pontus (d. 399) observed that: "If you are a theologian, you will pray truly; and if you pray truly, you are a theologian."[1] According to St Diadochus of Photiki (fifth century), theology is a "gift, which inflames our hearts and moves it to the love of his goodness more than any other [gift] . . . uniting it with God the Logos in unbreakable communion."[2] For St Peter of Damascus (eleventh–twelfth century), theology represents the final stage of spiritual contemplation, in which "God permits [the soul] to be seized in rapture, conferring on it the gift of true theology and the blessings of the age to be."[3]

[1] Evagrios the Solitary, "On Prayer: One Hundred and Fifty-Three Texts," in *Philokalia* I:62.

[2] "All God's gifts of grace are flawless and the source of everything good; but the gift which inflames our heart and moves it to the love of his goodness more than any other is theology. It is the early offspring of God's grace and bestows on the soul the greatest of gifts. First of all, it leads us gladly to disregard all love of this life, since in the place of perishable desires we possess inexpressible riches, the oracles of God. Then it embraces our intellect with the light of a transforming fire, and so makes it a partner of the angels in their liturgy. Therefore, when we have made ready, we begin to long sincerely for this gift of contemplative vision, for it is full of beauty, frees us from every worldly care, and nourishes the intellect with divine truth in the radiance of inexpressible light. In brief, it is the gift which, through the help of the holy prophets, unites the deiform soul with God in unbreakable communion." Diadochus of Photiki, *On Spiritual Knowledge and Discrimination* 67, in *Philokalia* I:275.

[3] "Once the intellect has freed itself from all things and, not content with hearing about

Thus in the Orthodox tradition there is no true theology that is not an act of worship: all authentic theology is liturgical, doxological, and mystical. It is a gift of God, a fruit of the internal purity of the theologian's spiritual life, and it leads to the immediate experience of the living, personal God. It is a deeply personal experience that transforms the theologian and results in the transfiguration of creation by the uncreated, divine grace of God.

> Dogmas, their interpretation and development are not the theoretical commentary on events in the history of salvation, for the purpose of constituting a more complete "metaphysics" than the metaphysics of the philosophers. Dogmatic frontiers express the experience of the Church. They separate the lived truth of the Church from the adulteration of heresy. That is why there is basically no difference between "ethos" and dogma. Dogma formulates the "ethos" of the Church. Theology [is ecclesial service] that expresses the experience of salvation.[4]

It is within this broad context of Orthodox theology that I will seek to develop a theology of mission. In doing so I will take advantage of a number of its unique characteristics. These include the following:

a) A Trinitarian Base

One of the most obvious features of Orthodoxy is its deliberately Trinitarian base. Almost everything in the Church is done with reference to the triune God. Every prayer ends with a Trinitarian doxology; every service begins with the "trisagion" prayers. This characteristic also applies to the Church's theology, of course. The Trinity is used as a conceptual framework for the development of every aspect of doctrine, including anthropology, soteriology, ecclesiology, and missiology.[5] For this reason

God at second hand, devotes itself to him in action and thought—God permits it to be seized in rapture, conferring on it the gift of true theology and the blessings of the age to be." St Peter of Damaskos, *Twenty-Four Discourses*, in *Philokalia* 3:277.

[4]Christos Yannaras, "Theology in Present-Day Greece," *St Vladimir's Seminary Theological Quarterly* 16.4 (1972): 195–214, 195.

[5]This is, in fact, the approach taken by Fr George Dragas. In one article he begins by recapitulating the Orthodox teaching that the Church is both catholic and local, both

our theology of mission must begin with the Father who sent the Son in the power of the Spirit, who is then given by the Father to mediate the continued presence of the Son in the world.

b) An Organic Unity

Another prominent characteristic of Orthodox theology is its organic unity. It is no accident that Orthodox theologians tend to shy away from the term "systematic" theology. This reluctance expresses, at least in part, an approach to theology that does not operate with a plurality of radically independent categories of theological content. Rather, it views theology as a single whole developed as a progression of interrelated doctrinal segments. For example, once the doctrine of the triune God has been articulated, Christology can be developed, which allows for soteriology and this, in turn, facilitates ecclesiology. Once one doctrine is established, it becomes the foundation for another. As a result, the Church avoids creating a collection of fragments—and indeed a theology of mission might fragment if it were not integrated into an organic whole. We need to keep the completeness of doctrine before us, allowing each part to inform the whole. For this reason it is impossible to write a theology of Orthodox mission apart from the dogmatic context established by our anthropology, soteriology, ecclesiology, and eschatology.

c) A Divine Gift

Theology is considered to be an undeserved gift of God's grace. St Thalassius speaks of it as "the desire of all desires, the grace of theology."[6] It is not simply our rational enquiries into the being and nature of God, but rather God's disclosure of himself (Jn 1.18). Theology is not so much a matter of examining or knowing God, as being searched out and known by God (Gal

invisible and visible, one and many, and he then states that "the Grace of the Trinity is the starting point for understanding the nature of the Church, and especially her unity in multiplicity, as the Holy Spirit shares one life and one being." Cf. George D. Dragas, "Orthodox Ecclesiology in Outline," *Greek Orthodox Theological Review* 26, no. 3 (1981): 185–92.

[6]St Thalassios the Libyan, *On Love, Self Control, and Life in Accordance with the Intellect*, in *Philokalia* 2:329.

4.9). It rests upon divine rather than human initiative. As Origen puts it, theology is "the knowledge of divine things"; he also affirms it as an "exhalation" (*atmis*), an "outflowing" (*aporroia*), and an "effulgence" (*apaugasma*) from God himself.[7] For that very reason theology presupposes personal faith. Human reason is essential, but reason can be effectively exercised only within the context of faith. *Credo ut intelligam*, states Anselm of Canterbury ("I believe in order to understand"). He speaks of *fides quaerens intelligentium* ("faith seeking out understanding"), not vice versa![8]

d) A Mystery

The fathers also speak of theology as a mystery: something revealed to our understanding and yet never completely revealed, because it "transcends the intellect."[9] As Met. Kallistos (Ware) puts it, theology seeks "to express in human language that which lies beyond all human comprehension."[10] He cites St Basil's words that "no theological term is adequate to the thought of the speaker. . . . our thought is weak, and our tongue weaker than our thought."[11] Further, Met. Kallistos adds, "According to the Cappadocians, once theology forgets the inevitable limits of the human understanding, replacing the ineffable Word of God with human logic, it ceases to be *theologia* and sinks to the level of *technologia*."[12] Because the knowledge

---

[7]Origin, *Fragments on Proverbs*, PG 13:17B-20A.

[8]"For I do not seek to understand that I may believe, but I believe in order to understand. For this also I believe—that unless I believed, I should not understand." St. Anselm of Canterbury, "Proslogium," I. ‹http://www.ccel.org/ccel/anselm/basic_works.i.html›, May 23, 2015. Some have wondered why we Orthodox would quote Anselm. Perhaps that is because his theology, in particular his soteriology, is in fact so very different than ours. But, then again, on this particular issue, he got it right. So why not give credit where credit is due?

[9]St Thalassios the Libyan, *On Love, Self Control, and Life in Accordance with the Intellect, Philokalia* 2:330.

[10]Metropolitan Kallistos Ware, "Theological Education in Scripture and the Fathers," in *Vth International Consultation of Orthodox Theological Schools* (Halki Theological School, Turkey, 1994).

[11]Basil the Great, *Letter 8, NPNF*[2] Vol. 8. ‹http://www.ccel.org/ccel/schaff/npnf208. ix.viii.html›, May 13, 2015.

[12]Ware, "Theological Education in Scripture and the Fathers."

of God remains a paradoxical mystery, our theological discourse must be both negative and positive, apophatic and cataphatic. A theology that lacks the apophatic is mere "technology." We must avoid the temptation of writing a theology of mission that is nothing more than a business plan, or a strategy for achieving a specific set of human goals.

On the path of affirmation (*kataphasis*), one approaches God by assuming that he can, at least in some way, be known, and that that knowledge can be expressed by means of positive (logical) affirmations in human language. Our underlying assumption, of course, is that because God is incomprehensible, we will know him only to the extent that he chooses to reveal himself. This revelation has taken place in what might be called an economy of theophanies.[13] By the mercy of divine condescension, we are granted a series of "appearances" within the created order. God reveals something of himself in nature (cf. Ps 19, Wis 13, Rom 1.20), in human beings as the image of God, in the miraculous, in the word of the prophets, in the incarnate Logos through the Holy Spirit, in the Church, and in the Holy Scriptures. As St Gregory Nazianzen puts it, "Reason that proceeds from God, that is implanted in all from the beginning and is the first law in us, and is bound up in all, leads us up to God through visible things."[14] On the basis of these revelations we are able, by the exercise of our rational capabilities, to formulate certain affirmations that express some knowledge of God. Orthodox believers make limited use of this cataphatic way of doing theology, drawing on sources such as the Scriptures, the liturgy, the writings of the Fathers, the lives of the saints, and the iconography of the Church.

On the path of negation (*apophasis*) we approach God by eliminating every concept, definition, and description that may limit the divinity of God. According to Lossky, "The negative way of the knowledge of God is an ascendant undertaking of the mind that progressively eliminates all positive attributes of the object it wishes to attain, in order to culminate,

---

[13]"Now, we cannot know God outside of the economy in which God reveals himself." Vladimir Lossky, *In the Image and Likeness of God* (London: Mowbrays, 1975), 15.

[14]Gregory Nazianzen, *The Second Oration* XVI, *Fathers of the Church*, ‹http://www.newadvent.org/fathers/310228.htm›, May 22, 2015.

finally, in a kind of apprehension by supreme ignorance of him who cannot be an object of knowledge."[15]

The classic statement of this path of negation is found in Pseudo-Dionysius' *Mystical Theology*. Its author suggests that if one wishes to understand "the mysterious things," one must leave behind "everything perceived and understood, everything perceptible and understandable, all that is not and all that is, and, with your understanding laid aside, to strive upward as much as you can toward union with him who is beyond all being and knowledge."[16] As St John of Damascus asserts, "It is plain, then, that there is a God. But what he is in his essence and nature is absolutely incomprehensible and unknowable. . . . All that is comprehensible about him is his incomprehensibility."[17] In light of this, the only appropriate approach to knowing God involves "the breakdown of human thought before the radical transcendence of God . . . a prostration before the living God, radically ungraspable, unobjectifiable, and unknowable."[18] If, in the divine economy of revelation, the path is based on a descending series of theophanies, then the apophatic represents an ascent of the soul raising itself above all knowledge derived from the created order to a knowledge of God's limitless, mystical presence. Moses' ascent into the divine darkness of Mt Sinai has come to typify all who embark on this apophatic path: "I was running to lay hold on God, and thus went up into the Mount, and drew aside the curtain of the cloud, and entered away from matter and material things, and as far as I could I withdrew within myself. And then when I looked up, I scarce saw the back parts of God. . . ."[19]

[15]Lossky, *In the Image and Likeness of God*, 13.

[16]Dionysius, "The Mystical Theology," ‹http://www.ccel.org/ccel/rolt/dionysius.v.html›, May 25, 2015.

[17]John of Damascus, *Exposition of the Orthodox Faith* 1, 4, *NPNF*² Vol. 9. ‹http://www.ccel.org/ccel/schaff/npnf209.iii.iv.i.iv.html›, May 23, 2015.

[18]Vladimir Lossky, *Orthodox Theology: An Introduction* (Crestwood, NY: St. Vladimir's Seminary Press, 1978), 24.

[19]Gregory Nazianzen, *The Second Oration*, 3.

e) Purification

Since theology is the vision of God, and since only the pure in heart see God (Mt 5.8), authentic theology is impossible without *katharsis*, or purification. Although theology remains a gift of God's grace, this free gift requires on the human side our active cooperation, our voluntary *synergeia*. All theology is, in this sense, *theanthropic*.[20] Thus, there can be no true theology without a personal and active commitment to holiness, which involves repentance (a constant turning to God), ascetic labor (overcoming the passions), and above all prayer. For this reason we should not speak of theology as a science, although theology, like all science, aims at accuracy and intellectual rigor. These qualities are never enough by themselves. Of more fundamental importance is the requirement of personal communion with God. Theology without personal communion with God is mere pseudo-theology. According to St Diadochus, "Nothing is so destitute as a mind philosophizing about God when it is without Him."[21]

f) Stillness

As observed by Met. Kallistos, "There can be no theology without *hesychia*", that is, "without inner stillness . . . of the heart. 'Be still . . . and know that I am God' [Ps 46.10]: theology, . . . the knowledge of God . . . is not merely talking about God but also listening to him."[22] St Gregory the Theologian, having stated that theologizing is neither for everyone nor for every time, then asks, "And what is the permitted occasion? It is when we attain a state of stillness from all exterior defilement and disturbance. . . . It is necessary to be truly in a state of stillness and so to know God."[23] As Met. Kallistos summarizes, "In other words, all authentic theology is mystical theology."[24] He goes on to cite Lossky:

[20]Kallistos (Ware), "Theological Education in Scripture and the Fathers."

[21]St Diadochos of Photiki, *On Spiritual Knowledge and Discrimination: One Hundred Texts, Philokalia* 1:254.

[22]Kallistos (Ware), "Theological Education in Scripture and the Fathers."

[23]Gregory Nazianzen, *First Theological Oration* 3, NPNF[2] Vol. 7. ‹http://www.ccel.org/ccel/schaff/npnf207.iii.xiii.html›, May 23, 2015.

[24]Kallistos (Ware), "Theological Education in Scripture and the Fathers."

It is not by chance that the tradition of the Eastern Church has reserved the name of "theologian" peculiarly for three sacred writers of whom the first is Saint John, most "mystical" of the four evangelists; the second Saint Gregory Nazianzen, writer of contemplative poetry; and the third Saint Symeon, called "the New Theologian," the singer of union with God. Mysticism is . . . the perfecting and crown of all theology . . . theology par excellence.[25]

g) A Corporate Scope

Finally, theology is never done simply for the benefit of certain individuals. It answers the Church's need to explain to all the faithful the various aspects of Christian belief. As the Church moves through history, the eternal truths of its teaching need constant reflection and re-articulation: reflection, because we will never exhaust the infinite content, and re-articulation in order to make these truths understandable in a constantly changing world. This approach, of course, is not driven by a desire for novelty but rather by an uninterrupted continuity, a faithful preservation and proclamation of which has been revealed. So it is in, for, and by the Church that theology, especially a theology of mission, ought to be done, if we are to provide the organic explications necessary for the spiritual growth of the faithful and the renewal and growth of the Church.

---

2. The Rich Missions Experience of the Orthodox Church

Even though its formal witness has for centuries been hampered by Muslim and communist domination,[26] the Orthodox Church has a vast

[25]Vladimir Lossky, *The Mystical Theology of the Eastern Church* (Crestwood, NY: St. Vladimir's Seminary Press, 1976), 9.

[26]A few, who themselves have not suffered for their faith, have suggested that this is just an excuse for inaction. However, I submit that the deliberate mass extermination of believers, priests, and bishops; the closing of theological schools; the confiscation of church properties (documented, for example, in the following source: Raphael Moore, "In Memory of the 50 Million Victims of the Orthodox Christian Holocaust," ed. Nektarios Serfes, last modified October 1999, *http://www.serfes.org/orthodox/memoryof.htm*); and official government policies that completely forbade missions and charitable activities of the Church

treasury of missionary experience gathered throughout sustained periods of remarkable evangelistic expansion. The following brief history documents the efforts of Orthodox missionaries who wrestled with the practical challenges of cross-cultural ministry, and in doing so developed sound missiological principles and practices long before they became the subject of academic study. Modern missiologists have taken an interest in topics such as contextualization, group conversion, education, the official authorization and instruction of missionaries, and human rights. As we shall see, most of these ideas were articulated long ago, and not in the academy but in the field.

a) Contextualization

During the late Byzantine era we find the stellar examples of Sts Cyril (827–869) and Methodius (815–884), who developed one of the earliest examples of the principle of contextualization for advancing the Church within other host cultures. These missionaries were appointed by Emperor Michael III in 863 to teach the faith to the Moravians in the local language. In order to do so, they developed a new alphabet, Glagolitic, and translated the Bible and liturgical books into Slavonic. As a result, they gained an understanding of the local cultures and effectively organized numerous church communities and schools throughout Moravia, Bohemia, and Hungary. These early pioneers established the missionary principle followed by the Church as it expanded across central Russia, Asia, Alaska, and America. Each new language that was encountered was immediately used to meet the liturgical needs of the expanding Church. This indicates an early and sustained use of concepts that have become part and parcel of modern missiological thinking, such as dynamic equivalence, the necessity of vernacular translations (Wycliffe), and the whole field of contextualization.

(such as a resolution of the USSR Central Committee 1929, article 13 of the Bolshevik Party Program, article 124 of the 1936 Russian Constitution, etc.) actually did make it nearly impossible for the Church to engage in missionary outreach. That is not to say that the valiant suffering of these believers did not inspire others and sow seeds that later bore fruit. But to suggest that they somehow shirked their responsibility is to dishonor their sacrifice.

b) Group Conversion and Missionary Education

The Byzantine era also witnessed the expansion of the Church into Ukraine and Russia, primarily through the efforts of St Vladimir. He developed another missiological principle, the concept of group conversion. Donald McGavran and the modern Church Growth Movement made much of this practice in the twentieth century. Here again, we have astounding examples of this principle from a much earlier age.

Prince Vladimir the Great (958–1015) was converted to Christianity in 987. Later, he organized what some have described as the unforgettable and singular event of the baptism of all the Kievans. On the evening before, St Vladimir declared throughout the city: "If anyone does not go into the river [Dneipr] tomorrow, be they rich or poor, beggar or slave, that one shall be my enemy."[27] In other words, Kiev experienced what today is called group or mass conversion.[28]

In order to advance the faith among these newly enlightened people and ensure that they had personally accepted Christ and his teachings, St Vladimir also "commanded fathers and mothers to take their young children and send them to schools to learn reading and writing," thus bringing them to a knowledge of the faith by "a multitude of schools of scholars and philosophers."[29] This represents a remarkably early example of concern for the importance of individual expression and grounding in the faith—something that missiologists have more recently labeled "multi-individual conversion."[30]

---

[27]"Equal of the Apostles Great Prince Vladimir, in Holy Baptism Basil, the Enlightener of the Russian Land," ‹http://oca.org/saints/lives/2013/07/15/102031-equal-of-the-apostles-great-prince-vladimir-in-holy-baptism-basi›, May 23, 2015.

[28]Jarrell Waskom Pickett and Donald A McGavran, *Church Growth and Group Conversion* (Pasadena: William Carey Library, 1973).

[29]"Equal of the Apostles Great Prince Vladimir, in Holy Baptism Basil, the Enlightener of the Russian Land."

[30]Donald A. McGavran and C. Peter Wagner, *Understanding Church Growth*, 3rd ed. (Grand Rapids, MI: W. B. Eerdmans, 1990), 227.

c) Come and See

Another period of missionary activity occurred in medieval Russia. One of the principles of Orthodox missions developed at that time might be called the "come and see" principle. This approach involved inviting people to visit churches and monasteries in order to experience for themselves the presence of Christ and the power of the gospel. In fact, it is probably the best explanation for the amazing expansion of Christianity across vast regions of central Russia and Siberia. While missionaries of this era such as St Stephan of Perm (1340–1396) continued to create alphabets and set up church communities and schools, the "come and see" approach was mainly practiced by an ever-expanding network of monasteries. These spiritual centers had a profound influence on popular piety, becoming destinations for pilgrims seeking relics, wonder-working icons, and the monks' spiritual wisdom. As more and more pilgrims settled in the villages that developed around the monasteries, the monks continually felt the need to move deeper into the forests in order to maintain solitude. At the same time, the Mongol conquests of the thirteenth to fifteenth centuries drove some monastic groups into the largely uninhabited areas of northern and central Russia. St Sergius of Radonezh (1314–1392) led a renewal movement with disciples in approximately 150 monasteries that leap-frogged their way across the great expanse of Siberia. Speaking of the fourteenth-century revival of hesychast spirituality in Russian monasteries, one author likens their spiritual power to "a magnetic field . . . [of] spiritual energy [which] attracted loose elements and filled the surrounding area with invisible powers," triggering "one of the most remarkable missionary movements in Christian history."[31]

d) Official Authorization and Instruction

In the Eastern Church, proper hierarchical authorization for missionary work has always been expected. However, at certain times even secular authorities were involved in initiating and developing missionary

[31]James H. Billington, *The Icon and the Axe: An Interpretive History of Russian Culture* (New York: Vintage Books, 1966), 52–53.

outreach. One example is the work of the eighteenth-century Russian Church. A remarkable missionary decree issued by Peter the Great in consultation with the Holy Synod begins as follows:

> In order to strengthen and expand the Orthodox Christian faith and in order to proclaim the holy Gospel among the idolatrous peoples; further in order to lead those indebted tribes in the region of Toblolsk and the other cities of Siberia to Christian faith and to holy baptism, his highness after consultation with the all-holy patriarch, the Kievan Metropolitan, has decided to. . . .[32]

There follows a series of specific instructions for the missionary work in Siberia and the Far East. Whatever we might think about this close relationship between Church and state, it is fascinating to see how the Church continued the ancient practice of having the hierarchy not only authorize missionary outreach, but also develop the specific plans needed for that work. This decree contains clear and quite sophisticated missiological thinking, coming once again not from the academy but from the practical structures of the Church.

e) Human Rights

This principle was clearly developed and applied by St Herman, through whom Orthodox Christianity spread to Alaska and then to continental America.[33] In September 1794, the first Orthodox missionaries arrived in Kodiak. By this time Russian businessmen, already established in Alaska for years, had violently dehumanized the local population. Almost immediately the leader of the mission, Archimandrite Joasaph, sent reports of abuse back to Russia. In retaliation for this "interference," the monks were placed under house arrest, cutting off their contact with the local people.

---

[32]Josef Glazik, *Die Russisch-Orthodoxe Heidenmission seit Peter dem Grossen: Ein missionsgeschichtlicher Versuch nach russischen Quellen Und Darstellungen*, Missionswissenschaftliche Abhandlungen und Texte (Münster: Aschendorff, 1954), 32. Author's translation.

[33]Mark Stokoe and Leonid Kishkovsky, *Orthodox Christians in North America (1794–1994)*, ‹https://oca.org/history-archives/orthodox-christians-na›, May 23, 2015. 8–10.

Nevertheless, the missionaries continued to defend the Alaskans[34] against the traders' abuses. They spent their lives teaching the Aleuts, nursing the sick, and raising orphans, honoring basic moral obligations and thereby enabling both defender and defended to become fully human. In the spirit of long-developed missiological principles, these missionaries also took traditional Aleut spirituality into account and presented Orthodox Christianity as the fulfillment of the Aleuts' religious heritage, rather than as its abolition. The Alaskan case study demonstrates that Orthodox anthropology provides an effective framework for upholding and defending human rights. Long before the theologically suspect "option for the poor" was developed by twentieth-century liberation theologians, Orthodox Alaska offered a truly positive missiology of justice and liberation.

The examples cited above represent just a small portion of the Orthodox witness down the centuries. From these experiences we will draw insight and help as we seek to formulate missiological principles to guide the Church today.

---

3. The Reawakening of Orthodox Missions Awareness

The reawakening of mission awareness within the Orthodox world makes this study particularly timely. For centuries the missionary voice of the Church was all but silenced, first by the oppression of Muslim conquerors since the fall of Byzantium in 1453, and then by the persecution of the Church at the hands of communists in Russia and Eastern Europe in the twentieth century. Not only was direct missionary activity nearly impossible, but Orthodox theologians also made very few contributions to the discipline of missiology that began to develop in the West. Noting the absence of Orthodox contributions to the *International Review of Mission* (*IRM*) during its first few decades, Athanasios N. Papathanasiou points

---

[34]It has been suggested that my use of the words "Alaskan" and "Aleut" is not technically correct. However, this is exactly the way in which these terms were used in the sources I am quoting here. So I will leave them as I found them used by Michael Oleska in *Alaskan Missionary Spirituality* (Crestwood, NY: St Vladimir's Seminary Press, 2010), and Stokoe and Kishkovsky.

out that "the Orthodox churches were considered to be non-missionary, and limited by their various national identities."[35]

At the dawn of the 20th century the Orthodox churches found themselves in a strange, even contradictory situation. On the one hand, they had a rich missionary past (the Byzantine and the Russian missions) and a dynamic theology, which accepted local cultures and stressed the importance of trinitarianism and pneumatology. Yet on the other hand, the Orthodox churches had turned inwards, locked in with the national identities of the traditionally Orthodox countries. Thus Orthodox theology was almost completely absent during the first two decades of the *International Review of Missions*. Then some Orthodox voices began to appear.[36]

One reason for this change was the post-revolution emigration of Orthodox theologians to the West and their subsequent interaction with Western Christians. This interaction led to the publication of several significant contributions by Orthodox thinkers in *IRM*. The first example cited by Papathanasiou was a 1934 introduction to Eastern Christianity by the Russian lay theologian Nicolas Zernov[37] (1898–1980). In 1942 Lev Gillet[38] (1893–1980), a French convert to Orthodoxy, proposed a new understanding of mission as dialogue. Another article by Nicolas Zernov[39] appeared in 1954, in which he related his experiences teaching in the Oriental Orthodox Church of India.

According to Papathanasiou, the real turning point came in 1961. In that year Syndesmos ("World Fellowship of Orthodox Youth") "established a

---

[35]Athanasios N. Papathanasiou, "Tradition as Impulse for Renewal and Witness: Introducing Orthodox Missiology in the *IRM*," 100, no. 2 (2011): 203–15, 204. Orthodox mission was not completely unknown. There was an article by Charles F. Sweet in 1913 in which he told the story of the work of St Nikolai Kasatkin in Japan. However, Sweet was not an Orthodox theologian.

[36]Ibid., 203. This quote is taken from the abstract that appeared above the article as originally published in the *IRM*.

[37]N. Zernov, "The Christian Church of the East," *IRM* 23 (1934): 539–46.

[38]Lev Gillet, "Dialogue with Trypho," *IRM* 31 (1942).

[39]N. Zernov, "Christianity in India and the Eastern Orthodox Church," *IRM* 43 (1954): 390–96.

pan-Orthodox missionary centre, called *Porefthentes*, or 'Go Ye.' This centre was a catalyst for awakening missionary consciousness in the Orthodox churches, for producing missiological theory and for participating
ecumenically."[40] That same year, the Russian Orthodox Church joined the
World Council of Churches (the Greek Orthodox Church had been there
at its founding). An additional impulse came from the publication of an
article by Anastasios Yannoulatos,[41] the first director of Porefthentes, who
was to become the best-known (Greek) Orthodox missiologist.

In the years that followed, the number of Orthodox contributions to
IRM increased markedly, with further contributions from Yannoulatos,[42]
Elias Voulgarakis,[43] the Russian theologian Nikita Struve,[44] and the Romanian Orthodox priest Ion Bria.[45] This obvious reawakening of Orthodox
missions awareness was noted by *IRM* in 1963.

> Eastern Orthodoxy is once again asserting its former interest in mis-
> sionary activity. This will come as a surprise to the majority of Prot-
> estants and Roman Catholics. It has long been assumed and accepted
> that Orthodox churches are nationalist churches and therefore lack
> the missionary concern necessary for them to break out from these
> self-imposed boundaries. . . .[46]

---

[40]Papathanasiou, "Tradition as Impulse for Renewal and Witness: Introducing Orthodox Missiology in the *IRM*," 207.

[41]Anastasios (Yannoulatos), "Orthodox Spirituality and External Mission," *IRM* 52
(1963): 300–02.

[42]Anastasios (Yannoulatos), "Monks and Mission in the Eastern Church During the
Fourth Century," *IRM* 58 (1969): 208–26.

[43]Elias Voulgarakis, "Mission and Unity from the Theological Point of View," *IRM* 54
(1965): 298–307.

[44]Nikita Struve, "Macaire Goukharev, a Prophet of Orthodox Mission," *IRM* 54, 308.

[45]Ion Bria, *Go Forth in Peace: Orthodox Perspectives on Mission*, WCC Mission Series
(Geneva: World Council of Churches, 1986); *Martyria/Mission: The Witness of the Orthodox
Churches Today* (Geneva: Commission on World Mission and Evangelism, World Council
of Churches, 1980); *The Liturgy after the Liturgy: Mission and Witness from an Orthodox
Perspective* (Geneva: WCC, 1996).

[46]C. Samuel Calian, "Eastern Orthodoxy's Renewed Concern for Mission," *IRM* 52
(1963): 33–37.

In the decades since those early days there has been significant missiological development in the Orthodox world. By way of example, consider the formation of missiological institutes around the world. In Russia we can point to the Orthodox Institute for Missiological Research in St Petersburg, the Moscow Center for Mission Studies, and the very active Missions Department of the Russian Orthodox Church.[47] In addition, there is the international and interdenominational Central and Eastern European Association for Mission Studies (CEEAMS), founded in 2002.[48] The United States has the Orthodox Christian Missions Center[49] and the Missions Institute of Orthodox Christianity.[50] Finally, there is the Lausanne-Orthodox Initiative, a consultation on mission; recently,

> at the gracious invitation of His Beatitude Archbishop Dr Anastasios Yannoulatos of Albania, 46 Eastern and Oriental Orthodox and Evangelical leaders from 20 different countries gathered at St Vlash Monastery in Albania from 2 to 6 September 2013. . . . Under the theme *The Mission of God* participants were reminded by His Beatitude that "The Spirit ceaselessly gives life to the Church and to each of the Church's members, transforming them into living cells of the mystical body of Christ, enabling it to partake in His continuing mission for the salvation of the entire cosmos."[51]

[47]Valentin Kozhuharov, "Developments in the Mission of the Russian Orthodox Church," *Acta Missiologiae* 2, no. 7-26 (2009).

[48]"The Central and Eastern European Association for Mission Studies," ⟨The Central and Eastern European Association for Mission Studies⟩, May 25, 2015.

[49]"As the official missions agency of the Assembly of Canonical Orthodox Bishops of North and Central America, it is OCMC's mission to make disciples of all nations by bringing people to Christ and his Church." "Orthodox Christian Mission Center (OCMC) – Make Disciples of All Nations," "Orthodox Christian Mission Center," ⟨http://www.ocmc.org⟩, May 25, 2015.

[50]"The goal of the Missions Institute is to promote a vibrant mission consciousness, especially within our Orthodox Christian Theological Schools in the United States. The primary focus is to instill an understanding of international cross-cultural missionary work. The Institute will also engender a missions consciousness for the local setting through understanding evangelism and promoting participation and support for international and domestic cross-cultural missions." "The Missions Institute of Orthodox Christianity," ⟨http://www.hchc.edu/community/institutions_and_centers⟩, May 25, 2015.

[51]"The Mission of God: The First Consultation of the Lausanne-Orthodox Initiative,"

In spite of—or perhaps because of—this reawakening and renewed activity, missiology as a discipline is still considered a very new idea among Orthodox academic institutions. As recently as 2010, Fr Chad Hatfield, the dean of St Vladimir's Seminary, called missiology a new academic discipline, noting that "'missiology' is one of those words that your 'spell check' will underline. Still, the study of the Church's mission and evangelization is gaining interest in academic circles as a new discipline."[52] This is indeed an opportune time to attempt a re-articulation of the place of mission theology within the overall discipline of missiology, and to do so from an Orthodox perspective.

4) The Present Project

But what is a theology of mission—or, for that matter, of anything else? A cursory survey of a theological library's holdings will reveal a virtual avalanche of various "theologies of. . . ." Sometimes the preposition "of" indicates the source of a theology. Such sources range from biblical books and authors (*Theology of St John*), to particular theologians (*Theology of St Athanasius*), and even institutions (*Theology of the Church of England*). "Of" may also point to specific content or subject matter such as prayer, history, education, artistic sensibilities, or even golf. "Theology of" may signal the use of figurative language, such as analogy. In some works, a link to theology is used to criticize or legitimize some particular person, institution, concept, or practice.

In the case of this project, the term "theology of mission" implies several things. First, it suggests a relationship between theology and mission, namely, that there exists a concrete, objective, and justifiable link between theology and the missionary responsibility of the Church. In other words, mission must be regarded as a legitimate aspect of theology proper. Second, it implies that we already have (or must now reformulate) an expression of this aspect of theology within the context and authority of the

⟨http://www.loimission.net/st-vlash-consultation/communique/⟩, May 25, 2015.

[52]Chad Hatfield, "Missiology: A New Academic Discipline," ⟨http://www.svots.edu/voices/on_our_minds/missiology-new-academic-discipline⟩, May 25, 2015.

Church, drawing upon all available sources: Scripture, liturgical texts, tradition, the work of councils, the lives of the saints, even icons.

Third, since books are not written in a vacuum, "theology of" implies that we begin with a working definition of mission, one that includes every aspect of the Church's responsibility to witness Christ to all peoples, with priority given to those who have never heard or accepted the gospel. My intended readers may already know something of missions. They will have read about the topic, met and engaged its agents, or perhaps prepared for and even participated in it. Our task will be to test current understanding against Orthodox theological norms.

Since I have neither been Orthodox all my life nor formally attended an Orthodox theological institution, the question may arise as to whether I am in a position to offer a truly Orthodox theology of mission. Indeed, I have hesitated to take on this project for a number of years. However, having been a member of the Church for twenty years, an active priest for seventeen, and a professor of Orthodox studies for twelve, I now believe that I have finally matured enough in my understanding of the Church to attempt this task. I have consistently tested my ideas by submitting them to other priests and Orthodox scholars. I have cautiously developed a measure of confidence that I will be able to present fairly an Orthodox position on mission. Perhaps my situation is not all that unusual. Paul L. Gavrilyuk points out

> Orthodox theology has shifted from diaspora theology to convert theology. Only thirty years ago, almost without exception, Orthodox scholarship in the United States was dominated by Slavs like Schmemann and Meyendorff and Greeks like Romanides. Some were educated and even born outside of their countries of ethnic origin, but their roots still ran deep in their respective ethnic traditions. Now, a deep immersion in the Orthodox tradition has led a number of noted scholars to join the Orthodox Church. These include McGuckin, Humphrey, Harvey, the late Jaroslav Pelikan, Richard Swinburne, Andrew Louth, and David Bentley Hart. All of them teach or have taught primarily at non-Orthodox schools.[53]

[53]Paul L. Gavrilyuk, "The Orthodox Renaissance," *First Things* 228 (December 2012): 33–37, 36.

He goes on to state

> that we are presently witnessing the first signs of a theological earth-
> quake that will bring about the new and more potent wave of the
> world-wide Orthodox theological renaissance. The epicenter is likely
> to be North America, the main areas affected are likely to be non-
> Orthodox schools, and the sources of the most potent shockwaves are
> likely to be converts to Orthodoxy.[54]

From my perspective as a convert, I hope to find ways to bridge the
gap between the Protestant and Orthodox worlds of mission. For most of
my life I have been involved in one form of mission or another. I spent
fifteen years church planting with the free Lutheran churches of Germany,
twenty years teaching about missions as an academic field, and another
seventeen years planting a local Orthodox parish. My goal here is to tap
into the riches of Orthodox missiology and bring its unique insights to
bear on the contemporary mission of the Church in an idiom that my
Protestant friends will also be able to understand.

Accordingly, Part I contains three brief chapters that address the general field of academic study known as missiology. I examine the subject,
nature, methodology, and purpose of the study of mission as it has developed in both the West (chapter 1) and the East (chapter 2). Chapter 3
then articulates a specifically Orthodox understanding of the discipline,
including a) a definition of mission theology's place within the discipline
of mission; b) an initial working definition of mission; and c) a proposal for
a methodological framework and an agenda for a theology of mission.

Part II explores the sources of data needed for a theology of mission from an Orthodox perspective. This includes a review of Old Testament (chapter 4) and New Testament (chapter 5) materials supported
by patristic and modern commentary. In chapter 6, I pursue additional
mission-theological principles among historical and traditional sources
by examining representative missionary endeavors and selected mission-
related ecclesial pronouncements and documents.

[54]Ibid., 37.

Finally, Part III contains a reformulation of a systematic, theological statement of the rationale and goal of mission (chapter 7), the ecclesial origin of missionary outreach (chapter 8), the basic content of the gospel and church education (chapter 9), and guidelines for the implementation of mission (chapter 10).

PART ONE

The Context:
On the Development of
the Study of Missions

Theology of mission is generally regarded as a subdivision of missiology, as the study of missions is called today. As the name implies, mission theology may also be considered a branch of any one of several traditional theological disciplines, such as dogmatic theology, church history, or practical theology. Identifying mission theology's place within missiology and the complex field of related disciplines requires us to trace its development as a discipline and define its nature and structure. Only then will it be possible to delineate its methodologies and tasks. However, the very attempt to locate mission theology involves several assumptions about the discipline, none of which has been held without objection.

First, assigning mission theology a place among the traditional theological disciplines assumes that it is in itself a legitimate and identifiable discipline. That, in turn, suggests prior agreement with respect to the obvious subject of study, i.e., mission. Unfortunately, the meaning of this term has been the object of considerable debate. On the one hand, mission has been defined in terms of Christian presence. Since "presence" includes the entire spectrum of human activity, anything done either in the name of Christ or by the Church could be referred to as mission. When applied to theology, this definition reduces mission to a general theme or leitmotif, to the extent that while it might be present in each theological subdiscipline, it is not likely to flourish as a separate field of study.

On the other hand, mission has been defined in terms of specific, clearly defined tasks intended to spread the Christian faith among those who have not yet embraced it. In the Orthodox world, where a church plant is often called a "mission," such attempts could take place within the boundaries of a single culture, or could be done in a cross-cultural context. We may not be entirely satisfied with this particular definition, but such an approach lends itself to a clearer understanding of mission, one that could become the subject of an autonomous field of study.

Second, the desire to locate the study of missions within the general context of theology assumes a formal relationship to one or more of the traditional theological disciplines. This continuity issues from the fact that, as with all theological study, mission theology's point of departure and ultimate standard is the tradition of the Church, and in particular the Holy Scriptures. Accordingly, it must submit to the authority of that which has been revealed to the Church and conducted in keeping with accepted theological methodology. The relationship to other theological disciplines is also established by the fact that mission is one of the Church's primary responsibilities. Christ was sacrificed as "the Lamb of God, who takes away the sin of the world for the life and salvation of the world," and the Church is called to bear witness in the world. As such, a theology of mission, as with all theological reflection, must be done within the context of and in the service of the Church.

Third, describing mission theology as a "discipline" assumes that it has an academic or scientific status. Referring to the study of mission as a "science" may sound strange to readers, who tend to associate that term with a particular epistemology, research methodology, and fields of study. Nevertheless, the term "science" is applicable to any discipline conducted in a systematic and logically consistent manner. This convention is particularly common in the European academy where, for example, the German term *Missionswissenschaft* (study of missions) incorporates the root word *Wissenschaft* (science).

1

The Development of Missiology in the West

I n the West, academic interest in the systematic study of missions developed as a result of a logical progression of thought.[1] The bridge to the academy was initially established as a response to the dramatic rise in missionary activity that grew out of early German pietism. Once the Reformation's initial reluctance[2] had been overcome and the first Protestant missionaries were commissioned, the need for additional training became apparent. One of the earliest Protestant attempts to integrate missions and academy came in the Netherlands. In 1622, the University of Leiden allowed the establishment of the *seminarium indicum*, which, as the name indicates, was to provide training for missionaries working in the Dutch East Indies. Prospective missionaries were required to complete courses in non-Christian religions and in the Malay language as well as all the regular courses in theology. Unfortunately, the seminary was forced to close after only ten years of service.

A similar idea was realized in 1702 when August Herman Francke established the *collegium orientale theologicum* at the University of Halle.

[1]In what follows I have largely followed Olav Guttorm Myklebust, *The Study of Missions in Theological Education* (Oslo: Egede Institut, 1955).

[2]This reluctance was based in part on dogmatic consideration as reflected, for example, in Johann Gerhard's statement that "*mandatum praedicandi evangelium in toto terrarum orbe cum apostolis desiit.*" Johann Gerhard, *Loci Theologici* 6:147, ‹https://books.google.com/books?id=tMdimyujz3kC&pg=PA147&lpg=PA147&dq=mandatum+praedicandi&source=bl&ots=qQ5Q9EqJni&sig=IiumSXXJYJhslBU66oV4WxjW6kw&hl=en&sa=X&ei=-VJkVfwvwp-DBIumgOAE&ved=0CEIQ6AEwCQ#v=onepage&q=mandatum%20praedicandi&f=false›, May 26, 2015.

Again the object of the new seminary was the training of missionaries, in this case for service in India.[3]

Interestingly, the personal involvement of theologians in missions does not appear to have impacted their work as theologians. Commenting on Francke's work, Myklebust writes,

> As far as we know . . . Francke's missionary interests and activities did not directly affect his work as a professor of theology in the University of Halle. His introduction to the study of theology contains no reference to the task of foreign missions.[4]

Nevertheless, continued missionary activity did capture the attention of the theological community. During the latter half of the eighteenth century, a growing number of professors began to weave missions-related topics into the fabric of their regular lectures.[5] By the beginning of the nineteenth century the formalization of missiology's position in the academy was well underway. A few professors began to offer lectures devoted solely to missions. In 1800, J. F. Flatt gave a lecture on the history of the Danish Halle Mission at the university of Tübingen. A few years later, in 1825, F. C. Kraft offered a series of lectures on the history of missions at the University in Erlangen.

Of even greater significance was the fact that the theological encyclopedia, which appeared at this time, provided a theoretical framework that afforded missions a legitimate place among the other theological disciplines. In his *Kurze Darstellung des theologischen Studiums*, published in 1811, F. D. Schleiermacher developed the science[6] of theology as an integrated whole, the primary value of which is to be seen in its relationship to the practical needs of the Church. He refers to theology as the "collective

---

[3]Yet another example of the effort to provide systematic training for missionaries in an academic setting is reported by L. Stampe, "Collegium de cursu Evangelii promovendo," *Dansk Teologisk Tidskrift* (1946): 65–88.

[4]Myklebust, *The Study of Missions in Theological Education*, 52.

[5]Ibid., 53–55.

[6]According to Schleiermacher's scheme theology is to be viewed as a positive science. Heinrich Scholz, *Schleiermachers kurze Darstellung des theologischen Studiums* (Leipzig: A. Deichert'sche Verlagsbuchhandlung, 1935). Compare Wolfhart Pannenberg, *Theology and the Philosophy of Science* (Philadelphia: Westminster Press, 1976).

embodiment of those branches of scientific knowledge and those rules of art without the possessions and application of which a harmonious guidance of the Church is not possible."[7] As he conceived of it, theology could be divided into three major areas: philosophical, historical, and practical. In the second edition of this work, he included the study of mission with catechesis under practical theology. "Conditionally the theory of missions might also find a point of connection here; a theory which, up to the present time, is as good as altogether wanting."[8]

Similarly Ehrenfeuchter, a professor of theology at the University in Göttingen, made missions a part of his *lectiones publicae* and included missions as a fundamental part of his *Praktische Theologie*. In the latter work, published in 1859, he develops a theological system based upon three functions of the Church: expansion, presentation, and preservation. Expansion is defined in terms of conversion of the heathen, sending, preaching, and church planting. Thus, mission is viewed as a basic, essential function of the Church.[9] On the integration of mission and Church he writes:

> The greater the degree to which a conscious awareness of the Church characterizes missionary work, the more likely it (mission) is to view itself as an activity which flows from and benefits the Church; on the other hand, the greater the degree to which the work of mission remains part of the Church's awareness, the more likely it (the Church) is going to recognize the fact that it owes its existence to the preaching of the gospel from which it has grown.[10]

---

[7] Scholz, *Schleiermachers kurze Darstellung des theologischen Studiums*, 2.

[8] Ibid., 114.

[9] Cf. Falk Wagner, "Über die Legitimität der Mission," *Theologische Existenz Heute* (1968): 154.

[10] "Je mehr das theologische Bewusstsein der Kirche die Arbeit der Mission begleitet, desto mehr wird sich dieselbe als seine Tat der Kirche erkennen, sowohl sie an dieser geschieht, als wie sie von dieser ausgeht; und andererseits, je mehr das Werk der Mission zum Bewusstsein kommt, desto mehr wird sie, die Kirche, ihr Werden verstehen, wird begreifen, wie sie aus der ersten Botschaft des Heils zu ihrer vollen Gestalt erwächst." A. E. Ehrenfeuchter, *Die praktische Theologie* 1:210, ⟨http://babel.hathitrust.org/cgi/pt?id=hvd. ah4xqf;view=1up;seq=230⟩, May 26, 2015.

At this time there was also a definite movement in the direction of instituting a formal chair of missiology at the academy. The first steps in this direction were taken at Princeton Seminary. In 1830, a special committee appointed to study the possibility of establishing a missions department recommended to the general assembly that a professor of Pastoral Theology and Missionary Instruction be appointed. It was resolved

> that the said Professor have committed to him the instruction in everything which relates to the Pastoral office, and that he be especially charged with collecting and imparting instruction on the subject of Missions; and with using all proper means, by public lectures, and private interviews, to promote among all the students an enlarged spirit of pastoral fidelity, of Missionary zeal, and of liberal preparation and active effort for the advancement of the Redeemer's Kingdom.[11]

With the implementation of this plan in 1836, Princeton became the first institution of higher education to support, at least in part, a chair of missions study. In a way analogous to Schleiermacher's scheme, the Princeton professorship of mission was included under and combined with practical theology. As such, it cannot be considered fully autonomous, i.e., the study of mission had not yet attained the status of an independent field of study.[12]

The Free Church of Scotland was the first to take that step. Free Church missionaries had promoted the idea of an academic study of mission for some time. During his studies at St Andrews from 1821 to 1829, Alexander Duff was struck by the absence of courses on missions and evangelism. He wrote:

> When passing through the theological curriculum of St. Andrews, I was struck markedly with this circumstance, that throughout the

---

[11]Myklebust, *The Study of Missions in Theological Education*, 147. This should not be taken to mean that interest in mission died out. Quite to the contrary, many of the Princeton professors (including Archibald Alexander and Charles Hodge) were enthusiastic supporters of foreign missions.

[12]Ibid., 149. By 1855 the subject of mission was no longer listed in the seminary's annual catalogue.

whole course of the curriculum of four years not one single allusion was ever made to the subject of the world's evangelization—the subject which constitutes the chief end of the Christian Church on earth.[13]

This concern was later translated into agitation for the idea of a missionary professorship. Duff, by this time a missionary in India, first aired the idea in a letter dated January 20, 1844. In it he hints "at a new professorship in the Free Church College." Not long thereafter Duff had an opportunity to fill the chair of theology vacated by the death of Chalmers in 1847. Duff refused the offer, not wanting to abandon his calling to missionary service. That sentiment was echoed by a number of his colleagues, who at the same time provided additional impetus for the idea of a professor of missions. For example, fellow missionary A. F. Lacroix wrote:

> I will not say either that I would not rejoice to see you some time hence appointed even Professor at the new Edinburgh University; but let me be well understood—not to one of the ordinary Chairs of Theology.
>
> Why, for instance should not a Chair be erected at its new University to be called the "Missionary" or "Evangelistic" chair, having for its object to impart information and instruction regarding that most interesting and important portion of the Christian system—the universal spread of our Lord's kingdom over the earth?[14]

After a long period of germination, the vision of a full professor of mission became a reality. In 1867, the general assembly adopted a committee report advocating the institution of a professorship for missions. Duff was appointed to that position and inducted into the office of Professor of Evangelistic Theology. In his inaugural address, Duff dealt with the question of the scope and subdivisions of evangelistic theology. Issues he proposed to incorporate in the curriculum included:

(1) The supreme importance of missions as variously shown from the revealed word of God.

[13]Ibid., 168. Proceedings and Debates of the General Assembly of the Free Church of Scotland (1867), 51.

[14]Ibid., 175. From an 1849 letter of Alexander Duff.

(2) The obligations which arise out of the preceding. . . .

(3) The obstacles and hindrances to the faithful discharge of these obligations within the Church.

(4) The work to be done among the heathen, and the various ways and modes of doing it. . . .

(5) Missionaries—their call; qualifications, natural and acquired; their training and employment. . . .

(6) The special duties which the Church at home owes to the missionaries. . . .

(7) Sketches of the history of missions. . . .

(8) The present aspects and prospects of the missionary enterprise throughout the world. . . .

(9) Misrepresentations and objections considered and removed.[15]

The installation of Duff was a historic occasion. For the first time, a full-time chair solely devoted to the subject of missions had been inaugurated.[16] In spite of whatever weaknesses Duff's teaching may have shown, and regardless of history's evaluation of his efforts,[17] the fact remains that a major academic institution had accepted in principle and practice the idea of the science of mission. Unfortunately, that success was not long-lived.

Duff passed away in 1878, and his successor was not appointed until 1880. At that time the discussion that preceded Duff's appointment resurfaced, and there was no consensus as to what the chair was established to do. There was a general feeling that the second occupant of the chair was likely to be the last.

---

[15]Ibid., 198–99.

[16]Ibid. At about the same time Karl Graul was appointed to be professor of missions history at the University of Erlangen.

[17]Based on student reaction, some historians suggest that Duff's work as a professor was a failure. K. Oepke, "K. Grauls Bedeutung Für die deutsche Missionswissenschaft und das deutsche Missionsleben," *Allgemeine Missions-Zeitschrift* (1917): 314–23.

Indeed, that was to be the case. A commission was appointed in 1891 to review the whole system of chairs at the three colleges. As a result, the concept of the chair of missions was weakened. The occupant was to be appointed for the limited period of only three years, with more emphasis placed on the subject of home missions. Funding was also gradually redirected to home missions projects. The chair was reduced to a lectureship and finally abandoned by decision of the general assembly in 1909.

At the University of Halle, Gustav Warneck achieved the final stage in the formalization of missiology's position at the academy. In 1897 he was appointed professor for *Missionswissenschaft*, becoming the first fully accredited professor to hold a chair devoted solely to the study of mission. He is said to have established the academic legitimacy of the discipline once and for all.[18] Part of his contribution may be seen in his efforts to establish a base of missiological literature. His own multi-volume *Evangelische Missionslehre* became a standard reference tool. Warneck in 1887 also inaugurated *Die Allgemeine Missionszeitschrift*, a journal of missiology, which established a public literary forum for the developing discipline.[19]

The way in which missiology developed in the West is rather typical of the way in which many new fields of study are introduced to the academy. Increased missionary activity led to the need for formal training designed to equip individuals for the missionary task. That, in turn, led a number of professors already personally involved in missions to incorporate missions-related topics into their regular lectures. Next came the introduction of formal lectures and, finally, professorships of mission. Thus missiology found its way into the academy, and with some reservation was counted among the sciences that could legitimately be taught at a university. Today there are few, if any, Protestant seminaries in which the systematic study of

[18] According to Warneck, missiology is related to the other disciplines in such a way "daß ihr nicht bloß ein Gast, sondern ein Hausrecht in der theologischen Wissenschaft gebührt und sie es also nicht als eine Gunst zu erbetteln, vielmehr ein Recht zu fordern hat, in den Organismus derselben eingereiht zu werden." Gustav Warneck, "Das Studium Der Mission. Wie Ist Es Am Praktischsten Einzurichten?" *Allgemeine Missions-Zeitschrift* (1907), 209.

[19] Since Warneck a number of theologians have continued the development of the discipline, e.g., Martin Kaehler, J. H. Bavinck, H. Kraemer, Horst Bürkle, and Peter Beyerhaus.

the Church's missionary responsibilities has not been accepted as part of the regular program and as an independent field of study.[20] In some cases this led to whole departments of mission, or even schools of mission and evangelism housed within an existing school—for example, the School of World Mission and Evangelism at Trinity Evangelical Divinity School, or the School of World Mission at Fuller Theological Seminary.[21]

[20]However, it must be pointed out that recent decades have seen a significant erosion of missiology's position in the academy due to a) a generally altered understanding of the missionary task, b) revived skepticism of the traditional theological disciplines that kept missiology at a distance, and c) intensified calls for increased specialization, which although understandable and in keeping with recent trends in education and research, have created difficulties for an activity which is, by definition, inter-disciplinary.

[21]There are, of course, any number of other institutions that have schools of mission, such as the E. Stanley Jones School of World Mission and Evangelism, and Asbury Theological Seminary. We might also point to extra-educational bodies such as the Overseas Mission Study Center in Hartford, Connecticut.

2

The Development of Missiology in the Eastern Church

A s noted in the introduction, the Orthodox Church has been actively involved in missionary outreach from its very inception. In doing so it developed and implemented a whole array of missiological principles and practices centuries before they were discussed by the missiologists in Western academies. However, an interest in mission as a university-based discipline has only recently surfaced in the East. The main reason for this is that missionary outreach in the East has always been done within the hierarchical structures of the Church. In the case of the general witness of the Church, when the presider (the priest) dismisses the faithful at the end of the liturgy, he also commissions them to go back into the world and bear witness to what they have seen during the service. This priestly blessing is the only authorization required for members of the laity to invite their peers to come and meet Christ. However, the more formal work of extending or planting the Church in places where it does not yet exist has always required specialized hierarchical authorization.[1] Christ officially conferred ministerial authority on his apostles, and they, in turn, passed that authority on to others: the next generation of bishops, without whom the work could not be legitimately continued.[2] Since the time of Christ,

---

[1]This is not to say that laypeople have never initiated the witness and then later called on the hierarchs to send clergy. That, however, seems to be the exception, and in any case, the point here is that in the end hierarchical authorization is always needed to establish a parish.

[2]While it does not involve mission per se, note the necessity of apostolic commissioning for the first deacons in Acts 6.5–6.

only those who receive this authorization from the unbroken chain of command, which starts with the apostles and continues through the succession of canonical bishops, can legitimately engage in the mission of the Church. For this reason the bishops, metropolitans, and patriarchs have always been the driving force behind new missionary outreach. Accordingly, most of the missiological material available in the Orthodox world comes not from academic faculties, but rather in the form of the decrees, instructions, and descriptions issued by the commissioning hierarchs and even at times the secular rulers of Christian nations, as well as the ongoing exchanges (letters) between the frontline missionaries and their hierarchs.

This pattern was established as early as the time of the Jerusalem Council described in Acts 15. Struggling with practical issues concerning the then-developing mission to the Gentiles, the apostles met, deliberated, and issued instructions in the form of a letter that was used to guide the work.

> The apostles, the elders, and the brethren, to the brethren who are of the Gentiles in Antioch, Syria, and Cilicia: Greetings. Since we have heard that some who went out from us have troubled you with words, unsettling your souls, saying, "You must be circumcised and keep the law"—to whom we gave no such commandment—it seemed good to us, being assembled with one accord, to send chosen men to you with our beloved Barnabas and Paul, men who have risked their lives for the name of our Lord Jesus Christ. We have therefore sent Judas and Silas, who will also report the same things by word of mouth. For it seemed good to the Holy Spirit, and to us, to lay upon you no greater burden than these necessary things: that you abstain from things offered to idols, from blood, from things strangled, and from sexual immorality. If you keep yourselves from these, you will do well. (Acts 15.23–29)

These verses may well be the very first missiological reflections on record in the Church, and the apostles themselves, under the guidance of the Holy Spirit, issued them. The letter contains a compassionate interaction with the cross-cultural implications of the Gentile mission. It seeks to maintain the basic principles of the new faith while at the same time adjusting its practice to fit the new situation. This type of decree or instruction became the primary vehicle of missiological thinking in the Eastern Church.[3]

For our purposes here, it will suffice to give just four examples of this kind of decree: 1) the Synodal Commission to Sts Cyril and Methodius (863); 2) the Missionary Decree of Tsar Peter the Great (1700); 3) the Missionary Instructions of St Innocent of Alaska (1858); and 4) the documents released through the Missions Department of the Russian Orthodox Church (1999–2014). At this point we are not interested in a detailed account of the missionaries or their activities,[4] but will rather focus our attention on the decrees and instructions themselves in order to highlight the advanced missiological thought they contain.

1. The Synodal Commission of Emperor Michael III (862)

St Cyril (827–869) and his brother, St Methodius (815–884), were born into a pious family in the city of Thessalonica. Methodius, the oldest of seven brothers, served in the military and became governor of one of

---

[3]This is not to say that schools have not played a significant role. As we will see, there were a number of famous examples of schools established by Byzantine (at Velehrad) and Russian missionaries. These schools were a reflection of the desire to develop a better-prepared class of priests, in particular, by a study of the language and the culture of the recipients, and especially raising up an indigenous priesthood. However, these few schools were a result of, and not the source of, missiological thinking already established and documented in hierarchical decrees.

[4]Adequate descriptions can be found in: Josef Glazik, *Die Islammission der russisch-orthodoxen Kirche; Eine missionsgeschichtliche Untersuchung nach russischen Quellen und Darstellung* (Münster: Aschendorff, 1959); Serge Bolshakoff, *The Foreign Missions of the Russian Orthodox Church* (London: Society for Promoting Christian Knowledge, 1943); Robert P. Geraci and Michael Khodarkovsky, *Of Religion and Empire: Missions, Conversion, and Tolerance in Tsarist Russia* (Ithaca: Cornell University Press, 2001); Konsti Kharlampovych et al., *Archimandrite Makarii Glukharev: Founder of the Altai Mission*, Studies in Russian History (Lewiston, NY: E. Mellen Press, 2001); Andrei A. Znamenski, *Shamanism and Christianity: Native Encounters with Russian Orthodox Missions in Siberia and Alaska, 1820-1917*, Contributions to the Study of World History (Westport, CT: Greenwood Press, 1999).

the Slavic principalities dependent on the Byzantine Empire (probably Bulgaria), which made it possible for him to learn the Slavic language. After living there for about ten years, he received monastic tonsure. Constantine (Cyril was his monastic name) was the youngest and studied science, theology, and several languages. Because of his sharp intellect, he was called "the Philosopher." After completing his education he was ordained to the priesthood, becoming curator of the patriarchal library at the church of Hagia Sophia. Because of his knowledge of both Hebrew and Arabic, he was sent on a diplomatic mission to the Caliph of Bagdad in 851. On the authority of a synod called by the Emperor, Cyril was commissioned with defending the Christian teaching of the Trinity among the Muslims.[5] Later, in 860, he was commissioned by Emperor Michael III and Patriarch Photius to lead a diplomatic mission to the mostly Jewish Khazars on the Caspian Sea. During that trip the remains of the martyred St Clement were recovered.[6] He then returned to teaching philosophy in Constantinople, but in 862 everything changed. In his *Vita* we read:

> As the Philosopher was happy in God, another commission and another task arrived which was in no way less important than the earlier ones. Rastislav the Moravian Prince, prompted by God, conferred with his princes and the Moravians and sent a message to Emperor Michael III, saying: "Since our people have turned away from our heathen ways and now keep the Christian law we have no teacher who could explain to us the true Christian faith in our own language.... So send us, O Emperor, a bishop and such a teacher...." After the Emperor gathered the Synod, he called the philosopher Constantine asking him to listen to the request and said: "Philosopher, I know that you are very busy, but it is worthy of you to go there. Because there is no one who can fulfill this commission like you can."
>
> The Philosopher answered: "Although I have things to do and am physically fragile, I will gladly go there so they will have a writing in their own language." The Emperor answered and said to him, "My

[5] Joseph Schütz, *Die Lehrer der Slawen Kyrill und Method* (St Otilien: EOS Verlag, 1985), 34.

[6] Ibid., 40–43.

grandfather and my father and many others have searched for that and have found nothing. How should I find something?" But the Philosopher said, "Who can write such a teaching on water or be labeled a heretic?" The Emperor together with his Uncle Bardas countered, "If you are willing, then God will give it to you just as he gives to all who ask without doubt and opens to those who knock."

The Philosopher withdrew and gave himself over to the ancient practice of prayer with his fellow workers. Soon God revealed himself and answered the prayer of his servant. And immediately he created letters and began to translate the gospel teaching.

The emperor was delighted and together with his counselors praised God. And he sent him out with many gifts and wrote the following letter to Rastislav: "God who commanded everyone to gain an understanding of the truth and to strive for great honor has recognized your faith, and has in our time done a great miracle and revealed the letters of your language, which from ancient days has not existed, so that you and your great people can praise God in their own language. And we are sending those to whom God revealed this, an honorable and pious and well-educated philosopher. And after receiving this gift, which is more valuable than gold and silver and precious stones and passing riches, go with him and fulfill this commission with all urgency, because all hearts long for God. Do not neglect the salvation of all, but encourage all not to miss but rather to embark on the true path so that you, too, who through your great act have led them to knowledge of God, will in the next life receive the reward for all who should believe on Christ our God from now until the end, in that you leave a memorial for distant generations just like the great Emperor Constantine."[7]

What we find so remarkable about this decree is its level of missiological sophistication. The negotiations between Michael, Photius, Rastislav, and Cyril show incredible insight into the dynamics of cross-cultural missions, in particular the importance of using vernacular languages. Not everyone recognized the wisdom of this approach. The adherents of the so-called "three language theory," for example, rigorously resisted the

---

[7]Ibid., 66–68.

whole idea of translating Scripture and liturgical books into local languages. According to this theory, God had given humanity only three languages in which they were to conduct Church business: Hebrew, Greek, and Latin. As proof of this idea, they pointed to the inscription in those three languages placed on the cross of Christ by Pilate. Even though the Byzantine authorities accepted the idea of a vernacular Bible and liturgy, there was strong opposition to the vernacular among Roman missionaries. For that reason Cyril went to Rome to discuss the matter. On the way he stopped for a debate in Venice. There the Philosopher put to shame all of his opponents with a rigorous, biblically based defense of using the local language.[8] The pope himself then warmly received him at the gates of Rome. Part of the reason for this positive reception was ascribed to the fact that Cyril had brought back the relics of St Clement. Once in Rome, the Byzantine missionaries proceeded to sing in Slavonic in a number of churches over the course of several days.

Finally, Pope Hadrian II approved the ecclesial use of the Slavonic language, as documented in his letter to the princes Rastislav, Sventopolk, and Kocel in 869, and in the papal bull *Industiae tuae* (880).[9] Once established, this practice became the norm for all subsequent missionary activity. In other words, something that we today take for granted was articulated in the negotiations between Emperor Michael II, Patriarch Photius, and Pope Hadrian. This gives clear evidence that missiology was being done early in the Church not at special academies, but by the hierarchs as recorded in their documents of commission. Based on these documents we see a clear commitment to respecting local social structures and, above all, to using local languages.[10]

[8]Ibid., 71–75.

[9]František Grivec, *Konstantin und Method: Lehrer der Slaven* (Wiesbaden: O. Harrassowitz, 1960), 76.

[10]This pattern of hierarchical authorization was also practiced in the Western Church. St Ansgar, who was sent to Rome to secure permission for his mission to Scandinavia, received confirmation around 846. "The Pope confirmed this, not only by an authoritative decree, but also by the gift of the *pallium*, in accordance with the custom of his predecessors, and he appointed him as his legate for the time being amongst all the neighboring races of the Swedes and the Danes, also the Slavs and the other races that inhabited the regions of the north so that he might share authority with Ebo the Archbishop of Rheims, to whom

2. The Missionary Decree of Tsar Peter the Great (1700)

According to Glazik, ever since the days of the apostles the Church has known itself to be responsible for spreading the gospel. It did so with great success until the schism of 1054. However, with the Crusades, the Muslim advances, and finally the fall of Constantinople in 1453, Byzantine Christianity was forced into a self-defensive stance that left few, if any, opportunities for geographic expansion. One great exception is the Russian Church. Beginning with the conversion of Kievan Rus', Christianity began to be spread throughout the vast region of Russia, central Asia, and the Far East. Russian missionaries successfully introduced Christianity to a region thirty times as large as the mission's European home base.[11] All this activity began with mission driven by the princes. From St Vladimir's time until the end of the eleventh century, Christianity moved to the northeast, something determined almost entirely by political constraints. There followed a phase of mission carried forth by Russian settlers who were forced to move north and east because of the Mongol invasions. They engaged in what Glazik calls indirect mission, colonization, and the expansion of the Church.[12] That led to an era of expansion led by monks and monasteries. Eventually there was a turn to a more organized form of missionary outreach, which seems to have come about as a result of three changes in the Russian worldview. First, there was the changing (and challenging) relationship with Islam that followed the destruction of Byzantium in 1453. The second change was that Moscow, as heir to the faith of Byzantium, came to be seen as the third Rome. Finally, the Russian conquest of Kazan by Ivan IV in 1552 opened up what seemed to be a missionary opportunity among the Muslims.[13]

In order to understand mission in this era, it is important to note the very close connection between Church and state. In the context of that

---

he had before entrusted the same office." Rimbert, *Life of Anskar, the Apostle of the North, 801–865,* ⟨http://www.fordham.edu/halsall/basis/anskar.asp⟩, May 26, 2015.

[11]Glazik, *Die russisch-orthodoxe Heidenmission,* 279.

[12]Ibid., 7–13.

[13]Ibid., 23–31.

relationship, it was, for example, "the most natural thing in the world for Ivan IV to mix matters of state and Church, and through the conversion of the Tatars push back and eliminate the influence of the Volga-Turkish elements."[14] Ivan saw the work of the Church as missionary outreach to the conquered people. In a detailed set of instructions, he laid out the basic principles that were to guide interaction with Tatars. This appears to be the first of the Russian missions decrees and, although it came from a secular source, there is no need to question the religious motivation of Ivan, who thought he could convert the Muslims to Christianity by means of love of neighbor.[15] He gave St Gurias, the archbishop of Kazan (1555–1563), detailed instructions on how to treat the unbelieving Tatars, suggesting that he draw the newly baptized to himself by feeding them, giving them drink, and removing every injustice so the nonbelievers, seeing his generosity and care, would convert and be baptized.[16] Moreover, Gurias was to instruct the upper-class citizens personally and take them to the monasteries. He is even given the power to release converts from past crimes at baptism, a move that was not very well received among the more upstanding citizens. Ivan's instruction included not only advice but also practical resources, such as assistance from the thirty-one new monasteries he established during the second half of the sixteenth century.

Following the succession of a number of bishops, St Hermogenes assumed office as the first metropolitan of Kazan in 1589. He found that the converts, who were continually under Muslim influence, did not know the basics of the faith and neither went to church nor wore their baptismal crosses, but had generally fallen back into their pre-Christian habits. Hermogenes tried everything he could think of, bringing to Kazan the relics of St Germanus (the second archbishop of Kazan), rounding up the lapsed Christians, and confining them in the cathedral for several days of intensive instruction. All to no avail! So he appealed to Tsar Feodor (1557–1598), who issued an edict on July 18, 1593, requiring all the newly baptized to be forcibly resettled in Russian villages.[17] Feodor's death in 1598 led to a

[14]Glazik, *Die Islammission der russisch-orthodoxen Kirche*, 44.
[15]Ibid., 47.
[16]Ibid..
[17]Ibid., 58.

period of great confusion and rebellion, during which the state resorted to external pressure (taxes, inheritance laws, denial of property rights, military escorts for missionaries) to force Muslims to convert. Many did, but only to circumvent the laws. One wonders what happened to Ivan's instruction to "remove every injustice."

In any case, "these methods of advancing Christianity held sway for the whole of the seventeenth century—until the inauguration of Peter the Great."[18] For over two hundred years missionaries had labored among the Muslims with little success. The situation was not that different in other parts of Russia. At the end of the eighteenth century the state-driven missionary activity of the Church collapsed, and large numbers of converts reverted to shamanism and Islam. The main reasons for this failure were the facts that a) missionaries concentrated on the externals of the faith and did little by way of ongoing catechesis; b) most of the missionaries were poorly trained; c) few missionaries knew the language or the culture of the recipients; and finally, d) the Church was considered an organ of the state, which sought to force conversion through external pressure.[19]

A new approach had to be found, and it seems to have come, again, in the form of an official decree. Issued this time by Peter the Great on June 18, 1700, it reads:

> For the strengthening and the expansion of the Orthodox Christian faith and for the proclamation of the holy gospel among the idol worshiping peoples; furthermore in order to bring the tribute-paying tribes in the region of Tobolsk and the other states of Siberia to holy baptism, after consulting with the all holy patriarch of the Kievan Metropolia, the highest official ordered the following:
>
> He should with vigor search out for this holy and God pleasing work, from among the minor Russian cities and Monasteries of his region, archimandrites and igumens or other outstanding monks, a man of discipline and learning. This one should be in the Metropolia of Tobolsk and with God's help gradually bring the blind and idolatrous and otherwise unbelieving people of China and Siberia to

[18]Ibid., 62.
[19]Ibid., 112.

knowledge, to service and to worship of the true living God. In addition he should bring with him two or three disciplined and learned, not too old monks, to learn the Chinese and Mongol languages and grammar, so that they may be able to recognize the false beliefs and bring firm proofs from the holy gospel in order to pull many souls from satanic darkness into the light of the knowledge of Christ. They should also live there and build churches, celebrate liturgy and so present an example to and move the Chinese Khan and his immediate circle and the whole people toward this holy goal.[20]

Once again we find a remarkable level of missiological insight in these instructions: careful attention to culture, social structure, language, religious systems, and the need for effective apologetics. There has been some discussion about Peter's real motives. Some have suggested that it was mainly a political move designed to counter the influence of China.[21] Others have maintained that his contact with the German philosopher Leibniz convinced him to use Christianity as a means of raising the level of general education in his territories.[22] There is probably no question that the Tsar's motives were mixed, but according to Glazik there is no reason to believe that his decades-long involvement in missions reflected anything other than a real and pious concern. In any case, his participation did, in fact, facilitate considerable missionary activity in Siberia, China, and Kazan. Furthermore, what is important for our present concern is that the organization, resources, and instructions of Peter and his hierarchs—and not some strategy developed in an academy—were being implemented on the mission fields.

Beginning with Siberia, Peter and the metropolitan appointed St Philotheus (Leshchinskij) (1650–1727) as metropolitan of Tobolsk in 1702.[23] Soon after he arrived, Philotheus began to fulfill his commission by making a number of missionary journeys to the initially resistant animistic and shamanistic tribes of western Siberia. During his travels he was

[20]Glazik, *Die russisch-orthodoxe Heidenmission*, 32.
[21]Ibid., 33–36.
[22]Ibid., 38–39.
[23]Ibid., 42.

guided by additional decrees from Peter. One of these edicts, issued on July 6, 1710, included specific instructions "to burn idols and their temples wherever they were found."[24] This direct confrontation, reminiscent of St Boniface,[25] had by 1715 led to the conversion of whole tribes, including their chiefs and shamans. By the end of his last journey (1721–1726), the full extent of his success could be seen. The number of churches in this region had grown from 160 to 448, with some thirty-seven of them mission stations. The number of baptized converts had reached 40,000, including 10,000 in 1720 alone.[26]

In China the Orthodox mission had very little success, but its early history once again illustrates the direct involvement of Peter the Great. The basis for this effort seems to have been laid down by the defection of a number of the Russian soldiers captured when the Chinese defeated the Russians at the fortress of Albazin in 1685. Some forty-five of these defenders joined the Chinese imperial guard. Although they took Chinese wives and were effectively denationalized, they staunchly maintained their Orthodox faith and received an old Buddhist temple to use as a church. Their company chaplain, Fr Maximus, served them until his death. At that point the Albazin community appealed to Metropolitan Philotheus in Tobolsk for a replacement. Nothing happened until 1715, when Peter decided to send a whole mission headed by Archimandrite Hilarion (Lezhajskij). These were appointed military chaplains for the guardsmen who actually received a stipend from the Chinese government. In 1719 Peter sought to establish a "See of Peking for the descendants of the Albazin Cossacks and for the conversion of China." To that end he consecrated Archimandrite Innocent, but when the Chinese refused him entry, he was moved and became bishop of Irkutsk. In 1728, the Russo-Chinese treaty

---

[24]Ibid., 44.

[25]"To show the heathens how utterly powerless were the gods in whom they placed their confidence, he felled the oak to the thunder-god Thor, at Geismar, near Fritzlar. He had a chapel built out of the wood and dedicated it to the prince of the Apostles. The heathens were astonished that no thunderbolt from the hand of Thor destroyed the offender, and many were converted. The fall of this oak marked the fall of heathenism." Francis Mershman, "St Boniface," in *The Catholic Encyclopedia*, vol. 2 (New York: Robert Appleton, 1907), 657.

[26]Glazik, *Die russisch-orthodoxe Heidenmission*, 47–48.

of Kyatcha was signed, allowing the Russian mission in Peking only ten persons: four priests and six scholars.[27] During this period, in which the spiritual mission was coupled to the diplomatic mission, the spread of Orthodox Christianity among the Chinese was accordingly limited to a few isolated conversions.[28]

Peter the Great was also involved in reestablishing a more active outreach to the Muslims of Kazan. He turned to Metropolitan Adrian to find a qualified missionary for the Volga region. They finally found a suitable candidate for Kazan in Metropolitan Tikhon III (1699–1724). Initially the mission had some success. One of Tikhon's helpers, Hieromonk Aleksej Raifskij, reported 3,700 baptisms between 1701 and 1705.[29] But the Muslims proved very resistant. Although 30,000 baptisms were reported before his time, Tikhon found that few people knew the faith, took the sacraments, or even came to church. As a result Peter was convinced to reinstate some of his less-than-spiritual tactics to force conversions, which only made things worse.[30] However, Peter did recognize that not only the dearth of missionaries led to failure, but also the lack of properly trained missionaries. In most dioceses there were no seminaries, and priests came from clergy families. They had no formal training, and most of the missionaries could not speak the local languages. As a result, the Church had little to show for its efforts. Accordingly, part of his reform included instructions for establishing religious schools in every diocese, especially for those who wanted to become priests—in fact, for them attendance was to be required. In 1722 Tikhon was instructed—not for the first time, for he had tried it in 1707—to open such a school in Kazan. This one, too, appeared to fail. He began with fifty-two students and proposed teaching them the basics of the faith, but by the end of the year he only had five students left. Not to be discouraged, he persisted, and by the next year had forty-four students.[31] This set a pattern for future efforts. In 1738 there was another attempt at improving education under the leadership

[27]Bolshakoff, *The Foreign Missions of the Russian Orthodox Church*, 62–65.
[28]Glazik, *Die Russisch-Orthodoxe Heidenmission*, 58.
[29]Glazik, *Die Islammission der russisch-orthodoxen Kirche*, 70.
[30]Ibid., 73.
[31]Ibid., 74.

of Bishop Luka (Konashevich), who had come from the Kievan Academy to establish the Kazan Seminary. He succeeded in attracting 183 students who were required to attend courses in philosophy, the worldview of other religions, and local languages, as well as the traditional theological disciplines of history, sacramental theology, and theology.[32]

Although we may not be completely convinced of the purity of his motives, Peter the Great was directly involved not only in promoting but also informing the missionary strategies of the Church during his reign. Not everything he proposed was in keeping with Christian teaching, nor was everything he suggested successfully implemented. But much of his instruction was sound missiological thinking that enabled, guided, and supported the mission of the Church.

Soon, however, state support for mission work began to erode. During her reign (1730–1740), Anna Ivanovna declared all Christian dogma to be myth and proceeded to murder many priests and monks.[33] Nevertheless, she recognized that the christianization of the people was really a form of russification, and did some things to support missionary work. In 1740 the Commission for the Newly Baptized was constituted under the leadership of the Moscow Academy.[34] In an attempt to reverse past abuses, this office developed a distinct method of mission work. Missionaries were to win converts through their enthusiasm, not through the use of force. In actuality not much changed. Missionaries were to be protected by a contingent of three soldiers. They were still allowed to offer privileges such as gifts, a year of immunity from taxes, settlement in Russian villages, schools, and even health care.[35] There was a "veritable hunt for success figures."[36] Missionaries were sent out to preach the gospel in every region of Kazan and met with considerable success, but not among the Muslims. In fact, the Muslims despised any convert who took gifts and began to counter the Orthodox mission with advertising and active teaching. They even separated their children from those who had converted. The situation

[32]Ibid., 81.
[33]Ibid., 77.
[34]Ibid., 83.
[35]Ibid..
[36]Ibid., 84.

deteriorated until in 1742 Russia retaliated by burning down most Muslim places of worship, destroying 418 out of 536 mosques in Kazan, 98 of 133 in Tobolsk, and 29 of 40 in Astrakhan.[37]

Catherine II reversed some of the abuses, but intensified the negative trend in missions outreach. In 1768 she called together a bishops' committee "to consider all questions that had to do with the conversion of the indigenous peoples to Christianity."[38] She supported the building of mosques, disbanded the Office for Converts, and refused to limit the activities of Muslim traders and missionaries. Her Edict of Religious Freedom (1773), which granted all religions equal standing, seemed to put an end to the missionary activities of the Church.[39]

During this epoch the christianization of Russia presented the Orthodox Church with a host of challenges. First, there was the sheer geographic size of the territory. Then there were the untold numbers of tribes, ethnic groupings, languages, and religions ranging from shamanism to Islam. Since the Church had already committed itself to the use of local languages, Russian missionaries invested enormous energy into learning those languages and translating Scripture and liturgical books. For example the Gurias Fellowship, founded in 1867, had by 1910 printed and distributed over one million copies of 558 translations.[40] The following passage in the Trebnik, one of the service books, captures this complex situation.

> Around us in Great Russia live heathen who do not know God, the teaching, and the Scriptures. They do not know the Law of Moses, circumcision, the prophetic statements concerning Christ or anything of the Christian Faith. . . . They live without God in this world and are like the ancient Greek idolaters. Some worship dumb pictures, others trees, bodies of water, stones, and wild and domesticated animals. Still others pray to demons and seek help through magic. . . . We must receive all of these . . . and teach them the Christian Law and the sign

[37]Ibid., 87.
[38]Ibid., 99.
[39]Glazik, *Die russisch-orthodoxe Heidenmission*, 112–13.
[40]Glazik, *Die Islammission der russisch-orthodoxen Kirche*, 141.

of the cross, and the prayer that says "Lord Jesus Christ, Son of God, be merciful to me a sinner."[41]

With the help of their hierarchs and a few pious rulers, Russian missionaries sought to fulfill their mandate for the most part by respecting indigenous cultures and treating people with respect. They won converts through clear preaching, by planting churches, by establishing the liturgical life of those churches, and by presenting examples of Christ's love. But they were hampered in all of this by their close relationship to, if not dependency on, the state. Perceived as an instrument of the state, and using the power of the state to force conversions, they forfeited much of what they sought to accomplish. Eventually various groups rebelled, and reverted to their former religions. But the most significant setback in the 1770s was the fact that the very state that had supported missions turned on the Church and made mission almost impossible. Still, something was changing, and the mission to the Far East and Alaska would point the way to a more effective and sound approach.

3. The Missionary Instructions of St Innocent of Alaska (1858)

The mission to Alaska began in 1793[42] when the Russian businessmen Golikov and Shelikov petitioned the Holy Synod to send "a good priest with the necessary assistants"[43] to Alaska. Metropolitan Gabriel of Novgorod, St Petersburg, and Olonets was given the task of organizing the mission. Knowing the ascetic life at the Valaam monastery, he asked the superior,

[41]Glazik, *Die Russisch-Orthodoxe Heidenmission*, 249. [Glazik cites the Nomocanon, found in the 1651 *Trebnik*. The penitential Nomocanon ascribed to St John the Faster was appended to the 1651 *Trebnik*, the last pre-Nikonian. This particular text is clearly a Russian addendum to the Nomocanon.—*Ed.*]

[42]This was not the first attempt. In 1789, Metropolitan Gabriel decided to send two monks to serve in America. At this time, the idea of sending monks to serve in America did not come to fruition.

[43]Sergei Korsum with Lydia Black , *Herman: A Wilderness Saint: From Sarov, Russia to Kodiak, Alaska*, trans. Daniel Marshall, Kindle ed. (Jordanville: Holy Trinity Monastary, 2012), 13.

Hegumen Nazarius, to select a few monks to fulfill this very important obedience. Six monks and four novices were chosen for the mission.

Metropolitan Gabriel also gave Abbot Joseph a document that contained instructions for the missionaries. Based on similar instructions given to Siberian missionaries in 1769, the document is of great historical significance. First, it shows that the missionaries were going to America not simply to serve the needs of the Russian colonists and merchants but to undertake missionary work among the natives. Second, the document emphasizes that Orthodox Christianity must spread among the natives chiefly through personal example and the love that the missionaries were expected to demonstrate. A portion of the instructions of Metropolitan Gabriel says: "When Jesus Christ leads you to meet those who do not know the law of God, your first concern will be to serve as an example of good works to them so as to convert them by your personal life into obedient servants of the Lord."[44]

After an arduous journey across Siberia, the Valaam monks arrived in Kodiak, Alaska, in 1794. After initial success in bringing some Native Alaskans to the point of conversion and baptism, they encountered practical challenges that required the missiological insight of their archbishop. Archimandrite Joasaph wrote to Metropolitan Gabriel:

Following your Grace's instructions for us, we tried, through translators, to give the Americans some elementary understanding of God and his holy faith. However, many problems exist which hinder the Americans from accepting Holy Baptism. Due to our demand that they abandon polygamy, they are deprived of many benefits. But, admitting the holiness of the Christian faith, they are agreeable to give their extra wives to others. I cannot baptize them until they have been introduced to the Gospel laws and they understand their meaning. Yet due to their ardent pleas, I do not wait until they are ready for baptism. I have also noticed, that those who were baptized before do not abandon their old

[44]Thomas E Fitzgerald, *The Orthodox Church* (Westport, CT: Greenwood Publishing Group, 1998), 15–16.

habits, but continue to respect shamans and use pagan rituals. They rightfully say of themselves that they cannot be baptized due to their behavior. They also condemn the bad behavior of those who have been recently baptized. . . . Therefore, I baptize everyone who comes to the settlement of Pavlovskaia Harbor and expresses a desire to be baptized. I only try to confirm how much they understand. I explain the rules of Christian life to them.[45]

Those were not the only problems the mission faced. There were also the challenges of the many tribal groups and their distinct languages. Again, Archimandrite Joasaph wrote to the archbishop for guidance.

If we are not able to speak the local languages, then our efforts to spread the Orthodox faith will run into great problems, but, unfortunately, even a translator is not able to properly express in his own words the reason for our teaching to the Americans in their own language. We have not had the opportunity to study their language. Each tribe speaks in its own dialect: Kodiak, Alaskan, Kenai, Chugash, Koliuzh, and other tribes which live along the shore, each speak in different languages and not one of them resembles the other.[46]

What interests us here is the fact that the missionaries turned to their bishop for missiological advice. He, and not the academy, was their source for instructions on cross-cultural ministry. As if underscoring this idea, Joasaph adds, "Unfortunately, I do not have the right, without your Grace's permission, to baptize or marry these Americans. Therefore I ask you to send me specific instructions about how to behave in these circumstances."[47] What we see here is another example of the missiological negotiations that take place between a hierarch and his missionaries as they try to implement his instructions in the field.

After a number of years, the missionary work in Alaska was turned over to the monk Herman. Upon leaving for St Petersburg in 1807, Hieromonk Gideon left a set of detailed instructions for Fr Herman to follow.

[45]Korsun and Black, *Herman: A Wilderness Saint: From Sarov, Russia to Kodiak, Alaska,* 25–26.

[46]Ibid., 26–27.

[47]Ibid., 28.

Reverend Father Herman! Departing now for St Petersburg to carry out my duties, I deemed it absolutely necessary to charge you with the leadership of the American-Kodiak spiritual mission, about which I have already informed his Honor, the collegiate counselor and chief manager of this region, Alexander Andreevich Baranov. I consider it both the best arrangement and my obligation to set forth my thoughts, beyond our private discussions, in a letter to you.

Knowing your virtues and practical zeal for the betterment of this region, I am sustained by the gratifying hope that you will not neglect to inculcate in the hearts of the Russians and Americans the rules of piety, Christian charity, and friendly ties among both groups using your well-tested exhortations. You know that the first responsibility of clergy is to give an example of Christian sanctity in their own lives; I do not doubt but that you will properly guide them in this way. The particular task before your Reverence is to see that everyone, in whatever responsibility he has, carries it out in a conscientious, honest, and God-pleasing manner.[48]

Echoing the bishop's instructions to "convert them by your personal life," Gideon impresses upon Herman the need to conduct the mission in a way that honors Christ. This may well be the most basic missiological principle of all: to win over the unbelievers by one's good example. Gideon goes on to show that this "good example" includes every aspect of missionary life from buildings to finances, and the efforts to improve the living standard of the Alaskans, that is, to address their social needs in a practical way.

There are a great many leaks throughout the entire church here, about which I have already informed the Kodiak office; so it is now your responsibility to insist on its being reroofed. Vestments, sacred vessels, and books are essential to conduct divine services; it is up to you to assign supervision to either Hieromonk Athanasius or monk Joseph and to take particular care for the conscientious preservation of all these things.

[48]Ibid., 70–71.

Upon my arrival I noted with pleasure your uncommon restraint in finances and exemplary management, such as your reliable means of preserving bread . . . just as with other property, I am entirely sure that in your zeal you will do all that can be done in such matters. . . .

After my arrival on the Neva to this wild and remote region, my entire being trembled with fear at the initial sight of both the harsh climate and the barren coarseness of the land. But when I saw the hard-earned fruits from your enthusiastic efforts applied to your good-natured relationship with the Americans, as well as in the agriculture and farming they have done, then this unexpected sight filled my soul with a pleasant calm. And, after his arrival, even His Honor [Rezanov] gazed with a similar satisfaction on these accomplishments of yours in this wild-looking country. For their even greater encouragement, in your presence, he personally rewarded those Americans you had nurtured for their industrious obedience to you. Then, for the development of this region, he deemed it best to place three principal elements at the foundation: 1—agriculture, 2—education, 3—population growth. He also asked me that everyone apply their minds to these principles, so as to more rapidly enrich this region.[49]

Education was another aspect of the work that had become a standard component of Orthodox missions. Accordingly, Gideon passes on to Herman the task of administering a children's school. He gives specific recommendations for the curriculum, assures him of the necessary resources, and points him to the personnel needed for the school. The most remarkable aspect of these instructions is the admonition to fill their young hearts with the faith and fear of God. The concern is not just education in general, but spiritual formation.

It is with pleasure that I entrust particular care to Your Reverence for the Russian-American school that I have been managing. In the first group, the children must be taught reading, writing, and the short catechism; in the second group, grammar, arithmetic, sacred history, and civil history, as well as geography. In addition to the sciences, do not

[49]Ibid., 71–72.

neglect subjects relating to agriculture; instead of taking breaks, study how to prepare gardens, to plant and to sow vegetables, to weed, to gather important herbs and roots, and to catch fish. The established order in the school must be maintained in the future; instructions from me have been left there. Ivan Kad'iakskii is the teacher; Christopher Prianishnikov, his colleague; and Alexei Kotel'nikov, their assistant. Paramon Chumovitskii, with the assistance of the others, has been charged with compiling a dictionary of the Aleutian language and a short outline of the grammar of that language. He should also be your translator. Likewise, maintain proper attention to and the diligence of the group of students who are farming. The company is responsible for supplying you with every means it has that is necessary for that. Most of all, be careful to fill their young hearts with the principles of faith, fear of God, and all morality; punish them for offenses. Your love for all that is good leaves me no doubt that you will carry out all of this in the best possible manner.[50]

Finally, Gideon gives Herman an indication of the importance of divine enabling and continuing to pass down instructions from one generation of missionaries to the next. This practice might not always be easy, but it was necessary for the integrity of the mission and the good example that the missionaries were supposed to set.

Most of all, try to keep peace, quiet, and harmony among the brotherhood. I hope that monk Joseph, as your spiritual son, will not scorn your instruction, although Hieromonk Athanasius, of course, will be difficult for you. . . . You, as an experienced and skillful spiritual doctor, will keep moderation in all things. I, for my part, ask and pray the Almighty Giver of gifts that he send down upon you the strength so that you can do his good will and more.[51]

These instructions offer amazing insight into both the daily workings of the mission and the principles that were to guide it. Fr Herman receives advice on everything from maintaining the church building to

[50]Ibid., 72–73.
[51]Ibid., 73–74.

relationships with the business community, internal relations among the brotherhood, and the practicalities of surviving in a harsh environment. While some of these topics may strike the contemporary reader as less than spiritual, or perhaps unworthy of missionary instruction, let us recall the incredible challenges of the whole Alaskan project. Rather than relying on secular powers, the mission was now required to sustain itself and was thus able to maintain a greater degree of independence. Furthermore, these practical missiological negotiations took place within the context of a relationship of trust between the missionaries and their ecclesial superiors. The hierarchs were shepherds and fathers who were directly involved in the lives of the missionaries.

The most astounding example of this kind of instruction came a few years later, in 1858. Metropolitan Innocent, the former archbishop of Kamchatka and the Kuril and Aleutian Islands, sent words of guidance to the Orthodox missionaries in Alaska. In this case his instructions also had the backing and approval of Tikhon, now bishop of Alaska and the Aleutian Islands. Innocent writes:

> To leave one's native country and seek out places remote, wild, without many of the comforts of life, for the sake of turning to the path of truth men who are still wandering in the darkness of ignorance; to illumine with the light of the gospel those that have not yet beheld this saving light is truly a holy and apostolic act. Blessed is he whom the Lord selects and appoints to such a ministry. . . . Therefore do I offer here for your guidance, a few instructions. . . . [52]

According to Innocent, the most basic instruction concerning the spiritual duties of a missionary is never to be hasty in the administration of baptism, but rather to take the time needed to "instill in [the converts] the force of Christian teaching, and to guide them towards all manner of good morals, without which baptism administered to savages can hardly be called anything but an abuse of one of the greatest sacraments of the

---

[52]Translated September 12, 1979, by the Very Rev. Vladimir S. Borichevsky; original text from the *American Orthodox Messenger* 20 (1904): 534–543; most readily available in Michael Oleksa, *Alaskan Missionary Spirituality*, 238–51.

Christian religion."[53] In order to do this, the missionary must prepare for the work through prayer and by developing a modest and lowly spirit; he should recognize that the conversion of a sinner is ultimately not the result of his own skill, but the grace of God. He goes on to remind them "that if the preacher does not have within himself love for his work and for them to whom he is preaching, the very best and most eloquent expounding of the doctrine may remain absolutely without effect."[54]

In the second section of his instructions, Innocent goes on to give very practical instructions on the way in which the preaching of the gospel is to take place, including the order in which biblical topics are to be presented. Again he admonishes the missionaries not to hurry, nor to administer any sacrament without first giving adequate instruction that uses the listeners' own belief systems, social structures, and native languages. The missionaries are also advised to adjust their message according to age, condition, and time.

> Methods of instruction vary according to the state of mind, age, and faculties of him who is to be instructed. Bear in mind, with regard to this, that those with whom thou shalt have to deal, are, in manners and ideas, heathens and erring, and in grade of culture—children.[55] To these facts should be adapted the method and order of instruction in the saving truths."[56]

The actual order of presentation was to be patterned after the universal model used by God himself. Innocent observes that the law was given earlier than the gospel, and that "before the written law of Moses, the unwritten natural law was known, and the author of it is God Almighty, the Creator. With this in mind the missionary should organize his instruction as follows."[57]

[53]Ibid., 239.

[54]Ibid., 240.

[55]In spite of this seemingly condescending attitude, the Orthodox missionaries did take the Alaskan cultures and religions quite seriously, using what was already in place to craft their own presentation of the gospel.

[56]Oleksa, *Alaskan Missionary Spirituality*, 241.

[57]These instructions reflect a remarkable understanding of the local culture and reli-

Starting with the existence and harmony of visible things, demonstrate the existence (which, however, none of those people appear to doubt); the almightiness, power, and glory of the Creator of the Universe; His goodness, knowledge of all things, etc. At the same time with this, tell them the story of the creation of the first man, and of his being the progenitor of all men and peoples, who, in this respect, are living monuments and visible proof of the Creator's supreme power and wisdom. Then, explain how man consists of soul and body, in what he differs from other animate beings, how he is possessed of an immortal spirit, and indicate the intent of God in crating man, i.e.,—blessedness.[58]

Note the clear connection to the cultural setting in which the missionaries were working. St Innocent is advising the missionaries to start with something they had in common with their listeners, i.e., something they shared. The Alaskan people were, for the most part, animists. As such, they already had some understanding of a creator and creation, and a very positive understanding of the created order. All beings, including animals, were thought to have spirits, and there were specific rules that governed human behavior, particularly in dealing with animals. The Native Alaskans could easily understand the concept of a creator and the inherent dignity of each creature. Their sacred tales, songs, and dances included stories of their origins and defined their identity as human beings, as "the people." They also believed that when the first human beings appeared, they were "given their own way to live appropriately, in harmony with the forces, spirit, and creatures with whom they share the cosmos."[59] On this basis they could appreciate the idea of a law or rules needed to regulate human life and preserve order between God and his world.

---

gion. The native peoples were animists who had no trouble with the idea of a creator, beneficent provider, and orderer of nature. They may well have had their own flood stories, their own understanding of what was right and wrong, a clear understanding of the role the ancestors played in their lives, and so on. So this presentation of the gospel starts with common understanding of creation, moves through similar and understandable concepts like the law and the effects of lawlessness, and then on to the offer made by Christ.

[58]Oleksa, *Alaskan Missionary Spirituality*, 241.

[59]Ibid., 8.

Innocent suggests that the second phase of evangelistic teaching should quite naturally include information about various aspects of divine law.

> Further, show them that the moral Law of Moses is the divinely writ-
> ten natural law; it is the means towards achieving blessedness. Do
> all this do simply and concisely. (Note:) When speaking of the law,
> thou shalt surely hear, from the crudest savages, things confirming
> the law, which is graven upon the tablets of every human heart. Thus,
> for instance, who does not know that a man should honor his parents,
> that he should not steal, kill, etc.? Try to arouse this feeling in them,
> and make use of it for thy purpose.
>
> When thy hearers shall have become convinced of the existence
> of God and the law, then (but not before) show them the necessity
> of observing the law, as being the will of God, and the visible conse-
> quences of not observing and of breaking it. Illustrate this with a brief
> narrative of the Great Flood (the tradition of the Deluge—(the tradi-
> tion of it, though confused, exists among savage races)—as being the
> consequence of not keeping the law of God: tell them of the blessing
> bestowed by God upon the Patriarchs after the Deuluge, and especially
> upon Abraham (whose descendants exist to this day)—as being the
> consequence of keeping the law.[60]

In other words, the missionaries were to tap into an existing world-view. They were to preach the gospel "without directly attacking the traditional shamanistic world view of the natives."[61] In fact, they were to present Christianity as the "fulfillment of what the Alaskans already knew."[62] With this foundation set down, the missionary was to move on to a presentation of Christ and the redemption he offers.

> Only now begin the Evangelical instruction proper, on the way that
> Jesus Christ Himself began it, i.e., by announcing repentance and con-
> solation, and the approach of the Kingdom of Heaven. Try to lead
> them to a feeling of repentance or something nearly akin to it. This

[60]Ibid., 241.
[61]Ibid., 13.
[62]Ibid.

can be accomplished by convincing them that they will inevitably be punished for disregarding the law written within their hearts, in this life and the next, or if not in this life, so much more heavily, and for all eternity, in the next; that no one can, of his own power, escape these punishments, etc.

Here thou shouldst shape thy speech so as to arouse in them a certain dread of the future; and when thou shalt have brought them into this frame of mind, then do thou announce to them Jesus Christ, the Savior, Redeemer and Hope of all men, to give them comfort.

Note. To bring souls to a state of repentance and contrition is one of the preacher's most difficult tasks. But this condition is one of the most important factors in the work of conversion; it is as the ploughed up soil, ready to receive the seed of Christianity, which then can sink into the very depth of the heart, and, with the later assistance of grace, can bear abundant fruit.

Having demonstrated the necessity of the redemption of the human race and shown the greatness of God's love towards men, thou shalt tell of the coming into the world of the promised Redeemer,—of His birth before the ages from the Father (this will be the time and the place to touch on the mystery of the Holy Trinity),—of the incarnation, nativity, and earthly life of Jesus Christ, of His teaching, sufferings, and death, of the resurrection of the dead (in which all American savages believe in their own particular way), of the future, and the retribution to be dealt to the good and the wicked, according to their deeds.

Lastly, shalt thou tell them that Jesus Christ, during His life on earth, had many disciples out of whom He chose twelve, imparting to them special grace and power, and whom He sent forth into the world, to preach the gospel unto all creation;—then tell them how all that those chosen ones taught, and all that Jesus commanded is recorded in their writings, which have come down to us, and which are known to nearly all the nations of the earth,—and how all good and simple-minded men to whom it has been given to hear their teachings have received them with joy and have followed, and are following in His steps. Tell them that such men are usually called Christians, and that

those among them who have strictly kept the commandments of Jesus
Christ have become saints, and the bodies of many among them have
reposed these many centuries exempt from corruption, etc.[63]

It was only after having reached this point of understanding that the
listeners were to be baptized and brought into the Church. This gives obvious significance to Innocent's advice not to hurry the process, but to take
the time needed for a real understanding of the Christian message before
the sacraments are administered.

> When thou shalt see that thy hearers have understood thee, and when
> they express a wish to be counted among the flock of Christ, then tell
> them: a) of the conditions upon which they may be admitted among
> the faithful; b) of Holy Baptism, as the means of regeneration of water
> and the Spirit, which opens the new Christian life, and of the other
> Sacraments as the means of receiving the grace of Jesus Christ; and,
> c) of the manner after which he should live who aims at being a true
> Christian and, consequently, at obtaining all the fruits of salvation.[64]

As for the conditions of reception into the Church, Innocent insists
that the convert "1) he must renounce his former creed, give up Shamanism and not listen to the Shamans; 2) he must not observe any customs
contrary to Christianity; 3) he must agree to perform all things that shall
be demanded of him by the new law and the Church; and 4) He must
confess his sins."[65] This, then, represents the initial proclamation of the
gospel, which should be sufficient for new converts. Once in the Church,
the convert's continued education should include "spiritual interpretation
of the ten commandments, etc., expounding the words of Christ written
down in the gospel, the teachings of the apostles, and (in part) the traditions of the holy Fathers."[66]

These instructions present a clear understanding of the goal of mission, and a culturally sensitive and practical implementation of that task.

[63]Ibid., 241–42.
[64]Ibid., 243.
[65]Ibid.
[66]Ibid., 244.

They represent remarkably insightful missiological thinking arising not in the confines of an academy, but rather from the hierarchs responsible for those in the mission field. Finally, we note that Innocent's instructions "were formally approved by the Holy Synod of the Russian Orthodox Church on November 6, 1840, and thenceforth had canonical authority for all missionaries under its jurisdiction."[67]

---

4. Documents of the Missions Department of the Russian Orthodox Church (1999–2014)[68]

Since its release from the bondage of communism, the contemporary Russian Orthodox Church (ROC) has renewed its commitment to missionary responsibility. In keeping with the traditional patterns, this revival of missiological thinking is taking place within the context of ecclesial structures and has been documented and disseminated by means of archpastoral instructions. In 1995 Bishop John of Belgorod was appointed head of the Missionary Planning Committee, a research group seeking ways to revive the missionary activity of the Russian Orthodox Church. That same year the Missionary Department of the ROC was established, with Bishop John chosen to become its head. Later that year, he issued the first in a series of important decrees "on the revival of the missionary activity of the Russian Orthodox Church."

Based on this preliminary work, the Russian Church began a season of vigorous missionary activity. However,

the more they advanced in doing mission, the more they found that their theological reflections on mission needed to be analyzed and summarized in theoretical missionary documents. Three important official writings give theological definition to the missionary practice

---

[67]Joseph Irvin, *St. Innocent's Missionary Instructions* (Lulu, 2013), Endnote 2, Appendix A.

[68]"The Official Information Resource of the Department of Missions of the Moscow Patriarchate," Synodal Department of Missions of the Moscow Patriarchate, accessed June 2, 2015, портал-миссия.рф.

that the church was already carrying out: the Concept of 1995, the Report of 2004, and the Concept of 2005.[69]

These documents reveal the evolving missiological thinking of the ROC. According to Valentin Kozhuharov, the 2005 document clearly defines mission as "the fulfillment of the Great Commission of Christ: 'Go into all the world and preach the gospel to all creation' (Mk 16.15)."[70] Preaching the gospel leads to the ultimate goal of mission, *theosis*. This vision of mission is set within a threefold theological context.

> Without understanding what the soteriological principle means in the lives of believers, no possible idea could ever explain the ardent wish for the salvation of ordinary faithful Orthodox Christians in the churches.
>
> Without understanding the ecclesiastical structure of the Church— its hierarchical, sacramental and liturgical constitution, no proper comprehension of the sacrificial ministry and faithful life of believers in the local churches and within the apostolic succession (ecclesiastical hierarchy) could be achieved.
>
> Without understanding the eschatological purpose of believers' lives and of the Church as a whole, no sound understanding of the mission of Christ and the mission of the Church could be reached, because the mission of the Church is "to announce the *eschaton*— salvation in Jesus Christ."[71]

This leads us to the ultimate purpose of missions, namely "building up eucharistic communities by the example of the one founded by Jesus Christ."[72] Between 1995 and 2005 there was a decade of intense activity that included many of the practical forms of mission defined in the documents. These included short-term missionary expeditions by train,

---

[69]Valentin Kozhuharov, "Christian Mission in Eastern Europe," *International Bulletin of Missionary Research* 37. 2 (2013): 73–76, 78, 73.

[70]Valentin Kozhuharov, "Christian Mission as Teaching and Liturgical Life: An Orthodox Perspective," *Baptistic Theologies* 2 (2010): 1–45, 8.

[71]Ibid., 8–9.

[72]Ibid., 9.

ship, and car, during which groups of missionaries ministered to diverse populations in various parts of the country, as well as training seminars at the local and diocesan level. In keeping with ancient practice, this recent revival of missionary activity in Russia was initiated by the Church and defined by the responsible hierarchs.

All of this activity was bound to have an effect on the academic community,[73] and indeed several seminaries—for example, the theological seminary at Belgorod, St Tikhon Theological Institute in Moscow, and the Pimen Orthodox Institute, St Petersburg—were given over to the training of missionaries through standardized courses and departments of mission. An expression of this budding academic interest was the publication of a textbook on missiology. This manual "was prepared by a team of authors: teachers of missiology in the theological schools of the ROC. That is, it is an expression of the conciliar missionary mind. . . . it consists of two parts: 'The Theology of Mission' and 'The Principles and Methods of Missionary Activity.'"[74] In circumstances where the mission was perceived by many Orthodox as "innovation," it sought to establish an ecclesial environment conducive to its cause.

In 2010, the Department of Mission of the Russian Orthodox Church held what it called the fourth Congress of Diocesan Missionaries. This was a continuation of a series of conferences held before the Revolution in Moscow (1887, 1891), Kazan (1897), Kiev (1908), and at the St Grigory Bizyukov missionary monastery in 1917. Two important documents were prepared by Archbishop John for the two preceding congresses: "Missionary Congresses and the Prospects of the Orthodox Mission in the XXI Century" for the second congress (1999), and "The Missionary Service of the Russian Orthodox Church and the Challenges of the Modern World" for the third congress (2002). Once again we see missiological reflection being done by the hierarchs. In the first document, Archbishop John directly addresses the need for missiological thought.

[73]The Missions Concept 2005 of the Russian Orthodox Church included a call for establishing missionary schools. Kozhuharov, "Christian Mission in Eastern Europe," 10.

[74]Panteleimon (Berdnikov), *Textbook Missiology*; ⟨http://www.portal-missia.ru/sites/default/files/Отзывы/www.portal-mis⟩. Cited text translated into English by Brenda Seah Mikitish for this book.

What we need today is the uncovering of the treasury of the Church's liturgical tradition, its development, and the entrance of the gospel truths into the heart of the life of the people—through instruction, education, and the attraction of as many laymen as possible to missionary activity. All this is a vital necessity to, and the anticipated result of, our mission.

Apostleship, or the witness of missionaries by their personal example in being "an example in speech and conduct, in love, in faith, in purity" (1 Tim 4.12), is the fruit of the long process of the education of future pastors. It is doubtless that the most outstanding missionaries were called by the Lord to the missionary service of apostleship. Recall the example of St Innocent (Veniaminov), who by his own account "was all aflame with desire" to preach among the Aleuts. However, the system of instruction in the missiological disciplines is only now beginning to be developed, and together with the already-begun reform of theological education, we need to focus as much as possible on the publication of training aids, specialized monographs, and theological studies on the problems of mission.

So that missionary work does not turn into an academic exercise for students of the academy, it is necessary to place the appropriate emphases in the process of preparing future pastors, combining their instruction with social service in hospitals, prisons, military units, and so on.[75]

This chapter has traced the path of mission activity and missiology in the Eastern Church. We have seen how the Russian Church has recently established a Department of Missions and initiated a new stage in missionary practice and theology. "Similar missionary tendencies are taking place in the other Balkan countries, as well as elsewhere in Eastern Europe."[76] But as Kozhuharov observes, the ROC started with missionary activity and only then tried to theologically define what Orthodox

[75] Archbishop John of Belgorod and Stary Osko, "Missionary Congresses and Prospects of the Orthodox Mission in the XXI Century," ‹http://www.portal-missia.ru›, June 3, 2015.

[76] Kozhuharov, "Christian Mission in Eastern Europe," 75.

mission was.[77] As it turned out the theology lying behind that practical activity fully corresponded with the teaching of the Holy Fathers and the modern Orthodox theological research in Orthodox mission.[78] In other words, recent activity confirmed "the true understanding of mission as interpreted and practiced in the Orthodox church for centuries, though it has never been called 'mission' but 'ecclesiastical discipline' and 'ecclesiastical tasks', and simply witnessing."[79]

Another way of interpreting these developments is to say that since the work of proclaiming the gospel has been the responsibility of ruling bishops, they are the ones who have contributed the most to the missiological heritage of the Orthodox Church. There have been schools and missionary training institutes, but until very recently we find little evidence of a university-based academic discipline dedicated to the study of the missionary enterprise.[80] Today we are witnessing the birth of just such

---

[77]"... to reflect theologically on what has been carried out by the church means to describe her practical activities in terms of the teaching of the church and her theology. It could be said that this is the more reliable way of theological reflection, i.e., from the church's practice to theological generalization, instead of defining where in the practice of the church the general theological considerations have been applied." "Theological Reflections on the Missionary Activity of the Russian Orthodox Church," *International Review of Mission* 95, no. 378-379 (2006): 371–82, 371.

[78]Today, when we see the fulfilment of this primary task in the Russian Orthodox Church (ROC), and when we call it "a mission", we do not presume that the church has undertaken something new or innovative to interest the people of the 21st century. Rather, it is the same church's catechetical and eucharistic activity that has been carried out for twenty centuries." Ibid.

[79]"Mission in an Orthodox Christian Context: Witnessing Christ as Pastoral Responsibility," ‹http://www.edinburgh2010.org/fileadmin/files/edinburgh2010/files/pdf/Valentin%20Kozhuharov%202009-4-30.pdf›, 10/25/2014. Interestingly, Glazik made the same point: "... the official Dogmatic, which developed late, as well as exegesis provided no specific guidance for a specifically Russian theory of mission. However, by way of contrast, a number of ideas could be inferred from the Liturgy." Glazik goes on to say that the word mission didn't even appear in Russian language until the middle of the 18th century and that in connection with the China mission, which was actually a diplomatic mission led by monks. On the one hand, the term developed in a rather narrow way as the responsibility of each priest for his own flock and, on the other hand, in a broader way as the spread of the Gospel in close connection with the development of the Russian State. Ibid., 249–50.

[80]"Mission as an active program of carrying the Gospel to lands or peoples where Jesus

a discipline. With its active involvement in missionary outreach, the Russian Orthodox Church has, like its Western counterparts, recognized the need for "scientific" study of the Church's mission to the world. Unlike in the West, however, this work remains firmly in the hands of the ecclesial authorities and hierarchs, even though some of it is now being done in the academy.

Christ is not known has not yet found its proper place in the practice of the Orthodox churches of Eastern Europe. For this reason there are no mission departments within those churches, with the exception of the Russian and the Romanian Orthodox Churches. For the same reason missiology is not taught in Orthodox theological schools, again with the exception of Russia and Romania." Kozhuharov, "Christian Mission in Eastern Europe," 74-75.

3

Points of Departure: An Orthodox Missiology

Missiology is not yet taught at most Orthodox theological schools, but there are few, if any, Protestant seminaries in which the systematic study of the Church's missionary responsibility has not been accepted as part of the regular program. Most of these institutions have incorporated missiology into the curriculum as an independent field of study, and not as a mere guest afforded only occasional treatment under one of the other disciplines. If this discipline were to catch on in Orthodox academies, what, in light of the historical developments, might it look like? Is missiology really an academic discipline? How would it differ from traditional theological disciplines?

1. A Working Definition of Mission

In order to answer that question, we need a working definition of mission. Based on our discussion thus far, an Orthodox definition would view mission as a function or activity of the Church that involves:

1) *Sending authorized delegates* to proclaim the gospel to all nations and ethnic groupings that have not yet heard it.

2) *Making disciples*, which includes bringing men to the point of conversion, teaching them all that Christ has commanded, and baptizing them.

3) *Establishing eucharistic-liturgical communities* to serve as bases of ongoing missionary operation.

4) *Teaching the fundamentals of the faith,* which encompasses all educational ministries of the Church.

5) Addressing social and humanitarian needs through the ancient practice of almsgiving.

6) *Re-evangelizing* peoples and areas that were once Christian.

Throughout its long history, the Eastern Church has done all of these things under the able leadership of its hierarchs. However, today there seems to be a desire and a need to authorize others (priests, theologians, scholars) to codify, summarize, and articulate the basic principles involved by producing textbooks and teaching classes at ecclesial academies and schools—in other words, by developing a whole new academic discipline, i.e., missiology, the scientific study of mission as a whole.

2. The Four Sub-Disciplines of Missiology

If the above-mentioned activities represent the essential tasks of mission, then the overall study of that work naturally falls into four distinct areas:

1) The *survey* of mission, which is a description of the current state of the Church's mission on the basis of reliable, verifiable information, with a view toward motivating the faithful to action.

2) The *history* of mission, which analyzes missionary activity in the past by asking how and under what conditions Christianity was spread, and what methods, forms, and principles were developed and applied.

3) The *theology* of mission, which delineates the biblical and traditional justification, nature, motive, and ecclesial resources for mission; establishes the eucharistic-liturgical context of mission; defines the content of the gospel and subsequent teaching; and provides guidelines or basic principles for the development of the various forms and practices of mission.

4) The *theory* of mission strategy, which involves applying the outcomes of historical and theological analysis to the development of practical strategies needed to accomplish the goals of all six aspects of mission: evangelism, discipleship, liturgy and Eucharist, teaching, social work, and re-evangelism.[1]

From what we can see at this early stage, this is in fact the way in which the Orthodox vision of the discipline is evolving. An example is the organization of the textbook on missiology produced by the ROC. It clearly covers both the theology and the theory of mission, and is divided into two sections.

In the first section one finds a theological conception of the foundations of missionary service in its various aspects (ecclesiological, canonical, soteriological, culturological, etc.), an understanding of the goals and objectives of mission, and a recognition of missiology's position within the system of theological disciplines. Importantly for future servants in the field of Christ, there is a correct placement of priorities in determining the strategies and tactics of missionary activity.

The second part presents very diverse material on missiology: mission in schools, in the media, on the Internet, among youths, soldiers, prisoners, migrants, and people of other faiths, as well as the organization of missionary congregations, camps, and expeditions. A range of other concerns, pertinent to missiology and very valuable and useful for future missionaries, is also discussed.[2]

We also observe a growing interest in the survey and history of mission. Apparently the history section of the aforementioned textbook was dropped from the second edition because a number of books on historical aspects of Orthodox mission were planned, such as *A Biographical Dictionary of the Missionaries of the Russian Orthodox Church*, and *Essays on History of the Missionary work of the Russian Orthodox Church*.[3]

---

[1] I first explored this approach to missiology in a paper given on my inauguration into the Naomi Fausch chair of missiology at Trinity Evangelical Divinity School. See Edward Rommen, "Missiology's Place in the Academy" (Deerfield: Trinity Evangelical Divinity School, 1991).

[2] "Textbook Missiology."

[3] Panteleimon (Berdnikov), ibid.

3. Is Missiology an Academic Discipline?

Even with this clearly evolving structure, we still have to ask whether missiology can really be considered an academic discipline. Is it, for example, on a par with dogmatics, church history, and exegesis? According to the Oxford English Dictionary, a discipline is "a branch of instruction of education; a department of learning or knowledge; a science or art in its educational aspect."[4] This usage is based on the term's development as an antithesis to "doctrine."[5] A doctrine or an abstract theory is the possession of a teacher, while the activity of imparting that material to students is what characterizes a discipline. This implies that any area of study that we are going to call a discipline in its own right must have

1) A limited or clearly defined scope, i.e., field of study;

2) A clear definition of its relationship to the area of knowledge of which it is a branch;

3) A clear methodology;

4) A special "doctrine" or set of theories, including a base of supporting literature;

5) A cadre of experts, trained in and able to impart those theories.

Each of the four subdivisions of missiology represents a clear and distinct field of study in that it deals with phenomena that are demonstrably discipline-specific. With regard to the specificity of the phenomena under consideration, we admit to a great deal of overlap with other theological disciplines. However, missiological disciplines, although they presuppose and depend upon traditional theological disciplines, are in a position to make unique contributions. In that sense, missiological disciplines may

---

[4]James Augustus Henry Murray, R. W. Burchfield, and Philological Society (Great Britain), *The Oxford English Dictionary; Being a Corrected Re-Issue with an Introduction, Supplement, and Bibliography of a New English Dictionary on Historical Principles*, 13 vols. (Oxford: At the Clarendon Press, 1978), s.v. "discipline."

[5]"Discipline, as pertaining to the disciple or scholar, is antithetical to doctrine, the property of the doctor or teacher; hence, in the history of the words, doctrine is more concerned with abstract theory and discipline with practice or exercise." Ibid.

be viewed as being derived from what we could call "parent disciplines." In the area of history, missiology derives from the general study of church history, but is particularly suited for the task of documenting the development of mission societies, providing biographies of missionaries, and analyzing the circumstances under which Christianity was introduced to various countries. In the realm of theology, missiology is derived from dogmatics and seeks, among other things, to provide a biblical justification for missionary outreach and to contribute principles that guide our interaction with the world, including non-Christian religions and cross-cultural situations. In each case, the work done by Orthodox missiologists, of which we now have quite a few, must be executed in a manner acceptable to the parent discipline. In other words, mission history would need to be recognized as legitimate history by the church historians.

As for a specific methodology, each of the four areas has, in fact, established its own "internal" set of principles for dealing with the phenomena they examine. The results of this work are usually formulated in terms of axiomatic summary statements, which can be evaluated in terms of generally accepted academic criteria. In other words, this work is carried out in a logically consistent and systematic way. Here, of course, is one area in which Orthodoxy has a great deal to contribute with its emphasis on and understanding of mystery and the mystical. Missiology, then, is a legitimate academic discipline. It is the systematic study of all aspects of the Church's missionary activity. The missiological sub-disciplines (history, survey, theology, and theory) function to facilitate the flow of data at the confluence of traditional theological activity and the "real time" execution of the Church's missionary mandate.

4. The Four Tasks of a Theology of Mission

We can now begin to see how a theology of mission, the particular concern of this volume, fits into the overall framework of missiology. Let us identify at least four essential tasks for that theological work.

First, the theology of mission will seek to articulate the biblical and traditional justification, nature, motive, and ecclesial resources for mission. This step will take us a long way toward a definitive clarification of the terminology needed to discuss, teach, and practice mission. In the almost anti-missionary[6] atmosphere of the modern world, such clarification becomes a most important task. Politics, the social sciences, economics, other religions, and sometimes even the Church itself are unified in their opposition to the missionary enterprise. Factors such as colonialism, which once facilitated missions, have now become the fuel of the missionary's chief critics. Walter Freytag captured the essence of the dilemma in his now well-known statement, "At one time mission had problems; today mission is itself a problem."[7] This, then, is a time in which mission is being called into question as never before, and only a missionary outreach solidly grounded in and based upon the word of God and the tradition of the Church can survive.

Second, the theology of mission will seek to establish the eucharistic-liturgical origin and context of mission. Here the missiologist will seek to demonstrate that all formal missionary work begins within the Church, and thus this work must be authorized, initiated, and overseen by the hierarchs. At the same time, mission theology will seek to elaborate on the general responsibility of all believers. The eucharistic assembly is the very heart of that general witness, since at the end of every liturgy the faithful are dismissed into the world as witnesses of what they have seen. This activity has been called the "liturgy after the liturgy,"[8] and it needs further theological elucidation.

Third, the theology of mission will define the content of the gospel and the subsequent teachings necessary for making disciples. This involves two main questions. First, just what is the gospel? What information has to be communicated in order for us to say that we have engaged in evangelism? Second, how might we establish a core curriculum—the basic

[6]H. D. Beeby, *Canon and Mission*, Christian Mission and Modern Culture (Harrisburg, PA: Trinity Press International, 1999), 40–42.

[7]Ibid., 39.

[8]Bria, *The Liturgy after the Liturgy: Mission and Witness from an Orthodox Perspective*.

biblical and theological content necessary for the ongoing education of a mature believer?

Fourth, the theology of mission will develop basic guidelines or principles for the practical implementation of the various aspects of mission: evangelism, discipleship, eucharistic communities, education, social concerns, and re-evangelization. These biblically based, theologically reasoned instructions will guide the Church's encounter with the world. What help, for example, does the theology of mission provide with regard to the confrontation with revitalized non-Christian religions? How do we approach the question of truth, especially the issue of Christianity's claim of absolute truth? What of our encounter with a multi-cultural world? What belongs to our cultural baggage, and what has validity across cultural boundaries? And what of the limitations placed upon us by non- or even anti-Christian political systems? To what degree is resistance justifiable? Can a missionary be involved in politics?

5. A Basic Missions-Theological Methodology

All of the above raises the question of just how we will approach these tasks. In light of the discussion of Orthodox theology in the introduction and these specific missiological tasks, we can now define a theological methodology in terms of three distinct steps.

First, theology involves gathering data relevant to the stated missiological tasks from all valid sources of Orthodox theology. The data needed by the theologian is available from a variety of sources, which we will discuss below. For now we can say that this data can be grouped into two general classes. One is divine revelation, i.e., the self-revelation of God as evident in creation, in the life and work of Christ, in Scripture, and in the tradition of the Church. The other source is the human situation: everything that is observable (experiential) in human existence, including both negative and positive, contemporary and historical aspects. As used here, the "positive" aspects of human experience are seen to issue from God's creative involvement in things human. They are reflected in individually expressed rational, emotional, and social traits, as well as their cumulative expressions, i.e., philosophy, science, art, community, and tradition. The "negative" aspects involve evidence of sin and its effects, and confront us with questions of evil, injustice, death, etc. This twofold categorization is not intended to imply parity between the divine and human classes of data, but rather some degree of correlation. We need to recognize that the theologian's cultural context will determine some of his preconceptions as well as the fundamental questions he asks. But these questions do not in any way dictate or alter the content of divine revelation; rather, they are ultimately subject to and informed by the absolute sufficiency of revelation.

Second, the theologian seeks to determine the meaning of each piece of data as it has been interpreted by the Church. To do that each element needs to be keyed to pertinent biblical data. Here we will make use of general exegetical tools and hermeneutical principles. However, this work also has to be subjected to the scrutiny of the "mind of the Church." We will not simply trust our own interpretive skills, nor those of our contemporaries. Since the Church, under the leadership of its bishops, is the proper context for interpretation, we will always want to ask how particular passages of Scripture are and have been understood by the Church. This provides a basis for evaluating our conclusions and enables further refinement or, where necessary, reformulation. These two steps in the theological process will be dealt with in Part II of this work.

Finally, the theologian must use these understandings to create a coherent system of axiomatic summary statements or principles that answer to the stated tasks of a theology of mission. These statements will become the blueprint of the actual execution of the missionary work. They will help us determine what we can and cannot do in the name of outreach. For example, our understanding of the nature of the Church will clearly prevent us from making use of secular business tactics, such as branding, marketing, etc., in our effort to expand and plant the Church. The development of this system of missiological thought will be taken up in Part III.

PART TWO

On the Sources for an Orthodox Theology of Mission

As indicated above, the first step of our theological work is to gather data on missiological concerns from valid sources of Orthodox theology. Our understanding of possible sources is derived from the Church's teaching on tradition, that is, from the several aspects of God's self-revelation. Here we make a threefold distinction similar to that used by St Paul (1 Cor 15.1–3 and 2 Tim 2.2). His approach is based on the verbs "to receive" (παραλαμβάνω, *paralambanō*), as in "I received from the Lord" (1 Cor 11.23); "to give" (παραδίδωμι, *paradidōmi*), as in "which also I delivered (gave) unto you" (1 Cor 11.23); and "to keep" (κατέχω, *katechō*), as in, "You keep the traditions just as I delivered (παραδίδωμι, *paradidōmi*) them to you" (1 Cor 11.2). He speaks of data that is given by the Lord, received by the apostles and their successors, and kept unaltered by the Church.[1] This gives us the three primary sources of theological data: revelation, tradition, and the Church.

[1]Nikos A Nissiotis, "The Unity of Scripture and Tradition," *Greek Orthodox Theological Review* 11.2 (Winter 1966): 183–208, 188.

1. Revelation (that which has been given by God)

Theology is best viewed as the pursuit of knowledge of—or rather, a vision of—God. While the necessary conditions for the acquisition of such knowledge are faith and personal purity, we also recognize that we are dependent on God's self-revelation; that is, we operate within a revelatory economy where there is a descending as well as an ascending movement. The descending movement is predicated on revelation, or a series of divine self-revelations that reveal knowledge about the divine being and person of God. Within this aspect of the revelatory economy two types of revelation can be identified: natural and supernatural. No sharp distinction is made between the two since one complements the other, i.e., both reveal the same God, although natural revelation is fully understood only in the light of supernatural revelation.

a) Natural Revelation

Natural revelation allows us to access the information contained in the created order. This is possible because, as Staniloae suggests, the cosmos is organized in a way that corresponds to our capacity for knowing.[2] The created order and human nature bear the stamp of divine rationality. Human beings have a reason capable of consciously knowing the rationality of creation as well as their own being. There exists, then, an intimate relationship between human beings and the Creator by way of the created order. As the only personal entities of creation, human beings are able to understand the meaning and reasons of creation as well as something of the supreme personal being, God himself. This communion with God is the ultimate end, the highest meaning of humanity. Therefore, it is to faith in God that the natural order is intended to move. However, the difficulty with natural revelation is that it is, at least with reference to the divine being, ambiguous and open to doubt. These inherent limitations

[2]Dumitru Staniloae, *Revelation and Knowledge of the Triune God*, trans. Ioan Ionita and Robert Barringer, vol. 1, *The Experience of God: Orthodox Dogmatic Theology* (Brookline, MA.: Holy Cross Orthodox Press, 1994), 1.

are exacerbated by human sinfulness, and have led to creatures distorting the knowledge of God and obscuring the true meaning of their own lives.

b) Supernatural Revelation

Supernatural revelation is provided as an aid to the darkened heart and mind of human beings. It specifies and realizes the goal of natural revelation. It is, in essence, a communicative process whereby God causes his word to appear directly in the mind of his creatures, bypassing their sin-distorted reasoning faculties. This process takes place by means of miraculous events and their explication, through the word given to the prophets and relayed orally and in writing, and ultimately in the incarnation of Christ—the Word of God with us. The incarnation represents both the deepest descent of God and the highest ascent of the creature, culminating, at least potentially, in full communion between the two.

In order for sinful human beings to fully apprehend the truth of supernatural revelation, their rational and spiritual faculties must first be sensitized by the Holy Spirit. The divine word is authenticated or validated by the Spirit. In fact, so vital is the Holy Spirit's contribution to the effectiveness of supernatural revelation that Jesus promises to send the Spirit to carry on this work after our Lord's ascension (Jn 16.5–15). One might say that the whole revelatory process culminates in the descent of the Holy Spirit at Pentecost. Revelation, then, is not merely a disclosure of theoretical information about God; it is God's act of descending to creation and raising creatures up to him, so that in Christ they might find the deepest possible union with God.[3] Supernatural revelation came to its close in Christ.[4] Nothing more is added because he is the fullness of revelation: in him is the fullness of the knowledge of God, and the possibility of *theoria*.

[3] Ibid., 34–35.
[4] Ibid., 37.

2. Tradition (that which has been received and handed on by the apostles)

Even though nothing more is to be added to revelation as fulfilled in Christ, the revelation already given continues to be active. It is to be put into effect, i.e., that knowledge is to be passed on to the lives of believers in order to bring them into union with God. To that end the fullness of divine revelation in Christ was entrusted to the apostles for further dissemination under the guidance of the Holy Spirit.[5] Viewed in this way, we see that tradition has two components: a) the totality of the various ways by which everything given in Christ passes over into the reality of human life, first via the apostles and then through them to others, and b) the actual process of transmitting these ways, this life in Christ, both verbally and in writing, from generation to generation.

a) Tradition as the Totality of Life in Christ

Tradition is not limited to mere doctrine, nor is it a set of commandments and moral rules or a collection of customs. Rather, it is that which has been given to us: the life in Christ,[6] the life of the Trinity as revealed by Christ and confirmed by the Holy Spirit. Christ gave to the apostles everything that the Church has today, including his teachings, his commandments, and all of his instructions for the practice of the faith. This initial deposit was not a static collection of doctrines and rubrics, but instead a living, dynamic baseline for engaging the world under the guidance of the Holy Spirit. We see this at work in the Jerusalem council (Acts 15). The decisions of that council were added to the apostolic deposit. The Church therefore has the possibility of becoming, of developing, but not of altering the baseline. Anything added must conform to the original deposit. Over time this deposit "developed," becoming what we call the collective consciousness

---

[5]Ibid.
[6]Abp Kokkinakis Athenagoras, Abp of Thyateira, "Tradition and Traditions," *St Vladimir's Seminary Quarterly* 7.3 (1963): 102–14, 103.

or mind of the Church. In this sense apostolic tradition is a "dynamic and active reality, which is lived by the people of God in the Church."[7]

b) Tradition as the Process of Giving, Proclaiming, Preserving

Tradition, then, is actively passed on from one generation to the next. However, it "does not mean merely transmission or transference of certain things or ideas from one person to another. In both biblical and patristic contexts it means gift, giving, offering, delivering, and even performing benevolences and charity."[8] In the broadest sense we can speak of an inner-Trinitarian tradition as evidenced in Matthew 11.27, where Jesus says, "All things have been delivered to me by my Father." In John 10.29, Jesus uses the word "I give" or "I offer" (δίδωμι, *didōmi*), often paired with "I take" or "I receive" (λαμβάνω, *lambanō*), to express the same thing. What is given and received within the Trinity is simply everything as such, in an eternal and infinite exchange.

A remarkable extension of this idea is found in John 17.8: "For I have given to them the words which you have given me; and they have received them." Here St John incorporates a communicative aspect, the verbalization (words) of divine truth. Not surprisingly, then, the basic term "I hand over," "I hand down," or "I entrust" (παραδίδωμι, *paradidōmi*) is frequently complemented by three synonyms throughout the New Testament: "I proclaim" (κηρύσσω, *kēryssō*), "I teach" (διδάσκω, *didaskō*), and "I bring or preach good news" (εὐαγγελίζω, *euangelizō*). These terms are often associated with the missionary outreach of the Church. What is most important here is that they clearly indicate that the truth that is given is supposed to be passed on.

In anticipation of this process, Christ promises the Holy Spirit (Jn 16, Acts 1.8), whose descent on Pentecost enables and guides the apostles. Indeed, this movement of truth from Christ to the apostles and to a succession of their followers is evident within the New Testament. In Hebrews 2.3 we read, "How shall we escape if we neglect so great a salvation, which

---

[7] George S. Bebis, *The Mind of the Fathers* (Brookline, MA: Holy Cross Orthodox Press, 1994), 10.

[8] Ibid., 5–6.

at the first began to be spoken by the Lord, and was confirmed to us by those who heard him. . . . ?" This idea also appears in 2 Timothy 2.2: "And the things that you have heard from me among many witnesses, commit these to faithful men who will be able to teach others also."

3. The Church (that which is kept)

As we have seen, tradition is the fullness of life in Christ as proclaimed by the apostles under the guidance of the Holy Spirit. The convergence of these two elements (the apostles and the Holy Spirit on Pentecost) generates the context of the Church, a context within which the fullness of the revelation in Christ actually and practically passes over into the lives of individual believers. Being the body of Christ, the Church is the place where new life is born, developed, and maintained, and from which it is proclaimed. Thus, it seems reasonable to suggest that one of the most important tasks of the Church is to preserve and advance that which has been received from the apostles and passed on into the lives of the faithful. To that end the Church has been given (and/or allowed to develop) what I would like to call "mechanisms of preservation and advancement." These include Scripture, dogma, apostolic succession, liturgical structures (services and sacraments), councils (creeds, canons), iconography, hagiography, and missions.

Note that these various mechanisms constitute neither a hierarchy nor an authority structure, but rather an organic synergy of separate and unique processes. Each is designed to facilitate the safeguarding of some aspect of the Church's life and contributes in a different way to that fullness which is life in Christ. The truths transmitted by each instrument are harmoniously fused together into a unified whole that defines the "catholic consciousness" or "mind" of the Church, an awareness guided by the Holy Spirit. Thus, if we were to speak of authority, it would have to be a) in connection with the Holy Spirit, who superintends the dynamic advance of the Church and b) with reference to the overall consciousness of the Church (Acts 15.28: "It seemed good to the Holy Spirit and to us . . .").

The service performed by Scripture, for example, cannot be accomplished by any of the other instruments. Similarly, the benefits of apostolic succession cannot be achieved through liturgical structures or iconography. Yet, taken together under the guidance of the Holy Spirit, they constitute a unity, the fullness of life in Christ. In other words, there can be no dogma that is not referenced in Scripture, preserved by apostolic succession, reflected in icons, lived out by the saints, facilitated by liturgical structures, defended by the councils, and proclaimed by missionaries.

Our search for missiologically relevant data will now take us to these three sources: revelation, tradition, and the Church. As a matter of practical implementation, revelation will be examined first in the Old Testament, and then the New (in particular the Gospel books), with a view toward understanding how the Church has interpreted the missiological data.[9] I will then combine our exploration of the other two sources—tradition and the Church—into a third step to see what principles the history of these other mechanisms of preservation yields for our theological task.

---

[9]This general approach to the Scriptures has been spelled out in Canon 19 of the Quinisext Council. "If any controversy in regard to Scripture shall have been raised, let them not interpret it otherwise than as the lights and doctors of the church in their writings have expounded it, and in those let them glory rather than in composing things out of their own heads, lest through their lack of skill they may have departed from what was fitting. For through the doctrine of the aforesaid fathers, the people coming to the knowledge of what is good and desirable, as well as what is useless and to be rejected, will remodel their life for the better, and not be led by ignorance, but applying their minds to the doctrine, they will take heed that no evil befall them, and work out their salvation in fear of impending punishment." *The Canons of the Council in Trullo* 19 (*NPNF*[2] 14:374–75).

4

Mission and the Old Testament

The Old Testament presents a particular challenge to those explor-
ing the biblical basis of mission because it contains very little that
either prescribes or describes the cross-cultural communication of a specific religious message. Nevertheless, there are some who are convinced
that the Old Testament affords ample evidence of overt missionary activity. The book of Jonah and several of the Servant Songs (Is 42.1, 49.5), for
example, appear to support this contention. This line of inquiry suggests
that Israel had a God-given mandate to make him known to other nations,
and that the paucity of textual evidence of such activity is nothing more
than a reflection of Israel's utter failure to fulfill its responsibilities to the
nations.[1]

Others suggest that any attempt to establish a clearly understood
"sending" or going out to the Gentiles in the Old Testament is based on
isolated proof-texts, and shows an eisegetic imposition of modern Christian concepts onto the text. Proponents of this approach point out that the
Old Testament emphasizes the activity of God, and insist on this basis that
Israel was never engaged in any form of missionary outreach. If anything,
God himself would convert the nations as a result of his exemplary dealings with Israel. These theologians maintain that Israel had no missionary
responsibility for the nations whatsoever.[2]

[1]Examples of this approach are found in Roger E. Hedlund, *The Mission of the Church
in the World : A Biblical Theology* (Grand Rapids, MI: Baker Book House, 1991). Walter C.
Kaiser, *Mission in the Old Testament: Israel as a Light to the Nations*, 2nd ed. (Grand Rapids,
MI: Baker Academic, 2012).

[2]As examples see Robert Martin Achard, *A Light Unto the Nations: A Study of the Old
Testament Conception of Israel's Mission to the World* (Edinburgh: Oliver and Boyd, 1962).

It is, of course, possible that this scholarly impasse results not from a lack of Old Testament data, but rather from the imposition of a contemporary conceptualization that limits mission to some form of cross-cultural outreach. Our own concept of mission may blind us to the missiological material that is in fact present in the Old Testament, if we are asking or framing our questions in the wrong way. If we accept the idea that the Old Testament is an integral part of redemption history, then discovering the Old Testament's missionary dimension requires a different set of questions. Does God's interaction with mankind give any indication of the presence, scope, and implementation of divine salvific will? What role might Israel have played in that scheme? What did that responsibility look like in practical terms? Such an approach avoids the "narrow basis" adopted by a few missions texts and endeavors to grasp the broad sweep of biblical testimony taken as a unified whole.[3] In keeping with this more general approach, I will consider three major Old Testament themes and demonstrate, albeit in a cursory fashion, the extent to which the idea of mission really does permeate the Old Testament.

1. The Universal Salvific Will of God

Let us begin with an attempt to assess the range or scope of God's salvific desire. Using only the New Testament, we have no difficulty concluding that God's desire for salvation is universal (1 Tim 2.1–6). He acts to reconcile the world to himself (2 Cor 5.19) and has gathered a people for himself from among the Gentiles, i.e., from all nations. (Acts 15.14). Most of the Old Testament, by contrast, seems to be the history of God's dealings with only one special people, Israel. Nevertheless, God's desire to save all men, of all nations, can be argued from several Old Testament perspectives.

Josef Müller, *Wozu noch Mission? Eine bibeltheologische Überlegung*, Biblisches Forum, (Stuttgart: Katholisches Bibelwerk, 1969).

[3]Johannes Blau, *Gottes Werk in dieser Welt* (Munich: Kaiser, 1967).

a) *The Universality of God's Interaction with Creation*

First, it should be noted that God's general interaction with the world has never been limited to any one part of humanity, as evidenced in the first eleven chapters of Genesis. Everything reported there is directed to all peoples and all of creation. Scripture clearly portrays God as the Creator and Sustainer of the world, and in particular of the human race (Gen 1.1–2.19, 14.19, Is 40.28). The intent of the command to "be fruitful and multiply" (Gen 1.28, 9.1) is obviously universal, as were the results. By the time of the events recorded in Genesis 10, seventy different nations had been formed. The multiplicity of human ethnicity is initiated by God's creative act, and unfolds as a result of obedience to his command. His inclusive ownership of all of creation is repeatedly affirmed (1 Sam 2.1–10, Ps 24.1, Ps 50). All peoples are his. All depend upon his custodial activity, that which sustains existence as we know it (Ps 104.14). This universal reign of God is the very foundation of the coming kingdom that it anticipates, the universal proclamation of salvation in Christ. Commenting on Psalm 24.2, Augustine notes that "when the Lord, being glorified, is announced for the believing of all nations, the whole compass of the world becomes his Church."[4] Summarizing this, Hippolytus speaks of the inclusivity of divine mercy:

> The Word shows his compassion and his denial of all preferential treatment among all the saints; he enlightens them and adapts them to that which is advantageous for them. He is like a skillful physician, understanding the weakness of each one. The ignorant he loves to teach. The erring he turns again to his own true way. By those who live by faith he is easily found. To those of pure eye and holy heart, who desire to knock at the door, he opens immediately. For he casts away none of his servants as unworthy of the divine mysteries. He does not esteem the rich person more highly than the poor, nor does he despise the poor person for his poverty. He does not disdain the barbarian, nor does he set the eunuch aside as no man. He does not hate the female

---

[4]Augustine, *Exposition of the Psalms*, ‹http://www.newadvent.org/fathers/1801024.htm›, June 11, 2014.

on account of the woman's act of disobedience in the beginning, nor does he reject the male on account of the man's transgression. But he seeks all and desires to save all, wishing to make all the children of God and calling all the saints to one perfect human person. For there is one Son (or Servant) of God, by whom we too, receiving the regeneration through the Holy Spirit, desire to come all into one perfect and heavenly human person.[5]

Second, we should note that God's response to sin was universal. The catastrophic effects of man's fall brought sweeping, inclusive divine condemnation. In Genesis 3, Adam, Eve, and the serpent are all called to account for their respective roles in the rebellion. No one was spared. "To the woman he said: 'I will greatly multiply your sorrow and your conception; in pain you shall bring forth children; your desire shall be for your husband, and he shall rule over you'" (Gen 3.16).

> Then to Adam he said, "Because you have heeded the voice of your wife, and have eaten from the tree of which I commanded you, saying, 'You shall not eat of it,' cursed is the ground for your sake; in toil you shall eat of it. All the days of your life, both thorns and thistles it shall bring forth for you, and you shall eat the herb of the field. In the sweat of your face you shall eat bread till you return to the ground, for out of it you were taken; for dust you are, and to dust you shall return" (Gen 3.17–19).

And to the serpent, "So the Lord God said to the serpent: 'Because you have done this, you are cursed more than all cattle, and more than every beast of the field; on your belly you shall go, and you shall eat dust all the days of your life'" (Gen 3.14).

When sin overtakes every nation (Gen. 6.5–8), God's response is again universal. He brings his judgment to bear on all men. "So God looked upon the earth, and indeed it was corrupt; for all flesh had corrupted their way on the earth. And God said to Noah, 'The end of all flesh has come

---

[5]Hippolytus, *Treatise on Christ and Antichrist*, ‹http://www.ccel.org/ccel/schaff/anf05.iii.iv.ii.i.html›, June 11, 2014.

before me, for the earth is filled with violence through them; and behold, I will destroy them with the earth'" (Gen 6.12–13).

When sin once again engulfs mankind, as reported in Genesis 10–11, God deals with it globally. Man's attempt to maintain a unity centered on an architectural object (the tower of Babel) meets with sweeping and universal condemnation. Chrysostom identifies the cause of the transgression as the insatiable human desire for ever more power.

> When they traveled from the east, they found open country in the land of Sennar [Shinar] and settled there. Notice how the human race, instead of managing to keep to its own boundaries, always longs for more and reaches out for greater things. This is what the human race has lost in particular, not being prepared to recognize the limitations of its own condition but always lusting after more, entertaining ambitions beyond its capacity.[6]

According to Augustine, however, it was more than an expression of general sinfulness. Mankind was deliberately defying God.

> After the flood, as if striving to fortify themselves against God, as if there could be anything high for God or anything secure for pride, certain proud men built a tower, ostensibly so that they might not be destroyed by a flood if one came later. For they had heard and recalled that all iniquity had been destroyed by the flood. They were unwilling to abstain from iniquity. They sought the height of a tower against a flood; they built a lofty tower. God saw their pride, and he caused this disorder to be sent upon them, that they might speak but not understand one another, and tongues became different through pride.[7]

In the end God disperses them by confusing their language. And why does God react this way? In his *Homilies on Genesis*, Chrysostom answers by pointing to the pattern already established by God in his dealings with human sin.

---

[6]John Chrysostom, *Homilies on Genesis* 30.5; ACCS OT 1:168.
[7]Augustine, *Tractates on the Gospel of John* 6.10.2; ibid.

This in fact is the way the Lord is accustomed to behave. This is what he did in the beginning in the case of the [first] woman as well. She had abused the status conferred on her, and for that reason he subjected her to her husband. Again, too, in the case of Adam, since he drew no advantage from the great ease he enjoyed and from life in the garden but rather rendered himself liable to punishment through the fall, God drove him out of the garden and inflicted on him everlasting punishment in the words "thorns and thistles let the earth yield." So when the people in the present case, who had been dignified with similarity of language, used the privilege given them for evil purposes, he put a stop to the impulse of their wickedness through creating differences in language. "Let us confuse their speech," he says, "so that they will be unable to understand one another's language." His purpose was that, just as similarity of language achieved their living together, so difference in language might cause dispersal among them.[8]

b) God's Universal Promise of Restoration (Genesis 3.15, 9.27, and 11.4)

At each stage of the human devolution into sin, God shows his desire to reestablish the broken relationship with humanity. Just as his condemnation of sin is universal, so is his promise of reconciliation.

First of all, it should be pointed out that God's response to sin is not limited to reacting on a case-by-case basis. There is evidence of an overall solution. Many have referred to Genesis 3.15 as the first statement (*protevangelium*) of God's ultimate answer to sin. Anticipating Christ's redemptive work on the cross, it is God's eternal " 'I will' with respect to salvation offered to the whole race, an immutable, unrescindable theme of the Bible and the history of Israel."[9]

> Christ completely renewed all things, both taking up the battle against
> our enemy and crushing him who at the beginning had led us captive
> in Adam, trampling on his head, as you find in Genesis that God said

[8]John Chrysostom, *Homilies on Genesis 18–45*, FC 82:229.
[9]Gerhard von Rad, *Theologie des Alten Testaments*, 2 vols., Einführung in die Evangelische Theologie (Munich: C. Kaiser, 1960).

to the serpent, "I will put enmity between you and the woman, and between your seed and the seed of the woman. He will be on the watch for your head, and you will be on the watch for his heel." From then on it was proclaimed that he who was to be born of a virgin, after the likeness of Adam, would be on the watch for the serpent's head. This is the seed of which the apostle says in the letter to the Galatians, "The law of works was established until the seed should come to whom the promise was made." He shows this still more clearly in the same epistle when he says, "But when the fullness of time was come, God sent his Son, made of a woman." The enemy would not have been justly conquered unless it had been a man made of woman who conquered him. For it was by a woman that he had power over man from the beginning, setting himself up in opposition to man. Because of this the Lord also declares himself to be the Son of Man, so renewing in himself that primal man from whom the formation of man by woman began, that as our race went down to death by a man who overcame, and as death won the palm of victory over us by a man, so we might by a man receive the palm of victory over death.[10]

The importance of Genesis 3.15 is that here God speaks of Eve's "seed." This archaic term has the same form in the singular as in the plural. Therefore, many believe that God is not referring to her entire progeny, but rather to one specific descendant (Christ) who is going to defeat Satan and provide salvation for humankind.

After the disaster of the flood, God enters into a covenant with the whole of humanity (Gen 9.9–17). That the covenant with Noah has universal salvific implications can be seen from the inclusive language (every living creature, all generations, all flesh) and from the fact that "the multiplicity of the entire world of ethnic groupings can be traced back to Noah's three sons."[11] None of them would ever be subjected to such destruction again. St Ephrem the Syrian captures this nicely in his commentary on Genesis 6:

---

[10]Irenaeus, *Against Heresies* 5.21.1, ACCS OT 1:91.

[11]Rad, *Theologie des Alten Testaments*, 1:175.

And his Lord spoke to [Noah], as he desired that Noah hear, "Because of your righteousness, a remnant was preserved and did not perish in that flood that took place. And because of your sacrifice that was from all flesh and on behalf of all flesh, I will never again bring a flood upon the earth." God thus bound himself beforehand by this promise so that even if mankind were constantly to follow the evil thoughts of their inclination, he would never again bring a flood upon them.[12]

What is important for our purposes is to note that this divine response to sin is matched by a similar concern for reconciliation, which also extends to every people (Ps 67.4; 82.8; 96.10; Is 2.4; Joel 3.12; Mic 4.3). The anticipation of fulfillment in Christ and by the apostles is typical of the patristic interpretation of these passages.

We can show you that this has really happened. For a band of twelve men went forth from Jerusalem, and they were common men, not trained in speaking. But by the power of God they testified to every race of humankind that they were sent by Christ to teach to all the word of God. And now we who once killed each other not only do not make war on each other, but in order not to lie or deceive our inquisitors we gladly die for the confession of Christ.[13]

Another element of God's response to this particular crisis can be seen in his reaction to the sinful incident that took place after the survivors emerged from the ark. We are told that Noah worked as a husbandman and became drunk with his own wine. The subsequent behavior of Canaan was quickly condemned and judgment meted out. In response to the righteous behavior of the two older brothers, "God enlarge[d] Japheth, and may he dwell in the tents of Shem; and may Canaan be his servant" (Gen 9.26–27). According to Kaiser,

this promise to "dwell" was most encouraging, for it assured mortals that despite God's transcendence, he would come to planet earth to

---

[12]Ephrem the Syrian, *Commentary on Genesis,* ACCS OT 1:155.

[13]Justin Martyr, in Oskar Skarsaune, *The Proof from Prophecy: A Study in Justin Martyr's Proof-Text Tradition: Text-Type, Provenance, Theological Profile* (Leiden: Brill, 1987), 159.

take up his residence with the line of Shem, the group of people we know as "Semites,"[14] and live in the midst of them.[15]

As Kaiser sees it, "God's antidote for the mess that humanity had managed to concoct was a promise. God chose a Hebrew Semite named Abraham to be his means of bringing the gospel blessing to all of the world."[16] Augustine observes:

> It is necessary, therefore, to preserve the series of generations descending from Shem, for the sake of exhibiting the city of God after the flood. As before the flood it was exhibited in the series of generations descending from Seth, now it is descending from Shem. And therefore does divine Scripture, after exhibiting the earthly city as Babylon or "Confusion," revert to the patriarch Shem and recapitulate the generations from him to Abraham, specifying the year in which each father gave birth to the son that belonged to this line and how long he lived. And unquestionably it is this that fulfills the promise I made. . . . [17]

2. The Universal Promise

As we have seen, God repeatedly blesses fallen creation with his words of promised restoration. In Genesis 12.1–3 he introduces a new promise and "repeats five times over his determination to 'bless' Abraham, his seed, and all the families of the earth."[18] "I will make you a great nation; I will bless you and make your name great; and you shall be a blessing. I will bless those who bless you, and I will curse him who curses you; and in you all the families of the earth shall be blessed" (Gen 12.1–3). This initial promise contains not only a promise for Abraham and his descendants, but for all nations. It unexpectedly frees Abraham from having to work to

---

[14]The English word "Semitic" comes from "Shemitic," from which the "h" was dropped as it came through Greek translation. Both words were adjectival forms of the Hebrew word *shem*, meaning "name." Kaiser, *Mission in the Old Testament*, 6.

[15]Ibid., 4.

[16]Ibid., 8.

[17]Augustine, *City of God* 16.10, ACCS OT 1:172.

[18]Kaiser, *Mission in the Old Testament*, 9.

make a name for himself, because God has promised to make his name great. But "the key purpose of the whole covenant of promise that was so surprisingly offered to Abram . . . was 'so that all the peoples on earth may be blessed through you'"[19] (Gen. 1.3). According to Bede:

> The promise of this blessing is greater and more important than the preceding one. That was earthly, this one is heavenly, since that one referred to the generation of the fleshly Israel and this one to the generation of the spiritual Israel; that one to the nation born from him according to the flesh and this one to the generation of the nation saved in Christ from all the families of the earth. Among these saved are included all those born from him according to the flesh, who wished also to imitate the piety of his faith. To all these together the apostle Paul says, "If you are of Christ, you are then the seed of Abraham." Therefore when he says, "In you will be blessed all the families of the earth," it is as if he were saying, "And in your seed will be blessed the families of the earth." Mary, from whom would be born the Christ, was present already when these things were said to him. This is what the apostle meant when he spoke of them [the descendants of Levi] as "in the loins of Abraham." How marvelous was the dispensation of the divine severity and goodness. The multitude of those who had gathered for a work of pride merited to be divided from one another into different languages and races. . . . This one man, who abandoned that region, going forth from it willingly by the order of the Lord, heard addressed to himself the promise that in one common blessing there would be reunited in him all the peoples divided into various regions and languages.[20]

This promise is reaffirmed and reiterated repeatedly: to Abraham (Gen 18.18; 22.18), to Isaac (Gen 26.4), to Jacob (28.14), to Moses (Ex 19.1–6; 34.10; Deut 28.9–10), and to Joshua (Jos 2.9–11; 4.23–24). Each generation

---

[19]Ibid., 10. This is Kaiser's translation of the passage. Significantly, he translates the last line as a purpose clause, "in order that. . . ." "Everything Abram was given was a gift to be shared for the enrichment of others."

[20]Bede, *On Genesis* 3, ACCS NT 2:5.

is reminded of God's promise, and there can be no doubt that this promise has a universal scope. Kaiser points out that in Genesis 18.18, 22, and 26.4 the Hebrew phrase in this identical expression is *kôl gôyê,* "all the nations," which the Greek translated as *panta ta ethnē,* "all the nations."[21] Of particular importance is the continuation of the promise during the reign of King David, as recorded in 2 Samuel 7. We sometimes speak of two distinct covenants, an Abrahamic one (Gen 15) and a Davidic one (2 Sam 7; 1 Chr 17). However, the linguistic parallels between the two passages are so striking that we can only conclude that one is, in effect, the continuation of the other. Kaiser spells out these similarities by pointing to six elements contained in each rendering of the divine plan.

"I will make your name great" (2 Sam 7.9, cf. Gen 12.2)

"I will provide a place for my people Israel and will plant them so that they can have a home" (2 Sam 7.10, cf. Gen 15.18; Deut 11.4–25; Josh 1.4–5)

"I will raise up your offspring [seed] to succeed you" (2 Sam 7.12, Gen 17.7–10, 19)

"He will be my son" (2 Sam 7.14, cf. Ex 4.22)

"You have established your people Israel as your very own forever, and you, Lord, have become their God" (2 Sam 7.24, cf. Gen 17.7–8; 28.21; Ex 6.7; 29.45, Lev 11.45; 22.33; 23.43; 25.38; 26.12; 44–45; Num 15.41; Deut 4.20; 29.12–13; et passim)

The exceptional use of *Adonai Yahweh* (2 Sam 7.18–19 [thrice], 22, 28–29; cf. Gen 15.2, 8)[22]

So what God says to David is nothing new, and the only conclusion these texts allow is that God has a single, unified promise of salvation for all peoples. As it developed throughout the Old Testament, this promise took on a very formulaic, threefold character. Basically God says, "I am

[21]Kaiser, *Mission in the Old Testament,* 11.
[22]Ibid., 25–26.

your God, you are my people, and I will dwell among you" (Ex 6.7; 29.45; 1 Kg 6.13; Lev 11.44; 26.12). As Augustine notes,

> God will be the source of every satisfaction, more than any heart can rightly crave, more than life and health, food and wealth, glory and honor, peace and every good—so that God, as St. Paul said, "may be all in all." He will be the consummation of all our desiring—the object of our unending vision, of our unlessening love, of our unwearying praise. And in this gift of vision, this response of love, this paean of praise, all alike will share, as all will share in everlasting life.[23]

This is certainly what the New Testament eventually calls *the* promise (Gal 3.15–18), the center that binds various Old Testament themes, concepts, and books together. A constellation of Old Testament terms, formulae, and metaphors refer to the "promise." According to Kaiser, the Old Testament uses a verb over thirty times which meant "to promise." "To these 'promises' God added his 'pledge' or 'oath,' thus making the immediate word of blessing and the future word of promise doubly secure. Men and women now had the divine word and a divine oath on top of that word" (see Gen 22; 26.3; Deut 8.7; 1 Chr 16.15–18; Ps 105.9; Jer 11.5).[24] Similarly, Thomas Edward sees the "promise" as the basis of God's gracious actions from the beginning of human history.[25] "The promise comprises the heart of the biblical teaching regarding the people of God. . . . The promise thus provides a theological continuum that spans all time. . . . The promise was placed in the form of a covenant [with Abraham] in Genesis 15 and continues in that form today."[26] For McCominsky, the "promise" is now in the "promissory covenant" of the Bible.

One of the most striking aspects of the prophetic promise is what appears to be a growing awareness of the divine inclusion of all peoples in redemptive history. As we have seen, references to all nations are

---

[23] Augustine, *City of God* 22.30, ACCS NT 3:204.

[24] Walter C. Kaiser and Lyman Rand Tucker, *Toward Rediscovering the Old Testament* (Grand Rapids, MI: Zondervan, 1987), 83–95.

[25] Thomas Edward McComiskey, *The Covenants of Promise: A Theology of the Old Testament Covenants* (Grand Rapids, MI: Baker Book House, 1985), 190–92.

[26] Ibid., 85.

included right from the first time the promise is issued. It then continues as an unwavering theme down through the days of the united kingdom. Moreover, the later prophets repeatedly point to the inclusion of the non-Israelite nations in the promise. We see this in the way God uses Jonah to rebuke Israel's narrow nationalistic understanding of the faith (Jon 4). Joel 2.28 speaks of God pouring out his Spirit on all flesh, a phrase that surely means all nations.[27] The prophet Micah (4.1–5) speaks of all nations coming to the holy mountain to find the God of Jacob. Jeremiah (3.17) foresees all nations gathered in Jerusalem to worship the Lord. Zechariah (2.11) sees many nations being joined to the Lord in that day. He even uses part of the promissory formula in saying that those nations "shall be my people, and I will dwell in the midst of thee."

A primary focus here is the notion of being or becoming a people of God. As long as Israel remained faithful, the people were called the chosen people of God, although they could lose that status (Hos 1.9). According to the prophets there were others who, at least at first, were not part of that people, who were going to be included in that designation. "I will have mercy upon her that had not obtained mercy; then I will say to them who were not my people (*lo-ammi*), 'You are my people!' And they shall say, 'You are my God'" (Hos 2.23, Rom 9.25). It would seem that God, who had all the nations in his purview from the beginning, is now making sure that they are included in his people. Commenting on St Paul's use of Hosea's words, Chrysostom writes:

> Here to prevent their saying that you are deceiving us here with specious reasoning, he calls Hosea to witness, who cries and says, "I will call them my people, who were not my people." Who then are the not-people? Plainly, the Gentiles. And who are the not-beloved? The same again. However, he says, they shall become at once people, and beloved, and children of God. "For even they shall be called," he says, "the children of the living God." But if they should assert that this was

[27]The reference to "all flesh" (Hebrew: kôl bāśâr) in Joel 2.28 (Hebrew: Joel 3.1) is used in other contexts to indicate a universal scope (e.g., Gen 6.12, 13, 17; Num 18.15; Isa 49.26). Johannes Blauw, *Gottes Werk in dieser Welt: Grundzüge einer biblischen Theologie der Mission* (Munich: Chr. Kaiser Verlag, 1961), 72.

said of those of the Jews who believed, even then the argument stands. For if with those who after so many benefits were hardhearted and estranged and had lost their being as a people, so great a change was wrought, what is there to prevent even those who were not estranged after being taken to him but were originally aliens, from being called, and, provided they obey, from being counted worthy of the same blessings?[28]

3. The Universal Mission of God (*Missio Dei*)[29]

Despite all this talk of the universal scope of God's activity, the twelfth chapter of Genesis seems to narrow the broad, all-inclusive activity of God to an extreme form of particularism. God enters a covenant with one person and his descendants. But as we will see, these developments alter nothing with respect to the universality of God's salvific will. In fact, the election of Israel is best viewed as a continuation of God's interaction with all nations. Deuteronomy 7.8 links Israel's election to the promise given to Abraham, which as we have seen was universal in its intent. So it seems fair to conclude that "the horizon of the election of the people of Israel is the peoples of the world, in relationship to which as a whole the

[28]John Chrysostom, *Homilies on Romans* 16, ACCS OT 14:13.

[29]Georg F. Vicedom, *The Mission of God; an Introduction to a Theology of Mission*, The Witnessing Church Series (Saint Louis: Concordia Pub. House, 1965). Several observations on Vicedom's use of the phrase are in order. 1) The term a) "mission" is God's work, he is the active subject of mission; b) if our assumption that God desires mission because he is himself involved in mission is correct, then the church can be God's instrument and tool only if it allows itself to be used by him (p. 13). 2) Mission through God: a) God is not only the one who sends; he is also the one sent; b) this is an inner Trinitarian activity (this is the use of *missio* through Thomas. Emphasis here is on grace *extra nos*). 3) Salvific work of God and mission (impersonal sending): a) mission is the continuation of God's salvific act by means of announcement of his work; b) God acts in history: he sends both sword (Jer 9.16) as well as grain, wine, and oil (Ps 57.41, Joel 2.19), therefore he is the God of Love, grace, and judgment; c) in this God is always present, therefore we can consider his very presence as mission. 4) Specific sending (personal) in Christ: a) ultimately mission is the decisive work of Christ, which requires a response; b) this *missio Dei* can be summarized in the idea of the reign of God (Herrschaft Gottes), i.e., the kingdom of God.

'individual' Israel was chosen. *Bhr* [Hebrew] as a technical term for the election of the people of Israel stands under the symbol of universalism."[30] This pan-national scope can be seen in the nature and the purpose of the election.

a) *The Basis of the Election, Deuteronomy 7.6–8*

The *locus classicus* for the concept of election is Deuteronomy 7.6–8 (see also 9.4–6, 10.14ff., 14.2). Here we see that Israel, in being chosen, is called a holy people (*am kadosh*) and treasured possession (*am segulah*). This description gives us significant insight into the nature of the election, that is, the reason Israel was chosen. No human standard was applied and used as the basis for the choice. We see that Israel is not chosen on the basis of special social characteristics, or its cultic and moral integrity. In fact we are told that it was the least among the nations. "The Lord did not set his love on you nor choose you because you were more in number than any other people, for you were the least of all peoples" (Deut 7.7). We also know that Israel was just as vulnerable to the effects of sin as other peoples, and certainly not the only nation to experience divine blessing. The Prophet Amos, for example, speaks about exodus events orchestrated by God among several nations. Israel made its own exodus out of Egypt the cornerstone of its national identity, and yet there were others. "'Are you not like the people of Ethiopia to me, O children of Israel?' says the Lord. 'Did I not bring up Israel from the land of Egypt, the Philistines from Caphtor, and the Syrians from Kir?'" (Amos 9.7).

The universal intent of the election is further underscored when we are told that the elect were considered God's own people, i.e., a *segulah* or treasured possession. [The Septuagint uses λαὸς περιούσιος, *laos periousios*.] This term *segulah* (Ex 19.5, 6; Deut 7.6, 14.2, 26.18; Ps 135.4; Mal 3.17) describes a portion of one's belongings that is aside or held in reserve for some special purpose. No devaluation of one's other possessions is implied. All nations still belong to God, but one small part of the totality

---

[30]Donald Senior and Carroll Stuhlmueller, *The Biblical Foundations for Mission* (Maryknoll, NY: Orbis Books, 1983), 94.

is set aside for a specific purpose. This word (used 146 times in the Old Testament) is the *terminus technicus* describing Israel's special status or belonging to God.

Several conclusions can be inferred from the use of the word *bhr* and the text's complementing terms *kadosh* and *segulah*. On the one hand, election must be viewed as a deliberate, careful choice occasioned by some specific need. By choosing Israel, God is executing his salvific plan, moving to accomplish his own redemptive purpose. On the other hand, while election sets Israel aside, this choice does not obviate God's relationship to the other nations. "In the case of this proposed covenant, God had nothing else in mind for his unique and holy nation but the salvation of all nations through Israel. By means of the practical and pastoral ministry of Israel, which itself was saved and taught by Jahweh, all peoples were to find their way back to God and be taught and sanctified by the Torah and the Cult."[31]

b) The Purpose of Election

Second, let us consider the purpose of election. As we have seen, the intended result was for Israel to become a blessing and a light for the nations (Gen 12.3, 18.18; Gal 3.8). Election does not imply privilege, but rather responsibility. This can be seen clearly in the various roles Israel was asked to play among the nations.

First, they were to be a nation of priests among the other nations. In Exodus 19.6, God says to Israel, "And you shall be to me a kingdom of priests and a holy nation." This command implies a twofold responsibility. On the one hand, Israel is to remain holy, maintaining communion with God and keeping his commandments. On the other hand, Israel is to collectively serve as a priest to the other nations. This activity necessarily means teaching the nations. St Peter uses this very concept (1 Pet 2.9) to remind the early Christians of their responsibility. "But you are a chosen generation, a royal priesthood, a holy nation, his own special people, that you may proclaim the praises of him who called you out of darkness into

[31]Heinz Kruse, "Exodus 19:5 and the Mission of Israel," *Northeast Asia Journal of Theology* 24–25 (1980): 129–35.

his marvelous light." Commenting on this verse, Bede reaffirms the missionary responsibility of God's people.

> The apostle Peter now rightly gives to the Gentiles this attestation of praise, which formerly was given by Moses to the ancient people of God, because they believed in Christ, who like a cornerstone brought the Gentiles into that salvation which Israel had had for itself. He calls them "a chosen race" on account of their faith, that he may distinguish them from those who by rejecting the living stone have themselves become rejected. They are "a royal priesthood," however, because they have been joined to his body who is their real king and true priest, who as king grants to his own a kingdom and as their high priest cleanses them of their sins by the sacrificial victim of his own blood. He names them "a royal priesthood" that they may remember both to hope for an eternal kingdom and always to offer to God the sacrifices of a stainless way of life.[32]

Second, Israel is to be the source of knowledge about God. The other nations are to see the blessing of God on Israel and thus come to know him. The Israelites' faithfulness to the commandments and their holiness will reveal God to the other nations. "The Lord will establish you as a holy people to himself, just as He has sworn to you, if you keep the commandments of the Lord your God and walk in his ways. Then all peoples of the earth shall see that you are called by the name of the Lord, and they shall be afraid of you" (Deut 28.9–10). At the same time, the mighty works rendered by God in their midst are to bring a knowledge of God to the nations. Rahab reveals that Jericho has heard how God dried up the Red Sea, among other things, and based on that knowledge recognizes that "the Lord your God, he is God in heaven above and on earth beneath" (Josh 2.11). Joshua expresses the same idea at the miraculous crossing of the Jordan river. He says that this was done so "that all the peoples of the earth may know the hand of the Lord, that it is mighty, that you may fear the Lord your God forever" (Josh 4.24). Similarly, David's defeat of Goliath is provided by God so that "all this assembly shall know that the Lord

---

[32]Bede, *Commentary on 1 Peter* 2.9, ACCS OT 3:95.

does not save with sword and spear; for the battle is the Lord's, and He will give you into our hands" (1 Sam 17.47).

Third, Israel was to "be a light to the Gentiles and mediate Jahweh's salvation to the ends of the earth."[33] The prophet Isaiah explicitly states this very thing in the following passages:

I, the Lord, have called you in righteousness, and will hold your hand; I will keep you and give you as a covenant to the people, as a light to the Gentiles, to open blind eyes, to bring out prisoners from the prison, those who sit in darkness from the prison house (42.6–7).

"You are my witnesses," says the Lord, "and my servant whom I have chosen, that you may know and believe me, and understand that I am he. Before me there was no God formed, nor shall there be after me. I, even I, am the Lord and besides me there is no savior. I have declared and saved, I have proclaimed, and there was no foreign god among you; therefore you are my witnesses," says the Lord, "that I am God" (43.10–12).

Indeed He says, "It is too small a thing that you should be my Servant to raise up the tribes of Jacob, and to restore the preserved ones of Israel; I will also give You as a light to the Gentiles, that you should be my salvation to the ends of the earth" (49.6).

The last passage raises the question of the Servant's identity. Is it Israel or Christ, a single individual or the whole nation? The Prophet Isaiah uses "servant" to refer to the whole nation of Israel (41.8–10, 43.8–13, 43.14–44.5, 44.6–8, 21–23, 44.24– 45.13, 48.1, 7, 10–12, 17) and also to Israel as an individual (42.1–7, 49.1–6; 50.4–9, 52.13–53.12).[34] Pointing out that

[33]Gerhard von Rad, *Old Testament Theology*, 2 vols. (New York: Harper, 1962), 2:253. "When Deutero-Isaiah describes Israel as a 'witness' for the nations (Is. XLIII. 10, XLIV. 8, LV. 4, he is not thinking of her sending out messengers to them. In the prophet's mind Israel is thought of rather as a sign of which the Gentiles are to become aware . . . They will come to Israel and confess that "God is with you only, and nowhere else, no god besides him" ; *"only in* Jahweh are salvation and strength"; "truly, thou art a God who hidest thyself" (Is. XLV.14C, 24)." Ibid., 249.
[34]Kaiser, *Mission in the Old Testament*, 56.

this term, like the term "seed," can have both individual and corporate meanings, Kaiser comes to the conclusion that the "'servant of the Lord' is a corporate term that embodies at one and the same time a reference to the One, who is the representative of the whole (i.e., the Messiah), and a reference to the whole group that belongs to that single whole or corporate term (i.e., Israel)."[35] It is clear that the "servant" is the messianic person, the descendant of the patriarchs to whom the promise was given (Abraham); those through whom it was carried forth (David, the Seed, God's holy one, the branch); and finally the Christ, in whom the promise is fulfilled. St Ambrose captures the essence of this argument:

> It is one thing to be named Son according to the divine substance; it is another thing to be so called according to the adoption of human flesh. For, according to the divine generation, the Son is equal to God and Father, and, according to the adoption of a body, he is a servant to God the Father. "For," it says, "he took upon him the form of a servant." The Son is, however, one and the same. . . . According to his glory, he is Lord to the holy patriarch David but David's son in the line of actual descent, abandoning nothing of his own but acquiring for himself the rights that go with the adoption into our race. Not only does he undergo service in the character of man by reason of his descent from David, but also by reason of his name, as it is written: "I have found David my servant"; and elsewhere: "Behold, I will send to you my Servant, the Orient is his name." And the Son himself says, "Thus says the Lord, that formed me from the womb to be his servant and said to me: It is a great thing for you to be called my servant. Behold, I have set you up for a witness to my people and a light to the Gentiles, that you may be for salvation to the ends of the earth." To whom is this said, if not to Christ? Who, being in the form of God, emptied himself and took on him the form of a servant. But what can be in the form of God, except that which exists in the fullness of the godhead?[36]

[35]Ibid.
[36]Ambrose, *On the Christian Faith* 5.8.106–107, ACCS OT 11:113.

But the Servant is, at the same time, no less than the whole people of Israel. This can be seen from the ways in which Isaiah uses the term. "My servant" is used in Isaiah 49.3 to address an individual, while in 44.21 it applies to the whole nation. The phrase "a light to the nations" is applied in 49.6 to an individual, and in 42.6 and 51.4 to the collective whole. So, both the nation of Israel and the coming Messiah (Lk 2.32) are to be a light to the nations. As Kaiser puts it, "salvation was to come to the Gentiles through the mediation of Yahweh's servant Messiah and Israel."[37]

What exactly does it mean to be a light? Was this a specific missionary task? Perhaps we can answer the question by citing St Paul's use of this very text. "For so the Lord has commanded us: 'I have set you as a light to the Gentiles, that you should be for salvation to the ends of the earth'" (Acts 13.47). Obviously St Paul understood this task as a "going out" to the nations in order to proclaim the gospel. If the servant can also be seen as the nation of Israel, can we not say that Israel bears the same responsibility? We find affirmation of this in Psalm 96.3 when Israel is called to "declare his glory among the nations, his wonders among all peoples." The verb "declare," or proclaim, implies that "an active proclamation of the good news exists for all the nations to respond."[38]

We may then conclude that the whole history of Israel is an unbroken stream of God's dealings with all the nations. Thus it comes as no surprise that others were allowed to participate in the benefits of that privilege, such as Melchizedek (Gen 14.18), Hagar the Egyptian (Gen 16.13), and the "mixed multitude" (Ex 12.38). Consider also the way in which the law governed the treatment of the so-called "resident aliens." "You shall neither mistreat a stranger nor oppress him, for you were strangers in the land of Egypt" (Ex 22.21, see also Lev 19.33). And were not the other nations included in King Solomon's dedication of the temple?

> Moreover, concerning a foreigner, who is not of Your people Israel, but has come from a far country for Your name's sake (for they will hear of Your great name and Your strong hand and Your outstretched arm),

---

[37]Kaiser, *Mission in the Old Testament*, 61.
[38]Blau, *Gottes Werk*, 33.

when he comes and prays toward this temple, hear in heaven Your dwelling place, and do according to all for which the foreigner calls to You, that all peoples of the earth may know Your name and fear You, as do Your people Israel, and that they may know that this temple which I have built is called by Your name. (1 Kg 8.41–43)

In fact, there is so much material of this sort in the Old Testament that we may safely infer a universal salvific expectation.[39] If God created all and provides materially for all, if he addresses man's sinfulness and reserves the right to guide, teach, and judge all, it can be reasonably inferred that he is also desirous of saving all. Indeed, he is presented as the God who saves both Israel and the nations. In Deuteronomy 33.29, for example, Israel is declared "blessed," saved by the Lord. (See also Is 43:3, 45:17, Zech 8.13.) That blessed hope, however, applies no less to the nations (Ps 72.8, 17, 19, Is 2.1–2, Is 45.21, 22, 52.10, Jer 3:17).

Typical of such passages are the following from Micah and Ezekiel:

Now it shall come to pass in the latter days that the mountain of the Lord's house shall be established on the top of the mountains, and shall be exalted above the hills; and peoples shall flow to it. Many nations shall come and say, "Come, and let us go up to the mountain of the Lord, to the house of the God of Jacob; he will teach us his ways, and we shall walk in his paths." For out of Zion the law shall go forth, and the word of the Lord from Jerusalem. (Mic 4.1–2)

"And I will sanctify my great name, which has been profaned among the nations, which you have profaned in their midst; and the nations shall know that I am the Lord," says the Lord God, "when I am hallowed in you before their eyes." (Ezek 36.23)

As Robert Hall Glover concludes, "The whole Old Testament lives in a missionary atmosphere, and is vivified with the love of the God of the whole earth for all his children."[40]

---

[39] André Rétif and P. Lamarche, *The Salvation of the Gentiles and the Prophets* (Baltimore: Helicon, 1966).

[40] Robert Hall Glover, *The Bible Basis of Mission* (Chicago: Moody Press, 1946), 22.

5

Mission and the New Testament

In contrast to the Old Testament, the New Testament is a patently missionary book. That is, the New Testament documents owe their very existence to the already active missionary outreach of the early Church. As such, they do not serve primarily as an apologetic for mission, but rather as a dynamic instrument of burgeoning missionary activity, which was largely the result of the completion of God's plan of redemption. With the coming of Christ we have the concretization of salvation, a new covenant, and a new people of God. As we gather missions-related data from these sources, it becomes obvious that the emphasis has shifted from that which will be the case (proto-descriptition and foundation) to that which is or is becoming the case (description and implementation). We will, of course, find some direct prescriptive instruction intended to guide the implementation of the new enterprise. In this chapter we focus on three stages of development: 1) the fulfillment of the promise in Christ; 2) the transition to a new covenant and a new people of God; and 3) the inauguration of Christian mission with its activation of witness.

1. Fulfillment of the Promise

Galatians 4.4–5 tells us that "when the fullness of the time had come, God sent forth his Son . . . to redeem those who were under the law." The idea here is not that time has simply run its course, but that an appointed time for the fulfillment of the promise has arrived. God himself initiates the final stage in redemption history by sending his Son into the world. The context for our understanding of these events is the one already established by the Old Testament, that is, the context of the Abrahamic promise, the covenants, and the anticipated blessing of all nations.

a) The Promise as Gospel (Gal 3)

Tying the incarnation and the passion of Christ to the promise made to Abraham is exactly the approach taken by St Paul in Galatians chapter three. In verses 1–5, he raises the fundamental question of just how the Galatian believers had received the gift of redemption, which is now a concrete reality for them. Their own experience provides the obvious answer. After beholding Christ crucified, they received the gift of the Spirit not through works of the law but by the hearing or obedience of faith (ἐξ ἀκοῆς πίστεως, *ex akoēs pisteōs*). In verses 6–9 Paul supplements this line of argument by appealing to Scripture, specifically Genesis 15.6, showing that it was Abraham's willingness to have faith in God's plan that led God to declare him righteous. That leads Paul to the conclusion (3.7–8) that the true children of Abraham are those including the Gentiles (τὰ ἔθνη, *ta ethnē*) who have faith (Gen 17.7, Rom 9.6ff.). Several observations are in order.

First, the promise made to Abraham (Gen 12.12) is referred to here as the gospel (προευηγγελίσατο, *proeuēngelisato*). So it is faith in Christ, and neither ethnicity nor keeping the law (3.10ff.), that leads to redemption. The law does not change the conditions of the promise (3.15), it only reveals sin as sin. Second, the object of this faith is God's plan as accomplished by Christ (3.10–14), which is precisely what the original promise envisioned. This fact is established by St Paul's highlighting of the singular form of the word "seed." "Seed," in the Abrahamic promise, does not refer to all descendants of Abraham, but only to a single descendant, Christ (3.16), and all those in him (3.26–29). Third, the scope of the promise has always been universal (3.8). Right from the beginning God envisioned the inclusion of all nations. All of them were to be blessed through the fulfillment of the promise made to Abraham (Gen 12.3). Fourth, the whole discussion is cast in chronological terms (Gal 3.23) "*before* [this] faith came."

This indicates that there was a certain sequence, a planned unfolding of these events. To begin with there was the law, and then, after the fulfillment of the promise, faith is revealed as the basis of our relationship with God. The period of time covered by the life and ministry of Christ is part of this unfolding; it is a transitional phase within redemptive history. For that reason it should not surprise us to find some tension or ambiguity caused by the mix of particularistic and universalistic elements in the Old Testament.

b) Universalism in the Ministry of Christ

The fact of universalism is clearly seen in the incarnation. As announced by the angel in Luke 2.10–14, Christ's birth is to bring joy to all peoples (παντὶ τῷ λαῷ, *panti tō laō*). St Simeon emphasizes the same thing when he says in verse 2.31 that his eyes have seen the salvation prepared for Israel and all peoples (πάντων τῶν λαῶν, *pantōn tōn laōn*). John the Baptist (Lk 3.6) likewise speaks of all flesh (πᾶσα σάρξ, *pasa sarx*) seeing the salvation of the Lord (καὶ ὄψεται πᾶσα σάρξ τὸ σωτήριον τοῦ θεοῦ, *kai opsetai pasa sarx to sōtērion tou theou*). The same universal intent can also be seen in statements about the goal or purpose of the incarnation. John 1.29 speaks of the Lamb of God who carries the sin of the world (τὴν ἁμαρτίαν τοῦ κόσμου, *tēn amartian tou kosmou*). John 3.16 assures us that God loves the world (ἠγάπησεν ὁ θεὸς τὸν κόσμον, *ēgapesen o theos ton kosmon*). Throughout John's Gospel we see that the world, the cosmos, is the addressee of divine revelation and attention. The Samaritan woman calls Christ the "Savior of the world" (4.42). Elsewhere he is called the bread of "God . . . who gives life to the world" (6.33).

Another indication of this universal vision is found in Christ's teaching on the approaching kingdom of God (Mk 1.14ff.). At the time when Jesus announced that the kingdom of God was near, Jewish expectations were running high. In the Old Testament, God is the king of Israel in particular and also king of all nations, the entire created order. In the New Testament we have an added dimension: God is now king also of the individual human being. The idea of kingship is expanded to include the heart of each individual as well as the Church (Acts 14.22, 19.8; Eph 1.22, Rom 12.5) and the world. So whenever Jesus talks about the kingdom, he has the whole world and all peoples in mind. His cleansing of the temple restores a worship space for all nations (Jn 2.13–14), and he explicitly promises salvation for all peoples (Lk 4.14–30, Jn 8.31–59), a message that is to be proclaimed to the whole world (Mk 13.10).

Based on the Old Testament idea of God as King of creation, however, many people expected God to intervene in history—to put an end to social injustice and political oppression, and to establish his reign. In Luke and Matthew, the term βασιλεία (*basileia*) refers not to a particular geographic region, but rather to the realm of God's active sovereignty. Further, there is no significant difference between Luke's "kingdom of God" and Matthew's "kingdom of heaven" (ἡ βασιλεία τῶν οὐρανῶν, *hē basileia ton ouranōn*), a more indirect, descriptive reference to God. The reference is not to some super-terrestrial region but instead to the reality of God's reign. Our understanding of this "kingdom" can be summarized in terms of several general characteristics.

It is eschatological in scope. The kingdom of which Christ speaks, although inaugurated in the present, will not be completed until the second coming or *Parousia*. His teaching includes such global elements as a new earth and a new heaven. There are also individual concerns such as the resurrection of the dead, the healing of the blind, and the liberation of the oppressed.

It is of divine initiative. Jesus' teaching about the kingdom does refer to human responsibility. We are to pray for the kingdom (Mt 6.10), implore God for it (Lk 18.7), strive to get into it (Lk 12.31), and hold ourselves ready for it (Mt 25.44). However, with our own resources we can do nothing to hasten its coming. God gives it (Lk 12.32), disposes it (Lk 22.29), and grants or denies admittance (Mt 8.11). The image is one of a kingdom that God alone can institute.

It is salvific. The purpose of Jesus' ministry is to announce and offer God's salvation to all of humanity. He does not speak of vengeance but of salvation, especially for the sinners. It is a message of peace offered even to publicans and prostitutes (Mk 2:15ff.). There is immediate forgiveness of sin, and prophecies fulfilled are signs of a new era.

It is exclusively spiritual. The salvation Christ offers entirely excludes any national or political-religious element. Evidence of this can be found in Peter's rejection of the passion announcement (Mk 8.32), the Zebedee sons' request (Mk 10.37), Christ's remark that "two swords . . . [are] enough" (Lk 22.38), and Peter's attack on the guard (Mk 14:17). Jesus clearly repudiates the widespread Jewish hope of a political kingdom.

It cannot be divorced from the person of Christ. The kingdom is necessarily linked to the person of Christ, who determines its contents in terms of his own sending. He is Savior and Victor. He will bring the ultimate victory of truth over all contradicting human ideologies, along with justice in the struggle between right and wrong, the healing of all wounds, and love and reconciliation.

It requires a response. "The preaching of conversion becomes fully intelligible only when a man is convinced that God's eschatological reign is operative in the word and deeds of Jesus, that it has the active power to bring about salvation now."[1]

We see a similar universal theme unfolding in Jesus' parables. According to Joachim Jeremias, some of these parables have to be interpreted in light of the Old Testament teaching on the appearances of God (Is 40.5, 51.4), the call of God (Ps 50.1), the parade of nations (Is 19.23, Zech 8.22), worship at a world-inclusive temple (Ps 22.28, Is 66.18, 45.23, Ps 96.8), and the feast of salvation on the world's mountain (Zech 9.10, Is 25.6–8).[2] With this vision in mind, we see that Jesus' talk of a city on a mountain (Mt 5.14) necessarily points to the meal of salvation planned for all peoples. Matthew 8.11's "many will come" echoes the eschatological parade of nations. The tree that grows from a mustard seed in Mark 4.32 is a great kingdom (Ezek 17.23) in which the birds of the air—that is, all the nations on earth (Ps 104)—nest. In these passages and others (Jn 10.16, Mt 25.32),

---

[1]Rudolf Schnackenburg, *God's Rule and Kingdom*, trans. John Murray, 2nd ed. (New York, NY: Herder and Herder, 1968), 106.

[2]Joachim Jeremias, *Jesu Verheisung für die Völker* (Stuttgart: Kohlhammer, 1956), 48-59.

we see that the approaching end times involve a universal salvation that includes every nation. Commenting on the Parable of the Great Supper (Lk 14.16–24), Cyril of Alexandria asks,

> What was the nature of the invitation? "Come, for look, all things are ready." God the Father has prepared in Christ gifts for the inhabitants of the earth. Through Christ, he bestowed the forgiveness of sins, cleansing away of all defilement, communion of the Holy Spirit, glorious adoption as children, and the kingdom of heaven. To these blessings, Christ invited Israel before all others, by the commandments of the gospel. Somewhere he has even said by the voice of the psalmist, "But I have been sent as a king by him," that is, by God the Father, "on Zion his holy mountain to preach the commandment of the Lord. . . ."
>
> The leaders of the Israelites remained aloof from the supper, as being obstinate, proud, and disobedient. They scorned a surpassing invitation, because they had turned aside to earthly things and focused their mind on the vain distractions of this world. The common crowd was invited, and immediately after them the Gentiles.[3]

The way Jesus refers to himself gives more evidence of his universal vision. The titles "Son of Man" (Mt 13.37, 41, 16.27, 19.28, 24.30–44; Dan 7.13),[4] "Servant of God" (Mt 12.15–21, Mk 10.45), and "Son of David" (Ps 110, Mk 12.35–37) all indicate a connection to and an authority over all of humanity.

Finally, we note Jesus' inclusive treatment of the people he encounters. Note the way he treats the Samaritan woman (Jn 4.1–42), the centurion from Capernaum (Mt 8.5–13), the Syrophoenician woman (Mt 15.21–28), the Gaderene demoniac (Mk 5.1–20), and the deaf man in the Decapolis (Mk 7.31–37).

The Great Commission, Jesus' command to make disciples, is the ultimate expression of this universalism (Mt 28.16–20, Mk 16.15–16, Lk

---

[3]Cyril of Alexandria, *Commentary on Luke* 104, ACCS NT 3:239.

[4]See article on υἱὸς τοῦ ἀνθρώπου (*huios tou anthrōpou*) in Geoffrey William Bromiley and Gerhard Friedrich, *Theological Dictionary of the New Testament*, 10 vols. (Grand Rapids, MI: Eerdmans, 1964).

24.47–48, Acts 1.8). Here Jesus specifically commands the apostles to take the message of his coming kingdom into the whole world. The grammatical structure of the passage is of special interest. Matthew 28.19–20 reads as follows in the Greek text: "πορευθέντες οὖν μαθητεύσατε πάντα τὰ ἔθνη, βαπτίζοντες αὐτοὺς εἰς τὸ ὄνομα τοῦ πατρὸς καὶ τοῦ υἱοῦ καὶ τοῦ ἁγίου πνεύματος, διδάσκοντες αὐτοὺς τηρεῖν πάντα ὅσα ἐνετειλάμην ὑμῖν" (*Poreuthentes oun mathēteusate panta ta ethnē, baptizontes autous eis to onoma tou patros kai tou hiou kai tou hagiou pneumatos, didaskontes autous tērein panta hosa eneteilamēn humin*).[5] What is so interesting here is that the command contains only one explicit imperative, namely the word μαθητεύσατε (*mathēteusate*), "make disciples." That word is followed by two participles, baptizing (βαπτίζοντες, *baptizontes*) and teaching (διδάσκοντες, *didaskontes*), which receive an imperative sense from the word μαθητεύσατε (*mathēteusate*). The whole construct is preceded by the term πορευθέντες (*poreuthentes*, "go forth"), which also acquires an imperative sense.

The command is to make disciples by baptizing and teaching—and to do so as and when the apostles go out into the world. It was not even entirely necessary to command them to go, since Christ might simply assume that once the faithful have beheld the resurrection and received divine grace, they will go out into the world and bear witness to what they have seen. Nevertheless, the aspect of "going" is of extreme importance. According to Bede,

[5]I am aware of some of the historical questions relating to the texts in Matthew and Mark, in particular the use of the Trinitarian formula in Matthew. Perhaps "formula" is saying too much, since this is simply the natural understanding of God's triune involvement in the world. This clearly indicates that the whole Trinity is involved in the redemption of humankind. Some have questioned this element of the text by calling it an anachronism. However, there is no reason to believe that this could not have been included. Given the prominent presence of the Spirit in the Gospels, especially in St John's Gospel, we can easily see that this pan-Trinitarian emphasis is not only possible but also sustained in the commission given the apostles. So I think that all of these objections have been adequately answered, and I accept the text as it has come down to us. Cf. Peter Stuhlmacher, "Mt. 28:16-20 and the Course of Mission in the Apostolic and Postapostolic Age," in *The Mission of the Early Church to Jews and Gentiles*, ed. Jostein Ådna and Hans Kvalbein (Tübingen: J. C. B. Mohr, 2000).

He who before his Passion had said, Go not into the way of the Gentiles (Mt 10.5) now, when rising from the dead, says, Go and teach all nations. Hereby let the Jews be put to silence, who say that Christ's coming is to be for their salvation only. Let the Donatists also blush, who, desiring to confine Christ to one place, have said that He is in Africa only, and not in other countries.[6]

Chrysostom affirms the pan-nationalistic emphasis of the Great Commission when he asks,

What does he finally say to them when he sees them? "All authority in heaven and on earth has been given to me." He is still speaking to them according to his humanity, for they had not yet received the Spirit which was able to raise them to higher things. "Go therefore and make disciples of all nations, baptizing them in the name of the Father and of the Son and of the Holy Spirit, teaching them to observe all that I have commanded you; and lo, I am with you always, to the close of the age." He gives them one charge with a view toward teaching and another charge concerning his commandments. He makes no mention of the future of the Jews. He does not scold Peter for his denial or any one of the others for their flight. Having put into their hands a summary of Christian teaching, which is expressed in the form of baptism, he commands them to go out into the whole world.[7]

Important for our missiological concerns is the fact that this command, as well as Acts 1.9, has a universal scope (they are to go to "all nations," πάντα τὰ ἔθνη, *panta ta ethnē*). It involves a specific message (the coming kingdom), is to be done in a specific order (baptism, teaching), has little to do with a specific time frame (until the end of the world), and depends on the empowering work of the Holy Spirit.

---

[6]Bede, *Homily on Mt. 28*, as cited by Thomas Aquinas, *Catena Aurea: Commentary on the Four Gospels*, vol. 1, *St. Matthew* (Oxford: J. H. Parker, 1841), 988.

[7]John Chrysostom, *Homilies on the Gospel of Matthew 90.2*, ACCS NT 1b:313.

c) Particularism in the Ministry of Christ

As mentioned above, the life and ministry of Christ fall into that time of transition between the finalization of the promise fulfilled in him and the inauguration of the new covenant, the Church and its mission. Although the basic tenor of his ministry is universalistic, we find some lingering evidence of an Old Testament particularism. We may read this in Christ's condemnation of the Jewish mission to the Gentiles: "Woe to you, scribes and Pharisees, hypocrites! For you travel land and sea to win one proselyte, and when he is won, you make him twice as much a son of hell as yourselves" (Mt 23.15). But is this really a narrowly defined particularism? Jesus seems to acknowledge the activity (proselytism) without condemning it; what he cannot accept is the end result. These hypocrites only make the state of the Gentile convert worse than it already was.

Another seemingly particularistic aspect of Christ's ministry is his refusal to allow the gospel to be proclaimed among the non-Jewish population (Mt 10.5ff., 15.24): "Do not go into the way of the Gentiles, and do not enter a city of the Samaritans. But go rather to the lost sheep of the house of Israel." On the basis of this passage, some have suggested that Jesus actually limited his activities to Israel. Certainly, he does not seem to have spent any significant time in Gentile territory (Mk 7.24). When he does cross that boundary, he enters areas that were formerly Jewish, or he traverses Gentile territory in order to reach another Jewish enclave. Likewise, some of Jesus' statements to and about the Gentiles seem unusually harsh. In Matthew 6.7, he says that the Gentiles' prayers are empty repetitions, while in verse 6.32 he describes them as earthly-minded and given exclusively to riches. In Matthew 18.17 he calls for an excommunicated brother to be treated as a heathen, i.e., separated and unclean. There is also the sharp comment about the dogs to the Syrophoenician woman in Mark 7.27. If we are going to claim that Jesus has a universal salvific vision from the beginning, how are we going to explain these apparently particularistic sayings?

d) Dilemma and Solution

Scholars have offered various suggestions for how to resolve this apparent dilemma. Most such proposals seem to reveal a pre-existing bias against the clear meaning of the New Testament texts. First, there is the "anti-Semitic" solution suggested by G. W. F. Hegel:

> The indifference with which his call was received soon turned into hatred. The effect of this hatred on him was an ever-increasing bitterness against his age and his people, especially against those in whom the spirit of his nation lived at its strongest and most passionate, against the Pharisees and the leaders of the people. In his attitude to them there are no attempts to reconcile them to him, to get at their spirit; there are only the most violent outbreaks of bitterness against them, the laying bare of their spirit and its hostility to him. Never once does he treat them with faith in the possibility of their conversion. Their entire character was opposed to him, and hence, when he had occasion to speak to them on religious matters, he could not start on refutation or correction; he only reduces them to silence. . . . After the return of his disciples (so it appears from Matthew 11), he renounces his people and has the feeling (verse 25 ["Thou hast hid these things from the wise and prudent and hast revealed them unto babes"]) that God reveals himself only to the simple-minded. From now onward he restricts himself to working on individuals and allows the fate of his nation to stand unassailed, for he cuts himself off from it and plucks his friends from its grasp.[8]

Obviously we must reject this approach, for it does not square with the facts as presented in the Gospels. Nowhere do we have any indication that Jesus hated his own people. Quite to the contrary, he invests himself in the lives of the masses and teaches them (Mt 5–6, Lk 5.17), even the Pharisees and scribes, until the end of his life (Mk 14.49). He has compassion on them (Mt 14.13), feeds them (Mt 14.19), and heals them (Mt 8.16, 14.14).

---

[8]Georg Wilhelm Friedrich Hegel, *On Christianity: Early Theological Writings* (Chicago: The University of Chicago, 1948), 282.

These are actions not of hatred or rejection, but rather of deep and abiding love. Moreover, the "anti-Semitic" theory does nothing to resolve the tension we see in the life and work of Christ. It simply ignores it.

Another theory proposes a form of "deliberate particularism." This position is presented by G. A. von Harnack, who writes,

> Jesus addressed his gospel—his message of God's imminent kingdom and of judgment, of God's fatherly providence, of repentance, holiness, and love—to his fellow-countrymen. He preached only to Jews. Not a syllable shows that he detached this message from its national soil, or set aside the traditional religion as of no value. Upon the contrary, his preaching could be taken as the most powerful corroboration of that religion.[9]

Once again we have a theory that simply does not do justice to the facts presented in the Gospels. If this proposal were true, what would we make of the many universalistic sayings and actions of our Lord mentioned above? How can Jesus proclaim the coming of many "from the east and the west" (Lk 13.29) without opening his vision to include other nations? Surely Jesus would have known that the promise made to Abraham included the eventual incorporation of the all nations, as mentioned by Zechariah (8.22). His awareness of this "parade of nations" is clearly evident in Matthew 8:11 ("And I say to you that many will come from east and west, and sit down with Abraham, and Isaac, and Jacob in the kingdom of heaven"). This position also fails to resolve the tension, since all it does is highlight one aspect of Christ's ministry to the exclusion of the other.

Von Harnack offers another alternative, which amounts to an "evolutionary scheme."

> Did the transition to gentile mission take place after Pascha of the year 29? Should we imagine the developments as follows? Jesus goes, forced, into the region of the Phoenician coastal plain; it is not his intention to

[9]Adolf von Harnack, *The Mission and Expansion of Christianity in the First Three Centuries*, trans. James Moffatt, 2nd, enl. and rev. ed., 2 vols., Theological Translation Library Vols. 19–20 (London: Williams and Norgate, 1908), 36.

carry out missionary work in the North, but rather to remain hidden (Mk 7:24), but the faith of the heathen woman shows him what God now has in mind. The sharp words he speaks to her are a last struggle against the decisive turn in his fortune, the transition to gentile mission, which had two periods in the life of Christ, up until Pascha 29 the proclamation to Israel and, in his last year, gentile mission.[10]

This approach has some promise, in that it sees movement from narrow nationalism to a universal expectation. However, the idea that Jesus' encounter with the Syrophoenician woman represents his struggle against the inevitable inclusion of the Gentiles seems difficult to accept. As Origen has it, "He was waiting for the time of his impending suffering—a time suitably and duly appointed."[11] In that case this event cannot be viewed as some kind of last-ditch effort to resist the inevitable. Rather, it is a deliberate transition to what has been promised, and to what is yet to come. As Chrysostom shows,

> Mark says that Jesus was not able to escape notice after he had come into the house. But, why did he go away to these parts of the region at all? When he released them from the observance of food laws, then he finally also opened a door to the Gentiles as he proceeded on the road. This anticipates the similar act of Peter, who first received a command to put an end to this law and then was sent to Cornelius.[12]

It seems, then, that the only solution is to assume a universal vision at the very beginning of Jesus' ministry. Here we can cite any number of scholars such as F. Hahn,[13] J. Jeremias,[14] and D. Bosch.[15] Hahn, for example, says that before Jesus could turn to an open mission to the Gentiles,

---

[10]Adolf von Harnack, *Die Mission Und Ausbreitung Des Christentums in Den Ersten Drei Jahrhunderten*, 2 vols. (Leipzig: Hinrichs'sche Buchhandlung, 1924), 36-43.

[11]Origen, *Commentary on Matthew* 11.16, ACCS NT 2:96.

[12]John Chrysostom, *Homilies on the Gospel of Matthew* 52.1 (ibid.).

[13]Ferdinand Hahn, *Mission in the New Testament*, Studies in Biblical Theology (Naperville, IL: A. R. Allenson, 1965), 31.

[14]Jeremias, *Jesu Verheisung für die Völker*, 61–62.

[15]David Bosch, *Die Heidenmission in der Zukunftsschau Jesu: Eine Untersuchung zur Eschatologie der synoptischen Evangelien* (Zurich: 1959), 115.

two prerequisites had to be fulfilled. First, the promise given to the fathers (Rom 15.8) and the sons of the prophets (Acts 3.25) had to be fulfilled by addressing the message to Israel (Mk 7:27). Hilary of Poitiers points out that this approach does not mean that "salvation was not to be imparted also to the Gentiles, but the Lord had come to his own and among his own, awaiting the first fruits of faith from those people he took his roots from. The others subsequently had to be saved by the preaching of the apostles."[16]

Second, there had to be a realization of the eschatological offer of salvation, which of course could not take place until the cross and the resurrection. In that sense, there could be no gospel for the whole world until Jesus had actually taken on the sins of the world. This idea is supported by Jesus' words at the Last Supper: "This is my blood of the new covenant, which is shed for many" (Mk 14:24), that is, for the countless individuals of all nations (Is 53:11f.). This new covenant is exactly what Jesus anticipates when he says, "Many will come from east and west, and sit down with Abraham, Isaac, and Jacob in the kingdom of heaven" (Mt 8.11). This approach comes close to what the Fathers teach. Commenting on Matthew 15.24, Augustine writes:

> How is it that we have come from the Gentiles to the sheepfold of Christ if he was sent only to the lost sheep of the house of Israel? What is the meaning of this puzzling dispensation? The Lord knew why he came—certainly to have a church among all the Gentiles—and he yet said that he was sent only to the lost sheep of the house of Israel? We accordingly understand that he had to manifest in due sequence to that people first the presence of his body, his birth, the display of miracles and then the power of his resurrection. It had thus been predetermined from the beginning, such and such had been foretold and fulfilled, that Christ Jesus had to come to the Jewish people and to be seen and killed and to win for himself those whom he knew beforehand. The Gentiles were not to be condemned but to be winnowed like grain. A multitude of chaff was there, the hidden dignity of grain

[16]Hilary of Poitiers, *On Matthew* 15.4, ACCS NT 1b:29.

was there, burning was to take place there, and a storehouse to be filled there. In fact, where were the apostles if not there? Where was Peter? Where were the rest?[17]

This idea of the progressively unfolding plan of redemption best resolves the tension we see in the life and ministry of Christ. We see such an unfolding in the Old Testament, where God gradually reveals the design of his plan to the faithful. In the promise to Abraham all nations are to be blessed. By the time of Isaiah and Zechariah, the nations are streaming to the holy mountain to worship the one living God, in anticipation of the ultimate fulfillment of the promise in Abraham's seed, Jesus. But it was not until his passion and resurrection that the curse of death and sin could actually be overcome. Accordingly his life, birth, and ministry were all working to that end, and thus represent the last stage of that unfolding plan. There is now good news for all nations.

2. Transition to a New Covenant

The book of Acts picks up the theme of unrestricted mission. In Acts 1.7–9, Jesus diverts attention from the question of the timing of the Parousia and places it among the disciples' responsibilities, which now include worldwide outreach. According to Chrysostom,

He had said earlier, "Go nowhere among the Gentiles, and enter no town of the Samaritans." What he did not say then, he added here, "and to the ends of the earth." Having said this, which was more fearful than all the rest, he held his peace. "When he had said this, as they were watching, he was lifted up, and a cloud took him out of their sight." Do you see that they preached and fulfilled the gospel? For great was the gift he had bestowed upon them. In the very place, he says, where you are afraid, that is, in Jerusalem, preach there. And afterwards he added, "and to the ends of the earth." Then again the proof of his words, "as they were watching, he was lifted up." Not "as they were watching," he

---

[17]Augustine, *Sermons* 77.2, ACCS NT 1b:30.

rose from the dead, but "as they were watching, he was lifted up," since the sight of their eyes was in no way all-sufficient then. For they saw in the resurrection the end but not the beginning, and they saw in the ascension the beginning but not the end.[18]

We can easily see similarities between this passage and the so-called Great Commission (Mt 28.19). What is now being described, however, is the actual implementation of that assignment. Before turning to that topic, let us briefly consider the new context established by the fulfillment of the promise and the coming of the Holy Spirit on Pentecost. The book of Acts presents the progressive, developing understanding by the early Church of the universal implications of the disciples' commission. This understanding develops with reference to a) a new covenant, b) a new people of God, and c) the new work of the Holy Spirit.

a) A New Covenant

Did the fulfillment of the promise end Israel's special relationship with God and the administrative structure of the law? No, but the change did require a new type of administration, a new covenant. Jeremiah 31.31–34 (Ezek 16.60–63, 34.25–31, 37.26–28) gives us the basic contours of this new structure.

Behold, the days are coming, says the Lord, when I will make a new covenant with the house of Israel and with the house of Judah—not according to the covenant that I made with their fathers in the day that I took them by the hand to lead them out of the land of Egypt, My covenant which they broke, though I was a husband to them, says the Lord. But this is the covenant that I will make with the house of Israel after those days, says the Lord: I will put My law in their minds, and write it on their hearts; and I will be their God, and they shall be My people. No more shall every man teach his neighbor, and every man his brother, saying, "Know the Lord," for they all shall know Me,

[18]John Chrysostom, *Homilies on the Book of Acts* 2, ACCS NT 5:10.

from the least of them to the greatest of them, says the Lord. For I will forgive their iniquity, and their sin I will remember no more.

This new covenant was based on the faith of the people and not just obedience to the law (Jer 31.32–34, Gal 3.21–25), a relationship to God defined in the terms of the original promise: "I will be your God, you will be my people, and I will dwell among you." This relationship, which is both individual and corporate (Jer 31.34), will include the absolute forgiveness of sins as mediated by Christ's sacrifice (Heb 9.15). Augustine confirms this:

> Because of the offense of the old Adam, which was by no means healed by the law that commanded and threatened, it is called the old covenant. The other is called the new covenant, because of the newness of the spirit that heals the new Adam of the fault of the old. Then consider what follows, and see in how clear a light the fact is placed, that people who have faith are unwilling to trust in themselves: "Because," says he, "this is the covenant that I will make with the house of Israel; after those days," says the Lord, "I will put my law in their inward parts and write it in their hearts."[19]

Christ and the apostles, of course, take up this theme. Jesus at the Last Supper speaks of the definitive—note the use of the definite article—and specific new covenant (Lk 22.20, Mk 14.24). The same idea is expressed by St Paul in his teaching on the Eucharist (1 Cor 11.25). Commenting on this verse, Chrysostom asks,

> Why does Paul mention that the cup is that of the new covenant? Because there was also a cup of the old covenant, which contained the libations and the blood of animals. For after sacrificing, the priests used to catch the blood in a chalice and bowl and then pour it out. But now, instead of the blood of beasts, Christ has introduced his own blood.[20]

---

[19] Augustine, *On the Spirit and the Letter* 35, ACCS OT 12:214.
[20] John Chrysostom, *Homilies on the Epistles of Paul to the Corinthians* 27.5, ACCS NT 7:113.

That this new arrangement is *the* new covenant mentioned by Jeremiah is made clear in Hebrews 8.7–13. Among the Fathers, St Leo the Great also affirms this connection.

> [The Lord] ascended into the retirement of a neighboring mountain and called his apostles to him there. From the height of that mystical seat he could instruct them in the loftier doctrines, signifying from the very nature of the place and act that it was he who had once honored Moses by speaking to him. He spoke with Moses then, indeed, with a more terrifying justice, but now with a holier mercy in order that what had been promised might be fulfilled when the prophet Jeremiah says, "Behold, the days are coming when I will complete a new covenant for the house of Israel and for the house of Judah. After those days, says the Lord, I will put my laws in their minds, and in their heart will I write them." He therefore who had spoken to Moses, spoke also to the apostles, and the swift hand of the Word wrote and deposited the secrets of the new covenant in the disciples' hearts. There were no thick clouds surrounding him as of old, nor were the people frightened off from approaching the mountain by frightful sounds and lightning. Rather, quietly and freely his discourse reached the ears of those who stood by. In this way the harshness of the law might give way before the gentleness of grace, and "the spirit of adoption" might dispel the terrors of bondage.[21]

b) A New People of God

This new covenant in Christ also defines a new people of God, which now includes the Gentiles. In Ephesians, St Paul says that before the coming of Christ the Gentiles were "aliens from the commonwealth of Israel and strangers from the covenants of promise. . . . But now in Christ you who once were far off have been brought near by the blood of Christ" (2.12). Thus the narrowness of the old covenant is expanded. As Tertullian puts it, "They were once far off from the Christ of the Creator, from the way of the Israelites, from the covenants, from the hope of the promise, from

[21] Leo the Great, *Sermons* 95.1, ACCS NT 10:127.

God himself. The Gentiles now come close in Christ to the things that were once far off."[22]

Participation in this new people of God is not a matter of the special election of just one nation, but is now open to all peoples who are reconciled and united into one body, not by keeping the law, but by faith in the redemptive work of Christ. Chrysostom points out that

> the Greek does not have to become a Jew. Rather both enter into a new condition. His aim is not to bring Greek believers into being as different kinds of Jews but rather to create both anew. Rightly he uses the term create rather than change to point out the great effect of what God has done. Even though the creation is invisible, it is no less a creation of its Creator.[23]

This close connection between the new people of God and Christ is also expressed in the fact that the faithful, collectively, are called his body. In 1 Corinthians 10.16–17, the image of a body is used for the entire believing community and its head, Christ (1 Cor 11.29). In Ephesians 2.16, this unified body is even referred to as Christ himself (1 Cor 12.12ff.). This identification with the Savior clearly shows that the redeeming presence of Christ is one of the things that makes this new people of God so new and so different. Now in him we all have access by one Spirit unto the Father (Eph 2.18).

This mention of the Spirit here is especially significant, since we are taught elsewhere that the new unified people of God is the result of the creative activity of the Holy Spirit (1 Cor 3.16–17, Eph 2.17–22, 1 Pet 2.4–7). The Holy Spirit both empowers and equips the new people for its work in the world by giving it a diversity of gifts or ministries. Underlying this charismatic structure of ministry is the concept of a royal priesthood of all believers, as described in 1 Peter 2.5, 9–10.

> You also, as living stones, are being built up a spiritual house, a holy priesthood, to offer up spiritual sacrifices acceptable to God through Jesus Christ. . . . But you are a chosen generation, a royal priesthood, a

[22]Tertullian, *Against Marcion* 5.17.12–13, ACCS NT 8:138.
[23]John Chrysostom, *Homilies on Ephesians* 5.2.13–15, ACCS NT 8:140.

holy nation, his own special people, that you may proclaim the praises of him who called you out of darkness into his marvelous light; who once were not a people but are now the people of God, who had not obtained mercy but now have obtained mercy.

In the New Testament, the entire people constitutes the priesthood. They are a nation of priests instead of a nation that simply has priests. According to Nicholas Afanasiev and Michael Plekon, "All the participants of the assembly together with their presiders constituted a single people of God, the royal priesthood."[24]

> The gift of the Spirit that every member of the faithful receives in the sacrament of initiation [baptism] is the charism of royal priesthood. In the Church there are no gifts of the Spirit without ministry, and there is no ministry without gifts. Through the charisma of the royal priesthood the Christian is called to priestly ministry in the Church.[25]

> The priestly ministry of all members of the Church finds its expression in the eucharistic assembly. . . . The eucharistic assembly was an assembly of the priestly people who offered sacred service to God "in Christ." Sacred service was an ecclesial ministry for the eucharistic assembly itself, was a manifestation of the Church of God in all its fullness. The Church is where Christ is, but Christ is always present in the fullness of the unity of his body in the Eucharist.[26]

c) The New Work of the Holy Spirit

This gifting of the Church leads quite naturally to a discussion of the new work that the Holy Spirit is to do within the new covenant and its people. Even a cursory reading of the book of Acts impresses one with the prominence and importance of the Holy Spirit. In fact, the role of the Spirit is so dominant that some have suggested calling Luke's work the "Acts of the

---

[24]Nikolaii Afanasiev, *The Church of the Holy Spirit*, trans. Vitaly Permiakov, ed. Michael Plekon (Notre Dame, IN: University of Notre Dame Press, 2007), 18.

[25]Ibid., 3.

[26]Ibid., 4.

Holy Spirit." In gathering our missiological data, we can specify the exact role of the Spirit either phenomenologically, by describing the things he did, or theologically, by relating that activity to the work of the Trinity.

On the descriptive side, we can point to three ways in which the Holy Spirit affected the mission of the early Church. First, the Holy Spirit generates a missionary spirit. This drive or urge toward spontaneous expansion comes to the Church only after Pentecost. The missionary mindset is first and foremost a willingness to sacrifice. The early Christians put their very lives on the line (Acts 15.26). They gave up everything familiar, even their homes (13.3), rather than keeping the best for themselves (see, for example, the prophets and teachers at Antioch in verse 13.1). This missionary spirit was also one of courage. Consider the way in which the apostles faced imprisonment, beatings, and a host of other privations. The challenges were, of course, not just physical. They were willing to confront existing paradigms and power structures (4.31, 21.2).

Second, the Holy Spirit actively guided and directed the missionary outreach of the early Church. On the one hand, the Holy Spirit is presented as the initiator of outreach (13.1ff.). The selection of an area of missionary responsibility is not just a matter of socio-demographic research, but based on explicit instruction from the Holy Spirit. The implication here is that we should not simply target needy areas, but rather ask the Holy Spirit to show us where the Church should be working. On the other hand, the Spirit inspires the actual proclamation of the gospel (Mt 10). Surely we have to have a very good idea of just what we need to communicate, and we will be prepared to do that to the best of our ability, aided by all available resources. However, even our best apologetic or catechetical efforts often fail to bring others to the faith. Instead we must rely on the validating and convicting work of the Holy Spirit, who alone knows the hearts of men and women, and who alone is able to move them to faith.

Third, it is thus the Spirit who actually achieves the results. In John 16.8, Jesus teaches that it is the Spirit who opens the eyes of the world to its own sinfulness. We see this at work in the sermons recorded in Acts. They clearly reflect a dependence on this aspect of the Spirit's work in that they call for a response (2.28), promise forgiveness (2.28), and warn of the coming judgment.

To this we might add the many ways in which the Holy Spirit supports the proclamation of the apostles through mighty and miraculous works. It seems that every time the Church moves into a new geographic area, the Spirit is there to confirm the advance with powerful demonstrations, validating the message of the Church. We see this first at Jerusalem (Acts 2–7), then in Samaria (8), Damascus (9), Caesarea (10–11), Antioch, and all the travels of St Paul (13–28).

On the theological side, we can relate the work of the Holy Spirit to the three offices of Christ (*munus triplex Christi*)[27] and show how he fits in perfectly with the overall divine plan of salvation. First, note how the Holy Spirit's work is related to Christ's prophetic ministry. This ministry situates Christ in the long line of prophets, past, present, and future, who have borne witness to the truth. They were guided by the Spirit to proclaim the word of God (Ezek 11.5). This tradition is carried into the New Testament through Jesus' ministry by means of the direct and immediate power of his status as the Logos, the word of the Word, the truth about the Truth.[28] Did he not need the overshadowing of the Spirit, like the other prophets? The Spirit's role is indeed confirmed by the fact that Jesus begins his public ministry only after his baptism and the Spirit's descent.[29] Jesus returns in the power of the Spirit after being tempted by Satan (Lk 4.14). Then, in the synagogue in Nazareth, he uses the words of the prophet Isaiah (61.1–2) to announce that the Spirit is upon him and that he is anointed to preach (Lk 4.18–19). After his ascension, Jesus asks the Father to send the Spirit to lead us "into all truth" (Jn 16.13), among other things. "He will teach you all things, and bring to your remembrance all things that I said to you" (Jn 14:26). The Spirit continues the ministry of proclaiming the word initiated by Christ by reminding us of everything that Christ said, and validating it. For that reason we can proclaim and teach with confidence, knowing

[27]Sergius Bulgakov, *The Lamb of God* (Grand Rapids, MI: Eerdmans, 2008), 321–441. See also Otto Weber, *Grundlagen der Dogmatik* (Neukirchen: Neukirchener Verlag, 1987), II, 276.

[28]Bulgakov, *The Lamb of God*, 324.

[29]Ibid., 325.

that the Holy Spirit, not our own apologetic skills, validates the truth of our Christ-given message.

Second, the Holy Spirit's work is related to the high priestly ministry of Christ.[30] According to Old Testament law, the consecration of a high priest involved an anointing with oil (Deut 29.7). This "anointing the high priest with oil denoted that he was to be filled with the influences of the Spirit"[31] (Lev 10.7, Ps 45.7, Is 61.1). Since the priest was a type of Christ (Heb 7.26), it follows that Christ, in his capacity as High Priest, was also anointed with the power of the Holy Spirit (Lk 4.18–19). Aided by that empowering, he accomplished our redemption by sacrificing himself, thereby freeing us, once and forever, from the twin curses of sin and death and establishing the foundation for the universal deification of man's creaturely being. Christ is our high priest not only because he offered a sacrifice for our sins, but also because he himself was that sacrifice (Heb 7.27). And this could only have been done by the power of the Holy Spirit. Note that this feat of redemption involved absolute sacrificial love, an accepting of the "cup" of suffering that involved the agony of separation from the Father, and the inevitable resistance of divine sinlessness to the collective sin of the world. Yet he voluntarily accepted the torment of the cross.[32] How could one individual accomplish this? "In his supernatural knowledge and co-experiencing, the God-man made the sin of the integral Adam his own, by suffering this sin to the end."[33] Such an act is possible only for one anointed by the Holy Spirit, strengthened by grace and by the union with the divine.

Third, the work of the Holy Spirit is connected to the royal ministry of Christ.[34] The kingdom of God is the foundation of that royal ministry. It has two distinct aspects. On the one hand, there is the work of preparation. Jesus is born king of the Jews—something anticipated in the concept

[30]Ibid.

[31]Commentary on Exodus 29.4, in Robert Jamieson, A. R. Fausset, and David Brown, *A Commentary, Critical, Experimental, and Practical, on the Old and New Testaments*, 6 vols. (Philadelphia: J. B. Lippincott).

[32]Bulgakov, *The Lamb of God*, 357.

[33]Ibid., 358.

[34]Weber, *Grundlagen der Dogmatik*, II, 286-91.

of "messiah" and then celebrated in the Palm Sunday entrance. On the other hand, his royal status is actually confirmed in his enthronement and glorification at the ascension. Although his royal power is still being actualized in the world, to be fully realized only at the second coming, the initial effects of this reign are already being mediated by the Holy Spirit. As St Paul puts it, "No one can say that Jesus is Lord except by the Holy Spirit" (1 Cor 12.3). Theodoret of Cyrrhus affirms the Holy Spirit's ongoing participation in the kingly ministry of Christ:

> There is no disharmony between the teaching of the only begotten Son and that of the Holy Spirit. In the Gospels, Christ the Lord taught us how great the Holy Spirit is, and the Spirit has proclaimed his lordship. No one who is truly moved by the Spirit can say that Christ is not divine.[35]

3. Inauguration of the Christian Mission

Our discussion of Acts brings us to one additional and obvious observation. The book shows how the early Christians actually implemented the commands of Christ, as issued in Matthew 28 and Acts 1. It documents the history of the shift from the particularism of the Old Testament community to the universality brought about by the fulfillment of the promise. As the text reveals, this shift did not take place suddenly, in one clean movement, but rather developed through at least three stages of implementation: a) the Jewish-Christian mission, typified by the Church in Jerusalem; b) the transitional phase, illustrated by Peter's dealing with Cornelius; and finally c) a completely unfettered mission to the Gentiles embodied in the work of St Paul, and affirmed by the Council at Jerusalem (Acts 15). We will continue gathering missiological data from these phases of growth.

---

[35]Theodoret of Cyrrhus, *Commentary on the First Epistle to the Corinthians* 242, ACCS NT 7:118–119.

a) The Jewish-Christian Mission (Acts 1–9)

The Church in Jerusalem (1.1–2.47). St Luke describes the scene as the disciples, after returning to Jerusalem, await the coming of the Holy Spirit. They are together and "continued with one accord in prayer and supplication, with the women and Mary the mother of Jesus, and with his brothers" (1.14). It is evident here that they are still very much caught up in the workings of the old covenant. Luke references the law governing the Sabbath when he points out that it was a Sabbath day's walk back to Jerusalem (1.12). And yet this too can be seen as an anticipation of what is to come. Bede finds both historical and allegorical meanings in this reference.

> According to the historical sense, this indicates that the Mount of Olives was a thousand paces distant from the city of Jerusalem, for the law did not permit one to walk more than a thousand paces on the Sabbath. According to the allegorical sense, however, anyone who becomes worthy of an interior vision of the glory of the Lord as he ascends to the Father, and of enrichment by the promise of the Holy Spirit, here enters the city of everlasting peace by a Sabbath journey. There will be for him, in Isaiah's words, "Sabbath after Sabbath," because, having been free of wicked works here [in this life], he will be at rest there in heavenly recompense.[36]

Another indication of the Old Testament perspective is their election of a replacement for Judas (1.15–26). One might say that they did so because they were already anticipating the universal work of the Church. According to some of the Fathers, it had to do with filling out the twelve (Lk 22.14) in order to maintain the full representation of the twelve tribes in the reconstituted Israel. Bede makes much of the numerical connection, saying that

> Peter restored the number of apostles to twelve, so that through two parts of six each (for three times four is twelve) they might preserve by an eternal number the grace which they were preaching by word, and so that those who were to preach the faith of the holy Trinity to

[36]Bede, *Commentary on the Acts of the Apostles* 1.12b, ACCS NT 7:119.

the four parts of the world (in line with the Lord's saying, "Go, teach all nations, baptizing them in the name of the Father and of the Son and of the Holy Spirit") might already certify the perfection of the work by the sacramental sign of [their] number as well.[37]

At the same time they may already be looking forward to the universal witness of the Church. For that reason, Chrysostom insists that Judas had to be replaced by

> "one of the men who have accompanied us," continues Peter. Note how he requires them to be eyewitnesses, even though the Spirit was about to come. There was still great care concerning this: "One of the men who have accompanied us," he says, "during all the time that the Lord Jesus went in and out among us." He means those who had dwelt with Christ, not simply been present as disciples. . . . "Until the day he was taken up from us—one of these must become a witness with us of his resurrection." He did not say a witness of the rest of his actions, but a witness of the resurrection alone. For indeed more trustworthy is the man who can say, "He, who ate, and drank, and was crucified, he rose again." Therefore, he must be a witness not only of the time preceding this event or of what followed it and the miracles: the thing required was the resurrection. The other matters were evident and acknowledged, but the resurrection took place in secret and was evident to these only. And they do not say, "Angels told us," but, "We have seen." Why is this evident? Because we perform miracles. For this reason they had to be trustworthy, especially then.[38]

Pentecost and the Coming of the Spirit (Acts 2.1–2:47). Of course the coming of the Spirit on Pentecost actually constituted the Church, propelling the apostles into a mission to all peoples. God visits his people, makes himself known, and gives them the spiritual power to fulfill the commission to preach the gospel. We have already seen how important the Holy Spirit was to the development of the Church, in particular

[37]Bede, *Commentary on the Acts of the Apostles* 1.16, ACCS NT 5:13.
[38]John Chrysostom, *Homilies on the Acts of the Apostles* 3, ACCS NT 5:17.

mediating the real presence of the ascended Christ in the Eucharist. But on this day of Pentecost the Holy Spirit provided something else, namely, an effective means of transferring the knowledge of God to others. On the one hand this involves facilitating communion with other members of the eucharistic community, and on the other proclaiming the *logos* to those outside that communion. As spiritually regenerated individuals, the apostles might begin to make proper use of the speech faculty among themselves, yet they still faced the language-degrading consequences of the fall and Babel—that is, unless God himself undertook to reverse those consequences. Indeed, the coming of the Holy Spirit at Pentecost was intended to do just that: to overcome the linguistic consequences of sin and to restore the possibility of using the faculty of human speech and language to facilitate communion. As illustrated in the two hymns below, the Church views Pentecost as a reversal of Babel:

> Once, when He descended and confounded the tongues, the Most High divided the nations; and when He distributed the tongues of fire He called all men into unity; and with one accord we glorify the All-Holy Spirit.[39]

> Thou hast renewed thy disciples with foreign tongues, O Christ, that they might therewith proclaim Thee, the immortal Word and God Who grantest our souls great mercy.[40]

In both hymns, the work of the Spirit is described as reversing the effects of Babel and enabling the disciples to effectively proclaim the gospel. The first hymn speaks of a renewed communion with God not based on a unified human language, but on the supra-linguistic unity of the Holy Spirit. This unity is most readily evident in the doxological oneness achieved by the eucharistic community in spite of its diverse languages. In the second hymn we encounter the idea of an effective proclamation of the gospel. There is no mention of the need for a single language, but rather for a renewal of the disciples with foreign tongues. Thus it is the

---

[39]Kontakion of the Feast of Pentecost, in *The Pentecostarion* (Boston: Holy Transfiguration Monastery, 1990), 412.

[40]"Lord I Call" verse of vespers of Pentecost, in *The Pentecostarion*, 404.

linguistically enabling work of the Holy Spirit, not a reunified single language, that reverses the effects of Babel. Christ comes into the world as the Word sent and authenticated by the Father (Jn 12.49, 14.10, 14.24), but the application of that witness to the human situation is the work of the Holy Spirit.[41] The Holy Spirit is, of course, not the Word. However, the Spirit facilitates the mediation of the Word by validating him and the Christian witness thereof. This is illustrated at the baptism of Christ, where the descending Holy Spirit confirms Jesus in his role (Mt 3.13, 4.1, Lk 4.1). St John tells us that the Spirit will remind us of everything Christ has taught (Jn 14.26) and guide us into all truth (Jn 16.13). In a more direct statement, the evangelist equates the word with the Spirit (Jn 6.63), explaining that the communion between the two makes the word effective and leads us to faith. St Paul insists that it is the Spirit of God who validates that which has been received (tradition) as the true words of Christ himself (1 Cor 7.10).[42] This historical word is given and, under the guidance of the Holy Spirit, passed on to successive generations without alteration.[43]

Summary Statement (Acts 2.42–47). It is only after Pentecost that we see the Church up and running, incorporating thousands from many nations who repent and believe, and who are by baptism incorporated into the oneness of the eucharistic assembly.

> "And they continued steadfastly and with one accord in the Apostles' doctrine and fellowship" (v. 42.) Here are two virtues, perseverance and concord. "In the Apostles' doctrine," he says: for they again taught them; "and fellowship, and in breaking of bread, and in prayer." All in common, all with perseverance. "And fear came upon every soul" (v. 43): of those that believed.[44]

The Growth of the Church in Jerusalem (3:1–9:31). The initial ministry (3.1–5.42) of the Church was centered on Jerusalem. There was some

---

[41]Weber, *Grundlagen der Dogmatik*, II, 276–79.

[42]Ibid., II, 278.

[43]Edward Rommen, "God Spoke: On Divine Thought in Human Language," *Pro Ecclesia* 15, no. 4 (2006): 387–402, 400–01.

[44]John Chrysostom, *Commentary on the Acts of the Apostles*, ‹http://www.ccel.org/ccel/schaff/npnf111.vi.html›, July 7, 2015.

interaction with the Hellenic population (6.1–8a), but the primary focus was on the Jewish population. Some cross-cultural activity occurred when Philip went to Gaza and Samaria (8.4–40). However, in the early Church these events seem to be the exception rather than the rule. As if anticipating the coming global outreach of the Church, we are also told about the conversion of Paul (9.1–30). Although at this point in its history the Church seems to have been centered in Jerusalem and focused on the Jewish population, that was about to change.

b) Transition to a Universal Mission (Acts 9:32–11:18)

Peter's encounter with Cornelius (chapter 10) represents the first step in opening up the mission's horizon. God himself pushes St Peter into witnessing to Cornelius, a non-Jew. Initially Peter resists, and it takes divine intervention to move Peter to accept Cornelius' invitation. Cornelius the centurion "was a devout man who feared God with all his house, which gave much alms to the people, and prayed to God always" (10.2). God responds by giving him a vision and directing him to Peter. Peter, for his part, is also given a vision, but one that signals an opening to a universal mission.

> [Peter] stood outside himself and saw the gospel linen sent down from above by four corners and holding the whole human race within itself in the myriad forms of birds and quadrupeds and creeping things and beasts formed according to the cults, whose beastly and irrational form the Word commanded Peter to sacrifice, in order that by being cleansed what was left would become edible. This cleansing is clear from the word of piety not being handed over naked, for the divine voice says not once that what God has made clean is not unclean, but this proclamation happens thrice, so that we may learn from the first voice that God the Father purifies and from the second that in the same way the God purifying is the only-begotten God and from the third that equally the God purifying all that is unclean is the Holy Spirit.[45]

---

[45]Gregory of Nyssa, *Homilies on the Song of Songs* 10, ACCS NT 5:126.

So Peter is directed by the Holy Spirit to accept the inclusion of the Gentiles in God's plan of redemption. God himself initiates this move toward a universal mission.

> At that time Peter saw a vision in which a heavenly voice answered him, "What God has cleansed, you must not call common." For the God who had distinguished through the law the pure food from the impure, that same God had cleansed the nations through the blood of his Son, and that is the God whom Cornelius worshiped.[46]

This God-directed universal scope is then extended and implemented in a further outreach that begins in Antioch (13.1–14.28). Here, the Holy Spirit sets aside Barnabas and Paul for the next stage of the Church's expansion. As St Luke describes it,

> "While they were worshiping the Lord and fasting, the Holy Spirit said, 'Set apart for me Barnabas and Saul for the work to which I have called them.' Then after fasting and praying they laid their hands on them and sent them off." What does "worshiping" mean? It means preaching. "Set apart Barnabas and Saul." What does "set apart for me" mean? It means for the work, for the apostleship. Remember who ordained him? Lucius the Cyrenean and Manaen, or rather, one should say, the Spirit. For the more lowly the personages involved, the more palpable the grace of God. Paul is ordained henceforth to apostleship, to preach with authority. How is it then that he himself says, "Not from men nor by men?" Because it was not humankind that called him or brought him over. This is what "or by men" means. For this reason he says that he was not sent by this man but by the Spirit.[47]

With that commission they set forth on their first missionary journey to Cyprus (13.4–12), Asia Minor (13.13–14.23), Iconium (13.51–14.6), and Lystra (14.6–19). On this journey the full and universal scope of the gospel is finally implemented. The gospel is now a message for all peoples.

---

[46]Irenaeus, *Catena on the Acts of the Apostles* 10.15, ACCS NT 5:128.
[47]John Chrysostom, *Homilies on the Acts of the Apostles* 27, ACCS NT 5:159.

c) The Unfettered Mission to All Nations (Acts 15–28)

The rest of the book of Acts documents the continued expansion of the early Church. This material, taken together with the New Testament epistles, shows how the Church moved out into the Mediterranean world and won an initial following for Christ. This did not occur, of course, without some difficulty. There were still believers who felt that the gospel was the reserve of the Jewish people. This dispute was resolved by the Church as described in Acts 15. What is significant here, as Chrysostom puts it, is that under the guidance of the Holy Spirit the assembled apostles come to the irrevocable conclusion that

> "it has seemed good to the Holy Spirit and to us." Why did they add "and to us," when "to the Holy Spirit" was enough? The latter prevents them from thinking it came of people, while the former teaches them that they too welcome [the Gentiles], even though they [as Jewish Christians] are circumcised. They have to speak to people who are still weak and afraid of them.[48]

And so the universal, unrestricted mission of the Church is launched. Throughout the remainder of Acts we are given significant insight into the ways in which the early Christian missionaries engaged various elements of the world around them. We have reports on encounters with the occult, other religions, different languages, economic pressures, hostile authorities, and even the challenges of nature. In each case we see how the apostles reacted under the guidance of the Holy Spirit, and turned these encounters into opportunities to preach the gospel and plant the Church. These pioneering events provide us with the initial data for establishing preliminary missiological principles to be further developed and applied to our own efforts. Consider the following examples:

The occult, encountered in the person of the sorcerer Elymas (13.6–12), represents a profound challenge to the gospel. He resists the apostles and seeks to turn others away from the faith. But instead of backing down, Paul, filled with the Holy Spirit, exposes his deceit and imposes temporary

---

[48]John Chrysostom, *Homilies on the Acts of the Apostles* 33, ACCS NT 5:191.

blindness. He does so not for revenge, but to prove the superior power of the gospel and to give the man an opportunity to come to faith.

> "And now, behold, the hand of the Lord is upon you, and you shall be blind." It was the sign by which [Paul] was himself converted, and by this he wished to convert this man. And the words "for a season" were spoken by one who seeks not to punish but to convert. For if he had wanted to punish, he would have made him blind forever. This is not what happens here, but only "for a season," so that he may gain the proconsul. For the man was prepossessed by sorcery, and he had to teach him a lesson by this punishment, just as the magicians [in Egypt] were taught by the boils.[49]

And indeed, this direct confrontation and refutation of the powers of evil results in the conversion of the proconsul. As we shall see, such dependence on the miraculous power of the Holy Spirit and the faith to use it becomes an important aspect of Christian mission throughout the ages.

Similarly, the apostles' encounters with other religions (14.12–13, 17.19) provide some insight into how the missionary is to deal with non-Christian belief systems. In the first instance, a crowd of listeners impressed by the healing of a crippled man mistake Paul and Barnabas for Zeus and Hermes, and set about to offer them sacrifices. This reaction was no doubt related to a local legend telling of a visit by Zeus and Hermes to Phrygia. According to the legend, only the one couple that received them survived, while the others were destroyed in a flood. Believing the miracle-workers to be gods, the Phrygians were not going to make the same mistake again. The apostles seem surprised by all of this, and we might draw the conclusion that a better advance knowledge of the local religious and cultural situation could have helped them avoid the misunderstanding.

That kind of pre-understanding certainly did play a role in the second instance, Paul's encounter with the philosophers in Athens. The apostle apparently knew of the local belief that sacrifices offered to an unknown god had stopped a plague. Since these altars were still present, Paul uses

---

[49]John Chrysostom, *Homilies on the Acts of the Apostles* 28, ACCS NT 5:161.

them as the basis for his speech. Chrysostom captures the essence of this approach:

> Did the words of the Gospels need to be declared? They would have mocked them. Or maybe the words from the books of the prophets or from the precepts of the law should have been talked about? But they would not have believed. What did he do then? He rushed to the altar and defeated them with the weapons of the enemies themselves. And that was what he said, "I became everything to everyone: to the Jews a Jew, to those outside the law as if I were outside the law."[50]

In both cases the apostles directly confront the false teachings of other religions, giving us some idea of how we should approach non-Christian belief systems in our own day. There is little in the way of the modern "live-and-let-live" approach, nor any hint of downplaying real differences in the name of tolerance or a misguided sense of love. In these examples from Acts, real love requires them to speak the truth, and they do so without reserve, but in a measured way that takes into account the intellectual place of their listeners. Consider Bede's description of the wisdom of St Paul's argument in Athens:

> First, he teaches that the one God is the originator of the world and of all things, and in him we live and move and are, and we are his offspring. Thus he demonstrates that God is to be loved not only because of his gifts of light and life but also because of a certain affinity of kind. Next, he disposes of the opinion that is the explicit reason for idols [by saying] that the founder and Lord of the entire world cannot be enclosed in temples of stone, that the granter of all favors has no need of the blood of victims, that the creator and governor of all people cannot be created by human hands, and finally that God, in whose image humankind was made, should not be appraised in terms of the value of metals. He teaches that the remedy for such errors is the practice of repentance. Now if he had chosen to begin by destroying the idolatrous rites, the ears of the Gentiles would have rejected [him].[51]

[50]Irenaeus, *Catena on the Acts of the Apostles* 17.23, ACCS NT 5:217.
[51]Bede, *Commentary on the Acts of the Apostles* 17.24, ACCS NT 5:218.

The events in Lystra also illustrate the importance of language. Apparently the apostles did not understand the dialect of Lyconia, and as a result they missed some important clues to the local culture and religion (14.11). This experience served to sensitize the missionaries to the issue and, as we have seen in the case of the three-language dispute,[52] the Church eventually decided to do all mission work in the vernacular.

Another early missiological principle had to do with economic interests that sometimes conflict with the mission of the Church. In Acts 16.16–19, we have the report of a young woman who has a spirit of divination. Greedy men who have exploited her ability and marketed her skill are making a great deal of profit. This economic circumstance does not factor into Paul's decision to cast out the evil spirit. He is not intimidated, but proceeds to set the girl free. Indeed, it costs her masters a great deal, and they seek to retaliate. However, the apostle's love for the girl and his commitment to the truth overcomes any consideration of financial loss or gain.

These are but a few examples of the ways in which the initial missionary encounters led to the development of the Church's basic missiological principles. As reported in Acts, these principles are still preliminary, still nascent, and yet they clearly show how the early Church responded to various challenges. Perhaps these principles are not yet fully articulated, but what we find is a clear indication of the initial inclinations. This information can guide us as we seek to formulate our own theology of mission.

Turning to the rest of the New Testament, we see that it provides not so much a description of as evidence of the struggle to establish the Church. The epistles give us a good idea of what the Church that was being planted was to be like, and the challenges it faced. For our purposes we need to summarize and highlight only three developments of significant missiological import: the evolution of the hierarchy; the pneumatic, charismatic structure of Church ministry; and the establishment of the eucharistic assemblies.

---

[52] A ninth-century belief that all Church work was to be conducted in one of only three languages: Hebrew, Greek, or Latin. With the help of Sts Cyril and Methodius, Pope Hadrian II approved the ecclesial use of the Slavonic language, and thereafter the vernacular, wherever mission work was done.

Evolution of the Hierarchy. One of the most important developments during this early period had to with the hierarchical structure of the churches being planted. This aspect is readily apparent in the New Testament when, for example, St Paul tells Timothy that the things he has heard should be passed on to faithful men who will be able to teach others as well (2 Tim 2.2). Note that this passage refers to three generations of apostolic succession: Paul's, Timothy's, and those that Timothy would teach. According to Irenaeus Kelly, the bishop, with the help of the Holy Spirit, maintains the

> identity of the oral tradition with the original revelation [which] is guaranteed by the unbroken succession of Bishops in the great sees going back lineally to the apostles. . . . [A]n additional safeguard is supplied by the Holy Spirit, for the message committed was to the Church, and the Church is the home of the Spirit. Indeed, the Church's Bishops are . . . Spirit-endowed men who have been vouchsafed "an infallible charism of truth."[53]

For every new region into which the Church expanded, new bishops were appointed. They in turn ordained priests to represent them in the local parishes. This allowed for an orderly and structured expansion that, in spite of being far-flung, retained its essential and defining link to the original apostolic deposit.

> Through countryside and city [the apostles] preached, and they appointed their earliest converts, testing them by the Spirit, to be the Bishops and deacons of future believers. Nor was this a novelty, for Bishops and deacons had been written about a long time earlier. . . . Our apostles knew through our Lord Jesus Christ that there would be strife for the office of Bishop. For this reason, therefore, having received perfect foreknowledge, they appointed those who have already been

[53]J. N. D. Kelly, *Early Christian Doctrines*, 4th ed. (London: Black, 1968), 37. This does not, of course, refer to any kind of papal infallibility, but is rather an expression of the conviction that those who are in succession from the apostles have received "the certain gift of truth," which would allow them to faithfully interpret the Scriptures and preserve the message handed down to them. Cf. Irenaeus, *Against Heresies*, IV, 26, 2. ‹http://www.newadvent.org/fathers/0103426.htm›, 1/20/2016.

mentioned and afterwards added the further provision that, if they should die, other approved men should succeed to their ministry.[54]

The Charismatic Gifting of the Church. The second missiologically important characteristic of the early Church was the charismatic nature of its structure of ministry. As mentioned above, the Holy Spirit enables and gifts us for ministry, that is, the Holy Spirit gives us the specific faculties needed for communicating Christ to the world. Perhaps the best way to see this is to take note of the so-called "gifts" of the Spirit mentioned in 1 Corinthians 12.5–12. Here we are told that the Holy Spirit gives the charism of a particular ministry to each and every member of the body, "to each one of us grace was given according to the measure of Christ's gift" (Eph 4.7). So the enterprise of mission does not require specialists accredited according to the world's educational and social standards, but rather ministers equipped and empowered by the Holy Spirit. Because these gifts are given to all believers, there are no non-charismatic members in the Church, no members who do not or cannot minister in it.[55] Whatever else the gifts are, they enable the individual members to reach out into the world and give witness to what they have seen in the Church. Establishing a new church thus means that we allow the Holy Spirit to create this structure; our participation in the charismatic structure of a local church's ministry is nothing short of doing mission.

The Development and Spread of Eucharistic Communities. The celebration of the Eucharist is one of the most ancient components of Christian worship.[56] The very reason the early Christians gathered at all was to celebrate communion, and all of the faithful partook of the sacrament. Faithful eucharistic practice was one indicator of the presence and the oneness of a Church. In other words, God is present in any group of believers that celebrates the Eucharist according to the Scriptures. This presence, being Christ himself, is the unifying presence of the tri-hypostatic unity of the Trinity. When the people of God gather for the celebration of the

[54]Pope Clement I, *First Epistle to the Corinthians* 42 and 44, in Kelly, *Early Christian Doctrines*, 37.

[55]Afanasiev and Plekon, *The Church of the Holy Spirit*, 16.

[56]Gregory Dix, *The Shape of the Liturgy* (Westminster London: Dacre press, 1945).

Eucharist, they constitute the Church: they are the body of Christ in the midst of which Christ is present (Lk 24.35). In the words of Afanasiev,

> Participation in the "sacrament of the assembly" is the revelation of the Church's life and life in the Church. The Eucharist is the center towards which everything aspires and in which everything is gathered. "This is my body," but the body is realized in the Eucharist. Where the body is, there is Christ. And the opposite: where Christ is, there is his body.
>
> The Eucharistic assembly is an assembly of all into one place for one and the same act. This axiom flows out of the very nature of the Eucharist, established by Christ. Christ is inconceivable without the Church just as the messiah is inconceivable without the messianic people. The people of God are called by God in the Body of Christ, which is the Church. This divine assembly of the People of God is realized each time in the Eucharist.[57]

We must not, of course, simply assume the continual spread of these eucharistic communities; we need also ask how the apostles went about establishing them. Did they have a plan, a strategy, for doing so? Is that plan evident in the documents of the New Testament? One very interesting response to these questions is found in David Hesselgrave's *Planting Churches Cross-Culturally*.[58] He begins with the question, "Did Paul have a strategy?" and answers with a qualified affirmative by quoting the words of J. Herbert Kane.

> Did Paul have a missionary strategy? Some say yes; others say no. Much depends on the definition of strategy. If by strategy is meant a deliberate, well-formulated, duly executed plan of action based on human observation and experience, then Paul had little or no strategy; but if we take the word to mean a flexible modus operandi developed under the guidance of the Holy Spirit and subject to his direction and control, then Paul did have a strategy.[59]

[57] Afanasiev and Plekon, *The Church of the Holy Spirit*, 9.
[58] David J. Hesselgrave and Earl J. Blomberg, *Planting Churches Cross-Culturally: A Guide for Home and Foreign Missions* (Grand Rapids, MI: Baker Book House, 1980).
[59] Ibid., 53–54.

As to whether such a strategy is normative for us today, Hesselgrave concludes that

> Paul's message is absolutely normative, and . . . his manner of life and missionary methodology are less normative. It is a matter of degree. There is room for adaptation in each case, but less in the case of his message and more in the cases of his lifestyle and methodology. Those of us who are two thousand years removed from the physical presence of the Master and his apostles would do well to learn from Paul's preaching, person, and program in dependence on the Word and the Holy Spirit.[60]

With that foundation established, Hesselgrave suggests that "the logical elements (steps) in Paul's master plan of evangelism and church development" are clearly visible in Acts and in Paul's epistles. On this basis he extrapolates a ten-step church-planting strategy that he calls the "Pauline Cycle."[61]

1. *Missionaries Commissioned* (Acts 13.1–4, 15.39–40). Hesselgrave first focuses on the churches in Jerusalem and Antioch, which have already been established, as the basis for further outreach. Three basic objectives are evident at this stage: fostering a willingness to participate in the God-given task of planting churches in both adjacent and more distant communities; mobilizing believers in a program of missionary outreach; and recognizing, preparing, sending, supporting, and cooperating with those whom Christ has appointed.[62]

2. *Audience Contacted* (Acts 13.14–16, 14.1, 16.13–15). Here we find four general missiological objectives: gaining the understanding and goodwill of the local citizens and their leaders; reaching unchurched Christians and inviting them into the church fellowship; reaching "prepared people" (those who might be favorably disposed toward the gospel); and getting as wide a hearing as possible for the gospel.[63]

---

[60]Ibid., 57.
[61]Ibid., 124.
[62]Ibid., 135–37.
[63]Ibid., 159–60.

3. Gospel Communicated (Acts 13.17–41, 16.31). The ultimate objective is a clear and persuasive presentation of the gospel. More specifically, the apostles' approach is to mobilize and deploy in order to evangelize the target area; to relate the gospel in a clear, convincing, and compelling way; to employ the most appropriate methods; and to utilize various and appropriate communication media in order to reach the unevangelized.[64]

4. Hearers Converted (Acts 13.48, 16.14–15). The goal is to facilitate conversion that grows out of understanding. It should be in keeping with the cultural patterns of decision-making, be genuine and lasting, and result in spiritual fruitfulness, heightening the possibility of others becoming Christian.[65]

5. Believers Congregated (Acts 13.43). "Once people have been converted, it is imperative that they feel themselves to be a part of the divine family, that they faithfully gather with other members of the family, and that they regularly participate in the activities of the family."[66] In Orthodox terms, this is the actual formation of the ecclesial context in which the sacraments can be celebrated, beginning with baptism.

6. Faith Confirmed (Acts 14.21–22, 15.41). By "confirming the faith," Hesselgrave means establishing believers in biblical teachings so they know what they are to believe and how they are to live, as well as providing opportunities for worship, service, witness, and stewardship.[67] In an Orthodox setting this would include not only the ongoing teaching ministry of the Church but also the catechumenate, which comes as part of the previous step and prior to baptism.

7. Leadership Consecrated (Acts 14.23). In this phase of the work, the missionary seeks to promote the spiritual maturity of all believers, recognize individuals who are gifted and spiritually qualified for leadership, and finalize an organizational structure.[68] In an Orthodox mission this might be expressed in the form of a parish council as well as in the deliberate implementation of the charismatic structure of ministries.

[64]Ibid., 201.
[65]Ibid., 233.
[66]Ibid., 269–71.
[67]Ibid., 302–05.
[68]Ibid., 349–51.

8. Believers Commended (Acts 14.23, 16.40). This aspect of the strategy involves the withdrawal of the church planter(s) and an orderly transition to new pastoral leadership. For the Orthodox faithful, this step would of course be overseen by the bishop.[69]

9. Relationships Continued (Acts 15.36, 18.23). This step includes establishing a continuing relationship between the church planter and the church; establishing a relationship between the new church and the larger Church, including the bishop, the diocese, and perhaps a deanery; and continuing the relationship between the new church and the founding mission or mother church that furthers the worldwide mission of the Church.[70]

10. Sending Churches Convened (Acts 14.26–27, 15.1–4). At this point the whole process starts over again, with the newly planted church now fully participating in a new round of missionary work originated and supported by the local church.[71]

Having established the basics of each step with the biblical texts, Hesselgrave seeks to incorporate the lessons and insights of the social sciences, linguistics, communications theory, and history to "modernize" and contextualize the actual implementation of the plan. We will look into this aspect in the final part of this book. While parts of Hesselgrave's strategy would have to be altered to fit an Orthodox setting, we find a considerable degree of overlap between his outline and the various strategies employed by Orthodox hierarchs and missionaries. The reason for this common ground, I believe, is the New Testament itself. The New Testament relays to us Christ's commission to the apostles, their early attempts to fulfill that assignment, and practical insights as to how they carried out their task. This information can now be taken and applied to our own missional situation in the form of specific principles of action. However, before we try to put those axioms in place, we still need to explore one more possible source of missiological data, namely, the tradition of the Church.

---

[69]Ibid., 383–85.
[70]Ibid., 401–03.
[71]Ibid., 427.

6

Mission in the Tradition[1] of the Church

W e have already looked at several elements of Orthodox tradition. The Scriptures have given us a wealth of data that we can use to develop our theology of mission. In addition, we have seen that the hierarchs have consistently contributed to missiological thinking by overseeing the missionary outreach of the Church. That leaves us with several other aspects of tradition to which we can turn for missiological data: the liturgical texts of the Church, the pronouncements of the canons and the councils, iconography, and finally, the Church's teachings on the saints.

1. Liturgical Texts of the Church

A great deal of theology is embedded in the texts of Orthodox services and commemorations. This fact reflects the unique character of Orthodox theology that I have referred to as its organic unity. Because all aspects of the Church form a unified whole, worship is understood to be a source of theology just as important as the Church's dogmatic assertions. For our purposes here, let us take a look at the text of the Divine Liturgy and also focus on a select number of festal hymns.

---

[1]In the Orthodox Church, "tradition" is everything that was passed down by Christ to his disciples and from them to each succeeding generation. It generally includes: 1) the Holy Scriptures, 2) apostolic succession, 3) liturgical structures, 4) councils (dogma and canons), 5) hagiography, and 6) iconography.

a) The Divine Liturgy

To begin with, we observe that the Orthodox liturgy is celebrated on behalf of the entire world. In other words, it is itself an instrument of mission and, as such, a rich source of missiological data. According to D. Passakos, "The Eucharist in Paul was understood not only as an icon of the *eschata*, but also as a missionary event with cosmic and social consequences. The Eucharist for him was not only the sacrament of the Church but also the sacrament of the world."[2] This perspective is expressed in several ways throughout the liturgy, which sets the context for the Eucharist. For example, during the service of preparation, the Lamb (a cube-shaped piece of the bread later fractured and distributed to the faithful) is cut cross-wise while the priest intones the words, "Sacrificed is the Lamb of God, who takes away the sin of the world for the life and salvation of the world."[3] Near the end of the preparation, the celebrant refers to Christ as the food of the whole world:

> O God, our God who didst send forth the heavenly Bread, the food of the whole world, our Lord and God Jesus Christ, Savior, Redeemer, and Benefactor, blessing and sanctifying us, do thou thyself bless this offering and receive it upon thy most heavenly altar; remember, as thou art good and the Lover of man, those who brought it and keep us uncondemned in the celebration of thy Divine Mysteries.[4]

The litanies and prayers of the liturgy include prayers for the civil authorities, the sick, the suffering, the captives; we beg God for plentiful harvest, the cessation of war, protection from natural disasters, mercy, peace, and salvation. Typical of these world-encompassing prayers is this one, intoned just after the anaphora:

> Remember, O Lord, the city in which we dwell, every city and country; those who in faith dwell in them. Remember, O Lord, travelers

---

[2] Cited in Hesselgrave and Blomberg, *Planting Churches Cross-Culturally*, 427.

[3] Petros Vassiliadis, *Eucharist and Witness: Orthodox Perspectives on the Unity and Mission of the Church* (Brookline, MA: Holy Cross Orthodox Press, 1998), 63, Note 13.

[4] *The Priest's Service Book*, trans. Archbishop Dmitri (Royster), 2 ed. (Dallas: The Diocese of the South, 2003), 103.

by land, by sea, by air, the sick and the suffering; captives and their salvation. . . .[5]

The choir responds with the words "and all mankind," affirming the universal intent of the prayer. Then, after the great entrance, the elements of bread and wine are placed on the altar and the great eucharistic prayers of thanksgiving are said. This is followed by a "remembering" of the saving works, the cross, the grave, the resurrection, the ascension, and the second coming, at which point the elements are raised in the air and presented to God "on behalf of *all* and for *all*."[6] In celebrating the Eucharist, we proclaim Christ's death and confess his resurrection until he comes.[7] This proclamation has as its intended recipients not only the faithful, but also the whole world, to which the gospel is addressed. The text of the liturgy explicitly states that this reasonable worship is being offered for the world,[8] implying that some benefit will accrue to the world because the liturgy has been celebrated. The liturgy and the Eucharist are an announcement to the world that Christ, the ascended one, is present. He is here with us, ready to engage anyone who approaches. And when the faithful are dismissed at the end of the liturgy, it is to go into the world as witnesses of what they have seen and received. As Archimandrite Meletios (Webber) puts it, "Having been touched by God, we go out into the world to proclaim the kingdom to all nations—not with our words or actions, but by who we are, or more correctly, who we have become through the actions of the Holy Spirit."[9]

The Divine Liturgy reminds us that the gospel is Christ himself; it mediates his very presence in the Eucharist. The prayers and hymns of the liturgy remind us of our responsibility to proclaim that gospel in the entire world. The liturgy is "undoubtedly one of the starting points for Orthodox mission, the springboard of the Church's witnessing exodus to

[5]Ibid., 111.

[6]Ibid., 151.

[7]Ibid., 146. This is taken from the Liturgy of St Basil the Great and references Christ's own words as reported by St Paul in 1 Cor 11.26.

[8]Ibid., 205.

[9]Meletios Webber, *Bread & Water, Wine & Oil: An Orthodox Christian Experience of God* (Chesterton, IN: Conciliar Press, 2007), 146.

the world."[10] It is a fundamentally missionary act, celebrated on behalf of the world and providing a context in which the living Lord can be personally encountered. If that presence is, at least in part, intended to benefit nonbelievers, then the liturgy becomes a place of missionary encounter with the immanent Savior. Mission, then, depends

> primarily on our being real witnesses to the joy and the peace of the Holy Spirit, to that new life of which we are made partakers in the Church. The Church is the sacrament of the kingdom—not because she possesses divinely instituted acts called "sacraments," but because, first of all, she is the possibility given to man to see and to "live" it in Christ.[11]

b) The Hymns of the Church

Another place to look for missiological data is among the many hymns of the Church. In a very general sense these hymns represent the moveable parts of our services, for they are usually associated with the feast or the saint commemorated on a particular day. The primary sources for these hymns are: a) the Octoechos (hymns used at offices throughout the week and composed according to an eight-tone system of religious chant); b) the Triodion (for services from the fourth Sunday before Lent to Easter, often including canons of three odes instead of the regular nine); c) the Pentecostarion (from Easter Sunday to the first Sunday after Pentecost); d) the Menaion (hymns for each day of the year, arranged by month); and e) the Horologion (the texts for the daily offices). We can tap into this rich resource by looking at the hymns for several major feasts and celebrations of the Church. In them we see the unfolding of divine redemption for all peoples and the commissioning of the Church as witness to every nation.

The Annunciation and Entry of the Theotokos into the Temple. The former feast celebrates the announcement of Christ's conception to Mary.

---

[10]Vassiliadis, *Eucharist and Witness*, 52.

[11]Alexander Schmeman, *For the Life of the World: Sacraments and Orthodoxy*, 2nd rev. and expanded ed. (Crestwood, NY: St. Vladimir's Seminary Press, 1973).

It refers to the incarnation of the Son of God and the salvation he is to bring. The festal hymn (troparion) speaks of salvation's beginning:

> Today is the beginning of our salvation, / The revelation of the eternal mystery! / The Son of God becomes the Son of the Virgin / As Gabriel announces the coming of Grace. / Together with him let us cry to the Theotokos: / "Rejoice, O Full of Grace, / The Lord is with You!"[12]

A similar theme is struck in the troparion for the feast of the Entry of the Theotokos, during which the Church celebrates Mary's presentation to the elders at the temple.

> Today is the prelude of the good will of God, / of the preaching of the salvation of mankind. / The Virgin appears in the temple of God, / in anticipation proclaiming Christ to all. / Let us rejoice / and sing to her: / "Rejoice, O Fulfillment of the Creator's dispensation."[13]

Nativity. The coming of Christ is a celebration of the fulfillment of God's promise of salvation. During the matins service, a verse in ode 4 of the canon highlights the connection to the ancient promise with these words: "You are the expectation of the nations, O Christ, foretold by Jacob in days of old."[14] This verse refers to Jacob's passing on the Abrahamic promise to his son, as recorded in Genesis 27.29: "Let peoples serve you, and nations bow down to you. Be master over your brethren, and let your mother's sons bow down to yu. Cursed be everyone who curses you, and blessed be those who bless you." This whole movement of God toward the world is captured and summarized in the troparion of the Nativity.

---

[12]"Troparion: The Annunciation of Our Most Holy Lady, the Theotokos and Ever-Virgin Mary," ‹http://oca.org/saints/troparia/2014/03/25/100884-the-annunciation-of-our-most-holy-lady-the-theotokos-and-ever-vi›, June 16, 2015.

[13]"Troparion: The Entry of the Most Holy Mother of God into the Temple," ‹http://oca.org/saints/troparia/2014/11/21/103357-the-entry-of-the-most-holy-mother-of-god-into-the-temple›, June 16, 2015.

[14]From the first canon of matins for the Nativity of Our Lord. Text found in the booklet *The Services of Christmas: The Nativity of Our Lord Jesus Christ* (Crestwood, NY: St Vladimir's Seminary Press, n.d.), 92.

Your Nativity, O Christ our God, / Has shone to the world the light of
wisdom! / For by it, those who worshipped the stars, / Were taught by
a star to adore you, / The Sun of Righteousness, / And to know You,
the Orient from on High. / O Lord, glory to You![15]

Pascha, the Feast of Feasts. The Paschal celebration is the apex of
redemptive history, since the passion and resurrection of Christ make
possible the salvation that has been promised. Reflecting on his death,
the ikos[16] from the canon of the midnight service anticipates the universal
implications with the words

He who holds all things together has been lifted up upon the Cross,
and all of ceation weeps at seeing him hanging, naked, upon the wood.
The sun hid its rays and the stars cast aside their splendor. The earth
shook with great fear, the sea fled, and the rocks were split asunder.
Many tombs were opened, and the bodies of holy men arose. . . . "This
is the most blessed Sabbath, on which Christ has fallen asleep to rise
again on the third day."[17]

Indeed, he did rise again, and this triumph of divine grace is captured
in the words of the famous paschal hymn: "Christ is risen from the dead,
trampling down death by death, and upon those in the tombs bestowing
life." The words of the canon exhort: "Let the heavens be glad, and the
earth rejoice. Let the whole world, visible and invisible, keep the feast. For
Christ is risen, our eternal joy."[18] This joy is universal because everything
accomplished by Christ on this day is to be offered to all nations, to every
people, to the whole earth. As expressed by the irmos of ode one, "This is
the day of resurrection. Let us be illumined, O people. Pascha, the Pascha
of the Lord. For from death to life and from earth to heaven has Christ our

[15]"Nativity of Our Lord God and Savior Jesus Christ: Troparion," Orthodox Church
in America, accessed June 16, 2015, http://oca.org/saints/troparia/2015/12/25/103638-the-
nativity-of-our-lord-god-and-savior-jesus-christ.

[16]A short text that follows the kontakion, between the sixth and seventh odes of the
canon.

[17]John Erickson and Paul Lazor, ed., *The Paschal Service* (Syosset, NY: Department of
Religious Education, Orthodox Church in America, 2006), 15.

[18]Ibid., 30.

God led us, as we sing the song of victory."[19] And again, "Today salvation has come to the world, for Christ is risen all-powerful."[20] This message is now to be proclaimed to the whole world, as affirmed by the hypakoe[21] of the paschal canon.

> Before the dawn, Mary and the women came and found the stone rolled away from the tomb. Thy heard the angelic voice: "Why do you seek among the dead as a man the one who is everlasting light? Behold the clothes in the grave. Go and proclaim to the world: The Lord is risen. He has slain death, as He is the Son of God, saving the race of men."[22]

Pentecost. Once the commission to "proclaim" has been issued, the need becomes apparent for an effective inter-human transfer of that knowledge, mediated by the *logos*. As we have observed, all missionaries face the challenge of the language-degrading consequences of the fall and Babel. This would have remained an almost insurmountable impediment to evangelism had not God himself undertaken to reverse those consequences. Indeed, the coming of the Holy Spirit at Pentecost was intended to do just that. As illustrated in the two hymns below, the Church views Pentecost as a reversal of Babel.

> Once, when He descended and confounded the tongues, the Most High divided the nations; and when He distributed the tongues of fire He called all men into unity; and with one accord we glorify the All-Holy Spirit.[23]

> Thou hast renewed Thy disciples with foreign tongues, O Christ, that they might therewith proclaim Thee, the immortal Word and God Who granteth our souls great mercy.[24]

---

[19]Ibid.

[20]Irmos of ode 4, ibid., 32.

[21]A hymn sung at matins on certain great feasts and Sundays: (1) On great feasts it occurs after the third ode of the canon; (2) on Sundays it comes at the end of the reading of the kathismata (i.e., after the Evlogitaria of the Resurrection and the small litany).

[22]Erickson, *The Paschal Service*, 31.

[23]Kontakion of the feast of Pentecost, in *The Pentecostarion*, 412.

[24]"Lord I Call" verse of Vespers of Pentecost, in *The Pentecostarion*, 412.

In both hymns, the work of the Spirit is described as reversing the effects of Babel and enabling the disciples effectively to proclaim the gospel. The first hymn speaks of a renewed communion with God, based not on a single, reunified human language, but on a supra-linguistic unity of doxological oneness in the Holy Spirit. This unity, of course, is most readily evident in the eucharistic community, which transcends the particular languages of its members. In the second hymn, we encounter the idea of an effective proclamation of the gospel. There is no mention of a single reunified language, however, but rather a renewal of the disciples with foreign tongues. It is thus the linguistically enabling work of the Holy Spirit that reverses the effects of Babel.

2. Canons and Councils

The councils of the Church were generally convened in order to meet some crisis or challenge to the integrity of the Church's teaching. Under the guidance of the Holy Spirit, their findings take the form of dogmatic statements (designed to articulate Church teachings), creeds, and canons (rules intended to regulate practical affairs of the Church). While the theological statements and the creeds tend to address missiological concerns indirectly by defining the theological boundaries of the Church, the canons seek to apply that faith and those moral principles to concrete, local, and historical situations: church order, baptisms, ordinations, church government, and the obligations of the hierarchy, clergy, and every Christian. As such, they are examples of the practical application and ongoing re-articulation of tradition to meet the ever-changing needs of the Church. Like dogma, the canons are a distillation of the principles of Scripture as they apply to human behavior. If we search the canons for references to the Great Commission, we find a number of instructions regarding making disciples, baptizing, and teaching. What is significant here is that these requirements are given as practical helps and re-affirmations of the already accepted teaching of the Church. We can lend some structure to our discussion by organizing examples of the canons according to the

Great Commission itself: a) make disciples by baptizing all nations, and b) teaching them "to observe all things I have commanded" (Mt 28.20).

a) Make Disciples by Baptizing All Nations

Canon 1 of the 85 Canons of the Holy Apostles.[25] The text of Canon 1 reads, "A Bishop must be ordained by two or three other Bishops." In his explanation, the commentator of the *Rudder* (St Nicodemus the Hagiorite) adds,

> . . . after the resurrection of our Savior from the dead and His assumption [*sic*] into heaven, the Apostles, who had been sent forth by Him, as He Himself had been sent forth by the Father, into all the world, and had received all authority to bind and to loose and all the gracious gifts of the All-holy Spirit on the day of Pentecost, they not only possessed the name of apostle by virtue of the facts themselves, but indeed even the name of bishop, or overseer, as sacred Epiphanius bears witness (Her. 27): "First were Peter and Paul, these two Apostles and Bishops." Likewise did all the rest, as the Fathers affirm. For this reason it was that they ordained, or decreed, that city bishops be ordained by three bishops or two. But also those who were preaching in the country and city, as sacred Clement says, in his first epistle to the Corinthians: "They appointed their firstfruits, trying them with the Spirit, as bishops and deacons of those who were going to believe in the future." Hence, too, Ignatius the God-bearer, in writing to the faithful in Tralles (a Greek city in Asia Minor), commands: "Respect your Bishop, too, like Christ, in accordance with what the blissful [*sic*] Apostles enjoined." Thus much is all we have to say concerning the word *bishop.*[26]

---

[25]See also Canon 4 of the First Ecumenical Synod; Canon 3 of the Seventh Ecumenical Synod.

[26]The canons also emphasized the fact that the teachings that came from Christ are to be passed down and preserved from generation to generation. Canon 1 of the Sixth Ecumenical Council reminds us that the Council ratified "the teachings set forth by the God-bearing Fathers who earlier assembled. . . ." Orthodox Eastern Church and Denver Cummings, *The Rudder (Pedalion) of the Metaphorical Ship of the One Holy Catholic and Apostolic Church of Orthodox Christians = or, All the Sacred and Divine Canons . . . As Embodied in the Original Greek Text* (Chicago, IL: Orthodox Christian Educational Society, 1957), 104–06.

What is evident here is that Christ did, in fact, commission certain individuals (the apostles) who were to initiate a sustained effort to proclaim the gospel in the entire world. In order to do that, they themselves commissioned the next generation of Church leaders (the bishops) who were to oversee the completion of the missionary task in each newly acquired region. What this canon does, then, is confirm the presence of worldwide evangelistic activity. It affirms that the basic hierarchical structures are part of that missionary strategy and gives legitimacy to the practice of second-stage, continuing commissioning of missionaries.

> *Canon 50 of the 85 Canons of the Holy Apostles.* If any Bishop or Presbyter does not perform three immersions (literally, "three baptisms") in making one baptism (literally, "one initiation"), but (*sc.* only) a single immersion (literally, "a single baptism"), that given into the death of the Lord, let him be deposed (*sc.* from office). For the Lord did not say, "Baptize ye into my death," but, "Go ye and make disciples of all nations, baptizing them in the name of the Father, and of the Son, and of the Holy Spirit." [27]

Once again, we see that the canon simply assumes the fact of and legitimacy of the apostolic task of making individuals disciples by baptizing them. What it adds are specific instructions for just how that rite is to be performed. This gave some uniformity or standardization to the then rapidly expanding Church. The interpretation of Canon 49 by Nicodemus the Hagiorite states:

> When the Lord sent forth His disciples to preach the Gospel, He told them: "Go ye, therefore, and make disciples of all nations, baptizing them in the name of the Father, and of the Son, and of the Holy Spirit" [Mt 28.19]. So the present Apostolical Canon prescribes that any Bishop or Presbyter who, instead of baptizing in that manner, in accordance with the ordinance of the Lord's, baptizes into three beginningless beings, into three sons, or into three comforters shall be deposed. For certain heretics, blaspheming against the Holy Trinity, were being baptized in such a manner notwithstanding that the Church of Orthodox

[27]Ibid., 668.

Christians had received instructions to say the Father on account of His being beginningless and unbegotten, even though the Son is also said to be beginningless as respects any beginning in point of time, as St. Gregory the Theologian theologically argues: and likewise to say the Holy Spirit, though not with respect to cause and natural beginning, for this character belongs only to the Father. Accordingly, the formula includes a Son on account of His ineffable birth, and a Paraclete (or Comforter), the Holy Spirit, on account of His super-rational procession out of the Father alone. Note, on the other hand, that all the Canons of the Apostles that relate to and speak of baptism mention only Bishops and Presbyters. For they alone have permission to baptize, and deacons and other clergymen have not.[28]

b) Teach Them to Observe Everything I Have Commanded

In each of the following examples, the authors of the canons simply assume that it is their Christ-given responsibility to teach everything that Christ has taught them.[29] In fact, the chief responsibility of a bishop is to preserve and disseminate that teaching. What the canons do is give us practical instructions on just how that teaching is to take place.

> *Canon 27 of the 85 Canons of the Holy Apostles:* As for a Bishop, or Presbyter, or Deacon that strikes believers for sinning, or unbelievers for wrong-doing, with the idea of making them afraid, we command that he be deposed from office. For the Lord has nowhere taught that: on the contrary, He Himself when struck did not strike back; when reviled, He did not revile His revilers; when suffering, He did not threaten.[30]

[28]Ibid., 30.

[29]This is affirmed in the Canon of St Gennadius, the Patriarch of Constantinople: "Our Lord and God and Saviour Jesus Christ, after handing over the preaching of the Gospel to His holy disciples and sending them forth over the whole inhabited earth as teachers, gave an express command that what they had received from Him gratis they were to impart the same to men gratis, without charging therefore any copper, or silver, or gold, or any other thing of material or earthly value whatever." *The Rudder*, 923.

[30]Cummings, *The Rudder*, 1668. Compare Canon 9 of the First and Second Synod; Canon 5 of Antioch; Canons 57, 62, 76, 106, 107 of Carthage; and 1 Peter 2:23.

In his explanation of this canon, Nicodemus adds,

In teaching His disciples His divine commandments the Lord used to say, "Whatever I say to you my disciples, I say also to all Christians" [Mk 13.37]. One of His commandments is to turn our left cheek to anyone that strikes our right cheek [Mt 5.39]. If, therefore, this commandment ought to be kept by all Christians, it ought much more to be obeyed by those in Holy Orders, and especially by bishops, regarding whom divine Paul wrote to Timothy that a bishop ought not to be a striker [I Tim 3.3]. That is why the present Canon says too: If any bishop, or presbyter, or deacon strikes those Christians who offend him, or unbelievers that do wrong to others, with a view to making others afraid of him with such blows, we command that he be deposed from office. For in no part of the Gospel has the Lord taught to do such a thing as that: in fact, He has taught us quite the contrary with His example; since when beaten by the soldiers and Jews, at the time of His passion, He did not lift a hand to beat them in return. When accused and insulted, He did not insult others, nor did He accuse them. Even when suffering on the Cross, He did not threaten to chastise them, but begged His Father to pardon them.[31]

In my opinion, if this canon had been known and observed, many questionable tactics—for example, locking people up in the cathedral for instruction—would never have been tolerated. In any case, this canon has clear missiological implications.

Canons 62 and 85 of the 85 Canons of the Holy Apostles. After giving careful instructions to the clergy on how they are to discharge their duties, Canon 85 legislates which books are to be used as sources for teaching in the Church. Canon 60 speaks negatively of heretical books that were banned (which would have included the so-called "Gospel according to St Thomas," "Revelations" of Abraham, Isaac, and Jacob, and the "The Alphabet of Alphabets").

[31]Ibid., 140.

If anyone reads to the public in churches the books of impious writers bearing false inscriptions and purporting to be holy, to the injury of laity and clergy, let him be deposed.[32]

To all you Clergymen and Laymen let the following books be venerable and sacred: Of the Old Testament, the five of Moses, namely, Genesis, Exodus, Leviticus, Numbers, and Deuteronomy; the one of Jesus of Nave (commonly called Joshua in English); the one of Judges; the one of Ruth; the four of the Kingdoms; two Paralipomena of the Book of Days; two of Esdras; one of Esther; three of the Maccabees; one of Job; one Psalter (commonly called the Psalms in English and also in Greek); three of Solomon, namely, Proverbs, Ecclesiastes, and the Song of Songs; twelve of the Prophets; one of Isaiah; one of Jeremiah; one of Ezekiel; one of Daniel; outside of these it is permissible for you to recount in addition thereto also the Wisdom of very learned Sirach by way of teaching your younger folks. Our own books, that is to say, those of the New Testament, comprising four Gospels, namely, that of Matthew, of Mark, of Luke, and of John; fourteen Epistles of Paul; two Epistles of Peter, three Epistles of John; one of James; one of Jude; two Epistles of Clement; and the Injunctions addressed to you Bishops through me, Clement, in eight books, which ought not to be divulged to all on account of the secret matters they contain[,] and the Acts of us Apostles.[33]

Both canons provide clear statements on the books that are allowed for teaching. Since they are limited to the recognized books of the Holy Scriptures, these canons clearly concentrate the content of our "teaching all things" on the story told by the Bible. From this we may conclude that the Church will not be using materials generated by secular philosophers, pop-psychologists, or businesspeople, no matter how good they might be, to fulfill this part of its missiological responsibility. I am not suggesting that there is no place in the Church for considering other sources, only

---

[32] Ibid., 102. See also Canons 2 and 63 of the Sixth Ecumenical Synod; Canon 9 of the Seventh Ecumenical Synod; Canon 51 of Laodicea.

[33] Ibid., 194.

that in the formal exercise of our commission to teach all things, we rely exclusively on the "grand narrative" of the Bible. So, until that work is done, there will be no "book" studies in the Church, only Bible studies.

Canon 19 of the Sixth Ecumenical Council. This canon describes the overall procedure for this teaching ministry, and shows how other sources of information, such as the writings of the Fathers, are to be used.

> We declare that the deans of churches, on every day, but more especially on Sundays, must teach all the Clergy and the laity words of truth out of the Holy Bible, analyzing the meanings and judgments of the truth, and not deviating from the definitions already laid down, or the teaching derived from the God-bearing Fathers; but also, if the discourse be one concerning a passage of Scripture, not to interpret it otherwise than as the luminaries and teachers of the Church in their own written works have presented it; and let them rather content themselves with these discourses than attempt to produce discourses of their own, lest, at times, being resourceless, they overstep the bounds of propriety. For by means of the teaching afforded by the aforesaid Fathers, the laity, being apprised of the important and preferred things, and of the disadvantageous and rejectable, are enabled to adjust their lives for the better, and do not become a prey to the ailment of ignorance, but, by paying due attention to what is taught, they sharpen their wits so as to avoid suffering wrongly, and for fear of impending punishments they work out their own salvation.[34]

Based on these few examples, we see that the canons of the Church maintain the concept of apostolic succession and the advance of the Church by means of ecclesial decree. They affirm the details of the baptismal process, as well as the necessity of teaching and the ways in which we are to teach. In a way, there is nothing new here. The canons simply explicate and affirm the process established by our Lord.

---

[34]Ibid., 240–41. See also Apostolic Canon 56; Canons 2, 16 of the First Ecumenical Synod; Canon 19 of Laodicea; Canons 79, 131, 132, 133 of Carthage; Canon 10 of Peter; Canon 6 of John the Faster.

3. Iconography

One of the best-known elements of Eastern tradition is the icon or holy image. Upon entering an Orthodox temple, the visitor is confronted with a whole universe of images. There is the image of Christ Pantocrator painted on the domed ceiling. The Virgin Mary with arms open in welcome greets one from the apse (Platytera). The icon screen (iconostasis), with its images of Christ, Mary, John the Baptist, angels, and feasts, serves as a portal between heaven (the sanctuary) and earth (the nave). The walls of the nave are host to numerous saints and biblical scenes. Before anyone sets foot in the temple, Christ and his saints already populate it. The same thing is true in the homes of the faithful, where icons establish prayer corners and occupy most of the rooms in the house. Because it is an element of tradition, the icon is also a source of theological data. So we can look to icons for instruction on the basic missiological aspects of the life of the Church, extracting the meaning contained in their many details. There are literally hundreds of icons that show the evangelistic work of the saints, including a few that depict and exemplify the commissioning of the apostles as well as the implementation of the mission given to them by Christ.

a) Commissioning of the Apostles (Mt 28)

The connection of this icon to Matthew 28 and Acts 1 is obvious. In it we see Christ sending his apostles (disciples) out into the world to make more disciples. Christ's hand, with its all-inclusive gesture, indicates that the whole world, everything beyond that place, is to be their audience. But his gaze is fixed on them, for He is transferring to them both the theological content and the practice of his teaching, and authorizing them to continue his work on earth. The depiction of the apostles is also instructive. Their faces are all intensely focused

The Great Commission
(contemporary icon)

on Christ, the giver of this commission and himself the very content of the gospel. Just as he is dominant in the icon, he would remain dominant in their lives. As they go out into the world, they learn to never take their eyes off him nor question the fact that he asked them to do these things. The apostles are presented as submissive and accepting: note how their hands are crossed on their chests or held out as if to receive something, especially in the case of Peter (in the orange garment) with both hands held out. These men will be sent out into a hostile world, but their demeanor in the icon is one of quiet acceptance and submissive agreement to the rigors that are to come. The icon affirms and restates the other missiological elements of tradition, i.e., the Scriptures, apostolic succession, and the fundamental hierarchical structure of the Church.

b) Commissioning of the Seventy (Lk 10)

The Seventy Apostles
(contemporary icon)

During his earthly ministry Jesus sent out seventy apostles to go before him, two by two, into the cities He would visit. He gave them the "authority to trample on serpents and scorpions, and over all the power of the enemy" (Lk 10.18). Later, with the coming of the Holy Spirit on Pentecost, the ascended Christ (seen in this icon) empowered and commissioned the Seventy to preach the gospel in various lands. Some, like the holy evangelists Mark and Luke, St Paul's companion Timothy, and Prochorus, the disciple of John the Theologian, accompanied the twelve apostles. The exapostilarion sung at the end of the matins canon on January 4 praises the Seventy, some of whom were martyred for following Christ: "O Word and Teacher, with fercent love the Seventy became your disciples, and they abandoned the world so that with faith they might cleanse the world of its ignorance."[35]

[35] *The Menaion* for January, ‹http://glt.goarch.org/texts/Jan/Jan04.html›, June 21, 2017; translated by Fr Benedict Churchill for this publication.

The icon thus confirms the very beginning of the post-apostolic, ongoing commissioning of the faithful and the legitimacy or authority of their mission. We have a visual confirmation of the way in which the number of apostles and bishops grew as the Church expanded.

c) The Church (Jesus, Apostles, Church Fathers)

This icon depicts the Church as a ship crossing the waters of history, with all of its dangers and obstacles. The ship in this icon is not bound to any particular time or place. It is a dynamic and living entity moving toward the kingdom of God. At its helm is Christ, actively involved in guiding the Church to its appointed destination. He is ascended, but still always present in the Church. Along with him are his disciples, that first generation of missionaries. In addition there are a number of the early Church

The Church
(contemporary icon)

Fathers, that second and third generation of hierarchs who authoritatively led the ongoing mission of the Church. And the Virgin Mary is there, her hands spread in prayer for the Church and its children.

This icon clearly teaches us that at any given moment the Church is situated in the long and unbroken continuity of apostolic tradition, and that Christ, Mary, and all the saints are to be taken into all the world in the form of eucharistic assemblies, for just as he is perpetually present in the icon, the assembly is and has always been the privileged place of Christ's manifestation in every generation. The icon also affirms the idea that this work can only be legitimately done by those "in the ship," that is, only by certain authorized representatives of Christ. This message, already familiar, is here confirmed in yet another way.

4. Hagiography

Literally thousands of saints have been involved in the spread of the gospel. Interestingly, Orthodox hagiography has given some saints special titles to indicate the type of work they did, or the reason for their canonization. One title of particular interest to us in our quest for missions-related data, is that of "Equal to the Apostles." This title is bestowed in recognition of certain saints' outstanding service in spreading Christianity, often in ways similar to those of the original apostles. As one might expect, these saints are spread out over all world and throughout all of history. Some of the saints included in this category are:

- Mary Magdalene (first century)
- Photine, the Samaritan Woman at the Well (first century)
- Thekla (first century)
- Abercius of Hieropolis (second century)
- Helena of Constantinople (ca. 250–330)
- Constantine the Great (ca. 272–337)
- Nino (ca. 296–338 or 340), baptizer of the Georgians
- Mirian III of Iberia (died 361), first Christian Georgian monarch
- Patrick of Ireland (fifth century)
- Cyril (827–869)
- Methodius (826–885)
- Boris I of Bulgaria (died 907)
- Olga of Kiev (ca. 890–969)
- Vladimir (ca. 958–1015)
- Stephen I of Hungary (969–1038)
- Sava I of Serbia (1175–1235)
- Cosmas of Aetolia (1714–1779)

- Herman of Alaska (ca. 1750–1836), cf. chapter 2

- Innocent of Alaska (1797–1879), cf. chapter 2

- Nicholas of Japan (1836–1912)

By examining the lives of some of these saints and the hymns dedicated to them, we tap into another source affirming the basic outline of the Church's mission as it now comes into view.

a) Saint Nino (ca. 296–338 or 340), Baptizer of the Georgians

The virgin Nino of Cappadocia learned that Christ's robe had arrived in Georgia, a country of pagans. She prayed that she might travel to Georgia to venerate the sacred robe. The Most Holy Virgin heard her prayers and appeared to Nino in a dream, saying, "Go to the country that was assigned to me by lot and preach the gospel of our Lord Jesus Christ. He will send down his grace upon you and I will be your protector." Patriarch Juvenal commissioned Nino to proclaim the gospel to the Georgians, asking God to enlighten her with the wisdom to proclaim the good news just as he did the apostles.

When Nino arrived in Georgia, she was greeted by a contingent of Mtskhetan shepherds near Lake Paravani. With God's blessing, she began to preach to the pagans of this region. Every place St Nino preached and performed healings, her listeners converted to the Christian faith in great numbers.[36]

The life of St Nino confirms and illustrates a number of the themes that have been emerging in our study. Her mission to Georgia began with both divine and hierarchical commission. She worked miracles and preached in a way that took into account the local culture (for example, asking permission to preach) and language. A hymn of praise by St Nikolai Velimirović commemorates her work.

---

[36]"St. Nino (Nina), Equal of the Apostles and Enlightener of Georgia," Orthodox Church in America, accessed Jan 31, 2017, https://oca.org/saints/lives/2017/01/14/100191-st-nino-nina-equal-of-the-apostles-and-enlightener-of-georgia.

A virgin most beautiful, noble Nina,

By providence became the Apostle to the Georgians,

In defiance of the persecution by Emperor Diocletian.

With the Cross she baptized Emperor Mirian,

His wife Nana and his son Bakar,

And through them, all the people and the elite of the leaders.

With the Cross of the Son of God she baptized them all.

Saint Nina, Apostle to the Georgians.

From her youth Nina prayed to God

That Djul (the Rose)—Georgia—be baptized by her;

And the good God granted that for which she prayed.

From Nina's hand the Cross shone

Upon gentle Georgia, where it shines even now,

Where Nina's hand blesses even now.

There is Nina's grave, over which a church glistens,

Glorifying Saint Nina and the Lord Christ.[37]

b) Patrick of Ireland (390–460)

What is remarkable about the life of St Patrick is that he was surrounded by the supernatural power of God. We have the following account from *The Life of St Patrick*:

> Now when the holy Patrick was born, he was brought to be baptized to the blind flat-faced youth named Gornias. But Gornias had not water wherewith he could perform the baptism, so with the infant's hand he made the sign of the cross over the earth, and a wellspring of water brake therefrom. Gornias put the water on his own face, and it healed him at once, and he understood the letters (of the alphabet), though he had never seen them before. Now here at one time God wrought a threefold miracle for Patrick, the wellspring of water from the earth, and his eyesight to the blind youth, and skill in reading aloud the order

[37]Nikolai (Velimirović), *The Prologue of Ohrid: Lives of Saints, Hymns, Reflections and Homilies for Every Day of the Year*, trans. T. Timothy Tepsić, ed. Janko Trbović, 2nd ed., vol. 1, *January to June* (Alhambra, CA: Sebastian Press, 2008), 52.

of baptism without knowing the letters beforehand. Thereafter Patrick was baptized.[38]

Around 432 St Patrick was commissioned to convert the Irish to Christ. His effective work was so successful that, within seven years, three bishops were sent from Gaul to help. This was no doubt the result of God's super-natural blessing. That he depended on this empowering is evident from the famous lines of his prayer, the Lorica, in which he asks for Christ's presence and supernatural protection against the evils of life, with the words: "Christ with me, Christ before me, Christ behind me, Christ in me, Christ under me, Christ over me, Christ to right of me, Christ to left of me, Christ in lying down, Christ in sitting. . . ."[39] The name Lorica is probably derived from Ephesians 6.14, wherein the apostle bids his readers stand, "having put on the breast-plate of righteousness," which in Latin reads *induti lorica iustitiae*. It is also called the "Cry of the Deer." Archbishop John Healy relates the reasons behind these names:

> This poem is called in Irish the Fead Fiada, or Cry of the Deer, because it was chanted by the Apostle and his companions, when they sought, under the appearance of a deer and her fawns, to escape the deadly ambushes prepared for them by King Laeghaire, on their way from the Hill of Slane to Tara, at the early dawn of Erin's First Easter Sunday morning. It is also called the Lorica, or Corslet of Patrick, because it was a shield to protect him and his against the wiles of Laeghaire and his Druids.[40]

So, blessed by God, Patrick enters a pagan country. Once again a hier-arch commissions him, he faithfully and effectively studies local culture and custom, language, and art, and uses these things in his ministry. Thirty

---

[38]"On the Life of St. Patrick," ⟨http://www.ucc.ie/celt/online/T201009.html⟩, June 17, 2015.

[39]Newport J. D. White, *St. Patrick: His Writings and Life*, Translations of Christian Literature Series V: Lives of the Celtic Saints (London: Society for Promoting Christian Knowledge, 1920), 66–67.

[40]John Healy, *The Life and Writings of St. Patrick with Appendices, etc.* (Dublin: M. H. Gill & Son / Sealy, Bryers & Walker, 1905), 560.

years later (461), the Christian faith had been firmly planted. The troparion and kontakion for the saint commemorate these aspects of his life.

> Holy Bishop Patrick,
> Faithful shepherd of Christ's royal flock,
> You filled Ireland with the radiance of the Gospel:
> The mighty strength of the Trinity!
> Now that you stand before the Savior,
> Pray that He may preserve us in faith and love!
>
> From slavery you escaped to freedom in Christ's service:
> He sent you to deliver Ireland from the devil's bondage.
> You planted the Word of the Gospel in pagan hearts.
> In your journeys and hardships you rivaled the Apostle Paul!
> Having received the reward for your labors in heaven,
> Never cease to pray for the flock you have gathered on earth,
> Holy bishop Patrick![41]

c) Cosmas of Aetolia (1714–1779)

Cosmas was a monk on Mount Athos who received written permission from Patriarch Seraphim II to preach the holy gospel. He began by preaching in the churches of Constantinople and in local villages. He then moved north into the Danube regions, continuing his work in Thessalonica, Verroia, Macedonia, Chimaera, Akarnania, Aetolia, and on the islands of Saint Maura (Lefkada) and Cephalonia. His preaching was simple, quiet, gentle, and yet filled with the power of God, who confirmed his words and miracles. He also preached in Albania, where Christian piety had all but disappeared. Through his preaching St Cosmas was able to lead the Albanians to repentance and, by his teaching, to advance their understanding of the Bible. He established church schools all over the region. At one point so many people were waiting to hear him preach that he, together with fifty priests, conducted services in the fields and

---

[41]"St Patrick the Bishop of Armagh and Enlightener of Ireland," ‹http://oca.org/saints/troparia/2014/03/17/100821-st-patrick-the-bishop-of-armagh-and-enlightener-of-ireland›, June 17, 2015.

town squares. He died a martyr's death in 1779, when he was seized by the Turks and strangled. The life of St Cosmas reflects the pattern we have seen elaborated in other aspects of tradition: arch-pastoral commission, sensitivity to the culture and language of his listeners, and the importance of continued education.

> Come from Aetolia, O God-bearing Father, thou didst become a righteous monk on Mount Athos; and as a true initiate of the glory of God, thou didst preach the word of truth to all men, O most blest one, and didst bring them all to Christ as a true emulator of the Apostles' choir, and thou didst prove a hieromartyr in shedding thy sacred blood.[42]

d) Nicholas of Japan (1836–1912)

Saint Nicholas the Enlightener of Japan was born in 1836. After his education he was ordained a priest and assigned to the consular church in Japan. Because of the many cultural differences, he spent eight years studying the people's language, manners and customs. In 1870 he was raised to the rank of archimandrite and began his ministry to the Japanese. In 1877 he began work in Tokyo on a building that was to serve as a church, a school for fifty men, and later a seminary. By this time there were 4,115 believers in Japan. In 1874, Bishop Paul of Kamchatka arrived in Tokyo to ordain a number of Japanese priests. Nicholas was consecrated bishop in 1880. He continued his apostolic work, completing the Cathedral of the Resurrection of Christ in Tokyo, translating service books, and compiling a special Orthodox theological dictionary in the Japanese language. By the time he died in 1912, the Japanese Orthodox Church had 33,017 members in 266 communities served by an archbishop, a bishop, and thirty-five priests. The troparion written in his honor clearly places him in the ranks of the apostles.[43]

---

[42]"Saint Cosmas of Aetolia, Equal to the Apostles," ‹http://www.goarch.org/chapel/saints_view?contentid=581&type=saints›, June 17, 2015.

[43]"St Nicholas, Equal of the Apostles and Archbishop of Japan," ‹http://oca.org/saints/lives/2015/02/16/100419-st-nicholas-equal-of-the-apostles-and-archbishop-of-japan›, June 17, 2015.

O holy saint Nicholas / The enlightener of Japan, / You share a dignity and the throne of the Apostles; / You are a wise and faithful servant of Christ, / A temple chosen by the Divine Spirit, / A vessel overflowing with the love of Christ / O hierarch equal to the Apostles, / Pray to the Life-Creating Trinity / For all your flock and for the whole world.[44]

This brief look at the liturgical texts, canons, icons, and saints has brought us clear evidence that, throughout its history, the Church has followed a very well-thought-out pattern, one passed on to us by Christ himself. We see missionaries, authorized by their canonical hierarchs, taking the gospel to every people and using indigenous cultures and languages to establish eucharistic communities. The next step in our journey will be to apply these data to our contemporary situation in a way that defines the task and provides adequate guidance.

[44]Ibid.

PART THREE

An Orthodox Theology of Mission

Now that we have gathered the raw data for our theology, we can set about the task of systematizing that information. Everything we develop will reflect the theological data that we have collected. Some years ago, when evaluating the mission theology of certain North American missiologists,[1] I suggested that one might readily see how the biblical data they had collected impacted the formulation of their theology. I pointed out that a) their understanding of Scripture provided the basis for their justification of missionary outreach; b) their emphasis on soteriology led to an almost exclusive emphasis on individual conversion as the goal of missions: c) the combination of their understanding of Scripture and an extreme pragmatism caused them to think of the execution of mission in terms of communication, contextualization, and dialogue; d) their ecclesiology allowed them to view the Church as both carrier and result of the Christian message; and e) their eschatology encouraged them to think in terms of an eventual completion of the missionary commission.

It is evident that the Orthodox pool of missiological data differs significantly from that of our Protestant friends, and therefore its impact on our understanding of the various aspects of mission will be just as pronounced. Our broad context as defined by our soteriological data will determine the ultimate rationale, task, and goal of missions. The specificity of our ecclesiology and our understanding of the eucharistic

---

[1] Edward Rommen, *Die Notwendigkeit der Umkehr* (Giessen: Brunnen Verlag, 1994).

community will determine the source, structure, and execution of that mission. Our understanding of Christ's incarnation, death, resurrection, and ascension will determine the basic content of the missionary's message. All of these biblical and historical data, as well as our conception of life in Christ (deification), will guide the ways in which we fulfill our missionary responsibilities.

Based on these data, I will now present an initial set of axiomatic principles for each of the five aspects of the Church's mission in the world: the rationale and goal of an Orthodox mission to the world (chapter 7); the ecclesial origin of missionary outreach (chapter 8); the basic content of the gospel and the nature of church education (chapter 9); and general guidelines for the implementation of mission (chapter 10).

7

The Rationale and Goal of Mission

The first set of questions we need to ask ourselves is why we engage in missions, and just what it is we seek to accomplish. The data we have gathered suggests that the rationale and the goal of the Church's mission are to be guided by two axioms.

1) Recipients Participating. The fundamental rationale or motive for Orthodox missionary outreach is rooted in the fact that each believer is a recipient of divine benefaction, and for that reason is to be an active participant in the ongoing mission of God to the world.

2) Making Disciples. The ultimate goal of the missionary endeavor is to introduce non-believing individuals to Christ with a view toward moving them by faith to enter into a personal relationship with Christ, which initiates the process of deification. The best way to summarize this task is to define it in terms of the more general concept of discipleship contained in the Great Commission itself.

1. Recipients Participating: An Orthodox Rationale for Mission[1]

The rationale for most Protestant missionary activity during the last 300 years has been based on the idea of obedience to the Great Commission

[1]I first explored these ideas in my Munich dissertation. Edward Rommen, *Die Notwendigkeit der Umkehr: Missionsstrategie und Gemeindeaufbau in der Sicht evangelikaler Missionswissenschaftler Nordamerikas* (Giessen: Brunnen Verlag, 1987).

(Mt 28.18ff.). This appeal to obedience was made popular by William Carey's famous *Enquiry (1792)*. *According to Carey, the command to make disciples has never been rescinded;*[2] it is still binding for us, and thus requires our obedience. This argument convinced many, and led to what has been called the "great century"[3] of Protestant missions. In rapid succession a host of new mission societies, such as "The London Missionary Society" (1795) and "The Church Missionary Society" (1799), were organized on this principle.[4] Obedience became the primary motive for the most successful epoch of Protestant missions.[5] To this day, especially among evangelicals, it remains the primary justification for missionary work, and it has even been adopted by a number of Orthodox organizations.[6]

Unfortunately, the concept of obedience has not fared well in the modern context. Both in the secular world and in the Church, it has proven an inadequate and misunderstood motivation for mission. There are two main reasons for this: obedience involves limiting personal freedom, and the once noble idea of obedience has been tainted by abuse.

First, any call for obedience is simultaneously an appeal to some operative authority, which by definition limits personal freedom. However, this individual freedom is arguably the most cherished and intensely defended component of the contemporary mindset. In fact, the desire for

[2]William Carey, *An Enquiry into the Obligations of Christians to Use Means for the Conversion of the Heathens* (Leicester, 1792).

[3]This is Latourette's designation for the nineteenth century, "the age of the most extensive geographic spread of Christianity." T. B. Ray, *The Highway of Mission Thought: Eight of the Greatest Discourses on Missions* (Nashville, TN: Sunday School Board, 1907), 9–17.

[4]Henry Venn, the then-leader of the CMS, speaking of the founders of the Mission, notes that "they were men who felt their individual responsibility to obey the command of Christ. . . ." In Kenneth Scott Latourette, *A History of the Expansion of Christianity*, 7 vols., Contemporary Evangelical Perspectives (Grand Rapids, MI: Zondervan Pub. House, 1970), 4, 1.

[5]Harry Boer suggested that the primary motive for the awakening of missionary energy during the century preeeding 1960 was "obedience to the command of Christ" based on the missionary's own experience of Jesus as savior and Lord and his conviction that Jesus was also the savior of all the lost. See Harry R. Boer, *Pentecost and Missions* (Grand Rapids: Eerdmans, 1961), 25.

[6]The Great Commission is prominently displayed on the OCMC home page. "Mission, Vision, & Values," ‹http://www.ocmc.org/about/index.aspx›, June 18, 2015.

freedom is so strong that it usually transmutes into a demand for choice, i.e., the ability to pursue the fulfillment of the desires of the will without coercion or restraint. And, as if to convince ourselves that we are free, we encourage an almost unlimited proliferation of choice, as if more choices actually secured more freedom. Another key aspect of this concept of personal freedom is the conviction that we are always entitled to express that freedom. This stance in turn leads to the chaos of unrestrained expression—the notion that we always have a right to a personal opinion, no matter the topic, and the right to express that opinion, regardless of the setting. This presumed right to choose and express is often extended into the moral and behavioral realms. As a result, the individual is seen as the primary or even sole arbiter of what is true and right,[7] and who thus needs no one's instruction.

Obviously this preoccupation with freedom conflicts not only with the gospel itself, but also with the idea of obedience in general. The gospel, first of all, offers a remedy to the human situation that has only one option: complete surrender to Christ. That effectively puts an end to the idea of unlimited choice. The relationship being offered cannot be demanded as a right, nor its terms negotiated. It is an invitation accepted only by an act of total submission to the Person of Christ. The gospel also limits our freedom of expression. In Christ we are no longer free to formulate personal opinions on every doctrine, every passage of Scripture, every pronouncement of the Church. Instead, we are to be of one mind with Christ. Rather than expressing our own opinions, we are taught to probe the collective consciousness of the Church for the interpretations, explanations, and directions we need. So accepting the gospel involves a self-restraint that will be difficult, to say the least, for the freedom-intoxicated inhabitants of the late modern age. If moderns, including even many Christians, are already uncomfortable with the freedom-limiting nature of the gospel, they will definitely resist the notion that they are required to announce a message that offers only one option. Thus, the limiting nature of the gospel

---

[7]Edward Rommen, *Get Real: On Evangelism in the Late Modern World* (Pasadena, CA: William Carey Library, 2009), 23–25.

itself has made it increasingly difficult to motivate believers to witness in an environment of unrestrained personal freedom.

The second difficulty with the idea of obedience is that it has been abused, that is, used to justify all manner of misbehavior by shifting responsibility away from oneself to some authority. For example, soldiers (and missionaries) may justify an atrocity by saying that they were just following orders. This kind of thing has happened so often that the idea of blind obedience is now viewed with some suspicion, especially if it is used to support activities that are considered wrong, intolerant, or in some other way unwelcome. In our freedom-loving world, any perceived disrespect for the beliefs, religions, and opinions of others—and especially any message that claims to be the only way to God—is going to be called into question. And when it is, it becomes difficult to get individuals to obey the command to engage in that activity. Moreover, even if a person is so motivated, there is a danger that obedience will become a sterile legalism displacing the moderating aspects of the Christian life such as compassion, love, and the warmth of the Spirit. The individual may instead become legalistic, insensitive, coercive, and even manipulative, further undermining the reputation of missions. Given the extreme individualization or personalization of religion in our world, most people simply do not want to be approached by a Christian witness, and Christians in turn have become less and less willing to press the issue. As a rationale for its implementation and reception, simple obedience to the Great Commission is all but incomprehensible in light of today's emphasis on individual independence.

What we need is a different rationale, one comprehensible to non-believers as well as believers. Perhaps we do not have to justify our missionary behavior to non-Christians, who will probably not agree with our actions anyway. However, we might be able to explain our desire to bear witness in terms that they might understand, thus forestalling some of their resistance. What would such a reason for witness look like? If we were to ask our contemporaries what kind of justification might be given for any form of good work, they would probably point to love, compassion, and, maybe more importantly, to the desire and ability to meet some real need, to alleviate some form of suffering. If we recognize the problems of hunger and poverty, then an acceptable, understandable rationale for combating those things would be a desire and an ability to contribute to a solution. Surely even the most jaded modern individual would acknowledge the nobility of active compassion in the face of suffering. On the part of a believer, we might also think of this in terms of an inner compulsion to help: I act not because I must do so, but rather because I want to help, and because I have the resources to do so.

So how might this idea of an inner compulsion translate into the context of the Christian mission? It begins with a recognition of the actual problem facing humanity. We can summarize this by saying the following: Human beings were created in God's image, possessing a free will that they used to turn away from life-giving communion and potential deification in God. This choice had two consequences: death and a propensity to sin, with ever-increasing levels of violence and evil. The incarnation, passion, and resurrection of the Son of God effectively addressed both problems. The solution, then, consists of a restoration of human nature, a healing of the human will, and the forgiveness of sin, available to the individual through faith in the resurrected Christ in the context of the Church.

We believers say that we understand the fundamental dilemma of human existence, that is, the source of all of its woes. Furthermore, we claim to know the answer to those problems, namely, the appropriation by individual faith of the work accomplished by the incarnate and risen Christ. Having experienced both the problem and its solution, believers quite naturally want to make this available to others. For that reason the Church issues an invitation:

> Come, all peoples, and learn the power of the awesome mystery. For Christ our Saviour, who is the Word from the beginning, was crucified for us freely suffered burial for our sake, rising from the dead that he might save all things.[8] Come let us worship him.[9]

---

[8] Some translations emphasize the universality of Christ's work with the words "to save the whole universe."

[9] Praises of Sunday Matins in Tone 3. In *The Octoechos or the Complete Book of Eight Tones*, ‹http://www.archdiocese.ca/rescs/liturgical-texts/OctoechosComplete.pdf›, March 12, 2017.

As beneficiaries of the redemptive acts of God, we are caught up into the flow of salvific history. Our new life in Christ quite naturally leads to the desire to participate in the completion of God's divine purpose. As Archbishop Anastasios puts it,

> It is not simply obedience, duty or altruism. It is an inner necessity. "Necessity is laid upon me," said St Paul, "Woe to me if I do not preach the gospel" (1 Cor 9.16). All other motives are aspects of this need, derivative motives. Mission is an inner necessity (i) for the faithful and (ii) for the Church. If they refuse it, they do not merely omit a duty, they deny themselves.[10]

We see this inner desire to witness at work in the early Church. Acts 8.4 reports that the scattered Christians "preached the word" in spite of being persecuted. This spontaneous expansion indicates an inner desire to do missions that was tied to various aspects of a relationship with Christ. Initially this relationship had more to do with individual experiences with Christ. The apostles were so impressed by what they had received that they felt obliged to make known everything they had heard and seen (Acts 4.20). However, they did not remain recipients of God's missionary intention but became co-workers with him, participants in the continued realization of his divine mission. The clearest example of this comes in the life of St Paul, who could not separate his own conversion from his call to Gentile mission (Gal 1.16). The divine grace shown to him became the foundation of his missionary service (Eph 3.7).[11] Divine condescension (Rom 5.5) moved him to the missionary act (2 Cor 5.14). The knowledge

---

[10]Anastasios Yannoulatos, "Purpose and Motive of Mission," *International Review Of Mission* 54(215) (1965): 281–97, 293.

[11]On the conversion of St Paul, see Jaques Dupont, "The Conversion of Paul, and Its Influence on His Understanding of Salvation by Faith," in *Apostolic History and the Gospel; Biblical and Historical Essays Presented to F. F. Bruce on His 60th Birthday* (Grand Rapids, MI: Eerdmans, 1970). Hahn, *Mission in the New Testament,* 80–83; Dean S. Gilliland, *Pauline Theology & Mission Practice* (Grand Rapids, MI: Baker Book House, 1983), 71–95; "Paul's conviction of the truth of the gospel and his call to proclaim it among the Gentiles resulted from one and the same divine revelation." Cf. F. F. Bruce, "Further Thoughts on Paul's Autobiography," in *Jesus und Paulus: Festschrift für Werner Georg Kümmel zum 70. Geburstag* (Göttingen: Vandenhoeck und Ruprecht, 1975), 21–29.

that what God had given him was available to all humanity caused Paul to think about the urgency of the missionary task (Rom 10.10–15), and also to consider himself indebted (Rom 1.14). This inner conviction expressed itself in Paul's concern for the lostness of the nonbelievers and in his willingness to sacrifice everything in order to enable others to benefit from the divine offer (2 Cor 4, Phil 1).

The evangelists of the early Church made every effort to adhere to the explicit command of Christ (Acts 1.9). But obedience, as shown in John 14.15, was always related to the person of Christ, i.e., directed not so much toward a specific command as to the person of Christ himself. Thus the motivation to bear witness has to be seen against the background of their own conversions and the resultant relationship with Christ. Rather than mechanistic obedience to some command, it was more a dynamic, spontaneous willingness to follow their Savior (Acts 5.29–32).[12] This is clearly demonstrated by the apostles, who could have answered their persecutors by claiming obedience to some command (Acts 5.20–21). Instead, they justified their deliberate disregard of the gag order issued by the Sanhedrin by appealing to God's salvific actions, of which they were the recipients (Acts 5.30–32). This explains the conspicuous absence of reference to the Great Commission in the book of Acts. Obedience does play a role, but it grows out of a relationship to the Savior.

Here we should also point out the motivating work of the Holy Spirit.[13] It seems to have been important to St Luke to demonstrate the active involvement and empowering function of the Holy Spirit. The outpouring of the Spirit on Pentecost is the spark that sets off the rapid expansion of the Church. Only after Pentecost does the inner compulsion to mission develop in the believers (Acts 2.43). The Spirit validates their witness: "We are his witnesses to these things, and so also is the Holy Spirit whom God has given to those who obey him" (Acts 5.32). The Spirit is presented as initiator (Acts 13.1–3), as enabling power (8.26, 11.2, 16.9–10), and as

[12]Roland Allen, *The Spontaneous Expansion of the Church and the Causes Which Hinder It*, 1st American ed. (Grand Rapids, MI: W. B. Eerdmans Pub. Co., 1962), 6–11.

[13]Ibid. Boer points to the same thing. "The Great Commission . . . derives its meaning and power wholly and exclusively from the Pentecost event." Ibid. Boer, *Pentecost and Missions*, 47.

generator of missionary breakthroughs (chapter 10). It was precisely the
coming of the Spirit that enabled the early Christians to relate their own
conversions to the idea of Christian witness.

This trend continued into the second century. A relationship to Christ
remained the primary source of individual motivation for mission. Aris-
tides, for example, says that after he read the Christian Scriptures and
accepted their truth, he felt "constrained to declare the truth to such as
care for it and seek the world to come."[14] He was evidently concerned for
the non-Christians.[15] For that reason the faithful engaged in a number
of activities—good works,[16] holy living, martyrdom—designed to communicate the gospel message and move others to faith.[17] In other words,
although they were determined to share Christ in word and deed,[18] they
did so without specific reference to the Great Commission. What determined their behavior was an understanding of the universal salvific will
of God, and the discrepancy between the fate of the nonbeliever and what
they themselves had received through faith in Christ. "Christian evangelism has its motivation rooted in what God is and what he has done for
man through the coming and the death and the resurrection of Jesus."[19]
For that reason, the actual motive for mission grows out of the realization
of divine salvific intent in the lives of individual believers. It develops into

[14]Aristides, *Apology*, XVI. ‹http://www.earlychristianwritings.com/text/aristides-kay.
html›, June 20, 2015.

[15]"And hell is a place where those are to be punished who have lived wickedly, and
who do not believe that those things which God has taught us by Christ will come to pass."
Justin, *First Apology*, 19. ‹http://www.newadvent.org/fathers/0126.htm›, June 20, 2015.

[16]Aristides, *Apology*, XV. Tertullian, *Ad Scapulam*, 4. ‹http://www.newadvent.org/
fathers/0305.htm›, June 20, 2015.

[17]Origen and John J. O'Meara, *Prayer. Exhortation to Martyrdom,* Ancient Christian
Writers: The Works of the Fathers in Translation (Westminster, MD: Newman Press, 1954),
141–98.

[18]"Thou shalt seek out every day the faces of the saints, either by word examining them,
and going to exhort them, and meditating how to save a soul by the word, or by thy hands
thou shalt labour for the redemption of thy sins." Barnabas, *Epistle of Barnabas*, 19, 10.
‹http://www.ccel.org/ccel/lightfoot/fathers.ii.xiii.html›, June 20, 2015.

[19]See also Michael Green, *Evangelism in the Early Church* (London,: Hodder & Stoughton, 1970), 273. Gerhard Rosenkranz, *Die christliche Mission: Geschichte und Theologie*
(Munich: Kaiser, 1977), 59–66.

a desire to participate in the ongoing implementation and the ultimate fulfillment of God's universal plan of redemption. From this it can be seen that believers have a twofold relationship to this work of outreach. Why should they do it? Because they are both recipients of divine grace and participants in the ongoing *missio Dei*.

a) Recipients Motivated by Divine Benefaction

In 2 Corinthians 5.11–18, St Paul defends his apostolic self-understanding. His answer to the question of what it means to be a servant of God gives us insight into his understanding of the foundation, motive, and task of missionary activity. He begins by recognizing that he, as a sinner separated from God, has been the "object" of divine salvific will. Because of his faith, he has now become the recipient of that salvation. In verse 17 he captures the new status that this change of allegiance has brought about by using the words "in Christ." The phrase clearly indicates his belonging to Christ and his incorporation into Christ's body.[20] Moreover, the result of this incorporation is described as "a new creation." This term is meant to express something concrete and decisive. The old has passed away, the oppressive weight of the law, that opinion claiming to be the only path to true teaching and a valid code of behavior. Forgiveness has removed the unbearable burden of sin. Fellowship with Jesus—incorporation—invalidates self-love, frees faith from the confines of a private religion, and compels Paul to witness. All this is the work of God, his creation; it is the very foundation of Paul's apostolic ministry.

From the moment he was seized by Christ, Paul became a fully transformed child of God, no longer living for himself, but for his Lord. Now his only desire is to speak to others about Jesus, the crucified one (1 Cor 2.2). Since Christ himself has seized Paul, there is nothing left in him to boast about. So he sees himself as one who has died with Christ (Gal 1.19–21) and is now dead to sin (Rom 6.6–11) and to the rule of his own will. For that reason any attempt at worldly recognition becomes unimportant. It is no longer necessary to promote himself, to prove what he can do or

---

[20]Ferdinand Hahn, "Zu 2. Kor 5,14–6,2," *Evangelische Theologie* 3 (1973): 244.

what he is. This attitude releases him from a desire for status and enables unconditional service to others.

> All this, in fact, blessed Paul had in mind, that fervent lover of Christ, who like a winged bird traversed the whole world. . . . See his uprightness, see the extraordinary degree of his virtue, see his fervent love. "The love of Christ," he says, "constrains us," that is, urges, impels, coerces us. Then, wishing to explain what had been said by him, he says, "convinced of this, that if one person [died] indeed for all, then all have died, he did die for all so that the living might live no longer for themselves but for the one who died and rose for them." Do you see how appropriate it was for him to say, "The love of Christ constrains us"? He is saying, you see, if he died for the sake of us all, he died for the purpose that we the living might live no longer for ourselves but for him who died and rose for us. Accordingly, let us heed the apostolic exhortation, not living for ourselves but for him who died and rose for us.[21]

When Paul begins to see himself in a different light, he is also able to view others differently. Race, ethnicity, riches, poverty, age, and status become completely irrelevant. This new way of seeing is the result of the fact that he has died for all (2 Cor 5.14). The love of Christ that now fills his heart, that determines his being, compels him to be a witness to this new life. So, for the Apostle Paul, the motive for missionary service grows directly out of that which he himself had received from Christ.

b) Participants in the Ongoing Mission of God

In 2 Corinthians 5.20–21, St Paul describes the twofold task of his apostolic service. On the one hand, he sees himself as one sent in Christ's stead.[22] This description of his work likens his role to that of an imperial legate who appears on behalf of his lord. When he speaks, he is not merely an

---

[21]John Chrysostom, *Homilies on Genesis* 34.15, ACCS NT 7:247.

[22]"Die stolzen Worte des Apostels Paulus (2 Kor 5.20 vgl. auch Eph 6.20) 'für Christus sind wir Gesandte erhalten ein ganz anderes Relief, wenn wir wissen, daß . . . 'Gesandter' im griechischen Osten die Bezeichnung für den Legatus des Kaisers war." Adolf Deissmann, *Licht vom Osten. Das Neue Testament und die neuentdeckten Texte der hellenistisch-römischen Welt*, 4., völlig neubearb. Aufl., ed. (Tübingen: J. C. B. Mohr, 1923), 320.

agent but also the representative of the commissioning authority. God himself speaks in the person of his first ambassador, Christ, and then through the apostles who succeeded him.

> The Father sent the Son to beseech, and to be his Ambassador unto mankind. When then He was slain and gone, we succeeded to the embassy; and in his stead and the Father's we beseech you. So greatly doth He prize mankind that He gave up even the Son, and that knowing He would be slain, and made us Apostles for your sakes; so that he said with reason, "All things are for your sakes" (2 Cor 4.15). "We are therefore ambassadors on behalf of Christ," that is, instead of Christ; for we have succeeded to his functions.[23]

The goal of the ambassador is not simply to relay a message, but to use every resource to assure that the message is accepted. For this reason the missionary is not engaged in a passive relaying of a message, but an active, urgent stretching out to the sinner. It is a battle, a struggle focused on the realization of the divine salvific intent of God. So on the basis of this new relationship "in Christ," the newly reborn person is naturally, internally compelled—not commanded—to participate in the ongoing realization of the *mission Dei*. As a result the Christian lives and moves in the space between the reception of God's grace and participation in God's ongoing mission to the world. Every motive necessary for the missionary activity of the believer can be drawn from the personal relationship of witnesses to their saving Lord.

2. Making Disciples: The Goal of Orthodox Mission

In one way or another, every missionary proclamation is an offer of salvation.[24] Obviously our understanding of what that offer entails will

---

[23]John Chrysostom, *Homilies on the Epistles of Paul to the Corinthians*, ‹http://www.ccel.org/ccel/schaff/npnf112.v.xi.html›, June 20, 2015.

[24]In almost every Christian confession, the doctrine of salvation is central to its teaching. This is, of course, also true of Orthodox theology. The following statement by Fr Michael Pomazansky is typical: "The dogma of salvation in Christ is the central dogma of Christianity, the heart of our Christian faith." Michael Pomazansky, *Orthodox Dogmatic*

determine how we go about making the offer. In other words, our soteriology goes a long way toward defining the actual goal, that is, the desired outcome of our witness. For some, the soteriological focus is cast in very narrow terms that emphasize just a few aspects of the doctrine. In Western theology the context for understanding salvation has been largely limited to the personal experience of the forgiveness of sin, that is, to the individual appropriation of redemption. For most such thinkers, salvation is an immediate change in a person's status before the judge of all things. Without Christ's sacrifice we are said to remain in a state of unrighteousness. When personal, individual faith is placed in the Savior—that is, if one believes that the just demands of an angry God are satisfied by the death of Christ—then all sin is canceled and one's status is changed to "justified." Due to the extremely individualistic focus of this approach and the accompanying judicial understanding of salvation, a person may be considered either saved or not saved. There can be no other state: no progress, no spiritual journey,[25] and no loss of that status.[26] Understandably, this reasoning has led to a mission strategy aimed almost exclusively at individual conversion.[27]

Theology (Palatine, CA: St. Herman of Alaska Brotherhood, 1994), 195. However, it should be pointed out that Orthodox theology has not produced a precise, logical system so typical of Western thought. See Jordan Bajis, *Common Ground* (Minneapolis: Light and Life, 1996), 230. "In the Eastern Church there is no official pronouncement on the doctrine of salvation. The tradition of the church concerning our reunion with God in Christ, our redemption or salvation or justification by God in Christ has not been challenged in the East. It is for this reason that one does not find any fixed doctrine even among the ancient Fathers, but only a common tradition." Savas Agourides, "Salvation According to the Orthodox Tradition," *Ecumenical Review* 21.3 (July 1969): 190.

[25]This despite the fact that the New Testament clearly speaks of salvation in the past, present, and future tenses, indicating that it is a process with a clear beginning and a definite goal. See Edward Michael Bankes Green, *The Meaning of Salvation* (Philadelphia, PA: Westminster Press, 1965).

[26]Not every Protestant group takes this never-to-be lost position. The Methodists, for example, do accept the possibility of "losing one's salvation." However, even for them, the act of conversion is so central that it becomes an almost permanent entry in the record of missionary failure or success.

[27]Rommen, *Die Notwendigkeit der Umkehr.*

The advantage of this approach is that it is, or seems to be, a relatively easy or convenient way to measure our compliance with the terms of the Great Commission. Certainly we all want to be faithful. This faith, it is said, can be measured in terms of our ability to fulfill the command by bringing new converts into the church. If our soteriology allows us to view each conversion as an unrepeatable, never-to-be-lost event, then it stands as a permanent part of our record of success. According to this thinking, a church is made up of countable individuals and statistics that reflect past and present increases in conversions, and which in turn indicate the successful completion of our missionary responsibility. No doubt many of us, no matter our soteriology, are tempted by the convenience and practicality of this way of measuring our effectiveness and find ourselves thinking this way, at least some of the time. But what if our soteriology pointed us in a different direction, away from a single aspect or moment of salvation and toward the broad expanse of the process as a whole? Such a perspective might explain why some of us find the "conversion-based" approach deficient. By narrowing the missiological "perspective to individual salvation [it has] thus kept neither the Church, as such, nor God's universal salvific order sufficiently in view."[28] How, then, does an Orthodox soteriology inform our understanding of the missionary's task? How are we to determine if we have been successful and faithful? Before we discuss the goal itself, we need a brief overview of the Orthodox doctrine of salvation.

a) The Orthodox Understanding of Salvation

In Eastern Christian thought, salvation has always been discussed in the broad context of creation and deification. In the beginning God created the heavens and the earth, and out of the dust of that earth He created the human frame and breathed life into it. Thus the universe and humanity are irrevocably related in that they share a material nature. As Gregory of Nazianzus puts it, "In my quality of earth, I am attached to life here below, but being also a divine particle, I bear in my breast the desire for

[28]Josef Glazik, "Meaning and the Place of Missiology Today," *International Review Of Mission* 57, no. 228 (1968): 459–67.

a future life."[29] For creation, mankind offers the hope of receiving God's grace and being reunited with him. However, human beings also represent the danger of failure and fallenness. And so creation "eagerly waits for the revealing of the sons of God" (Rom 8.19–21). "It is indeed to vanity that creation was made subject, not willingly, but because of him who subjected it; with, however, the hope that creation would also be liberated from the slavery of corruption to participate in the glorious liberty of the children of God."[30] In other words, the universe can only be what it was intended to be if humanity becomes what it was intended to be.

What is this God-intended goal of humanity? Scripture teaches that God created man in his own image and after his own likeness (Gen 1.26–27). Many modern exegetes do not accept the distinction between the two, suggesting that in Hebrew the two terms are synonymous.[31] However, in Orthodox theology the terms "image" and "likeness" are considered to be distinct, and that distinction provides an important baseline for the development of Orthodox soteriology. The image of God is that which reflects God's nature in human beings.[32] It is that which all human beings have in common, and constitutes human existence. It presupposes the divine prototype. In that sense this aspect of creation is indeed special—not only

---

[29]St Gregory of Nazianzus, as quoted by Lossky, *Orthodox Theology*, 71.

[30]Ibid.

[31]Keil and Delitzsch, for example, state that "modern commentators have correctly observed, that there is no foundation for the distinction drawn by the Greek and after them by many Latin Fathers, between εἰκών [eikōn] (*imago*) and ὁμοίωσις [homoiōsis] (similitudo), the former of which they supposed to represent the physical aspect of the likeness to God, the latter the ethical; but that, on the contrary the older Lutheran theologians were correct in stating that the two words are synonymous, and are merely combined to add intensity to the thought. . . ." Carl Friedrich Keil and Franz Delitzsch, *Biblical Commentary on the Old Testament*, trans. James Martin, vol. 1, *The Pentateuch* (Edinburgh: T & T Clark, 1872), 63. They go on to compare the difference to certain German word pairs, such as *Bild* and *Abbild* or *Umriss* and *Abriss*. Two comments are in order. First, the physical/ethical distinction they read into the Fathers is inaccurate. Second, although the terms are similar there are subtle differences in the German pairs, which do in fact translate into the English as "likeness" and "copy," and "outline" and "sketch."

[32]Or as Zizioulas insists, in the image of the Trinity, *imago Trinitatis*. Jean Zizioulas and Paul McPartlan, *Communion and Otherness: Further Studies in Personhood and the Church* (London and New York: T & T Clark, 2006), 248.

does the earth give rise to the body, but it is by the inbreathing of divine breath that the human being becomes a person. Again we have the idea of God releasing something of himself, of his person, in order to create. Put differently, God replicates himself in the human being. Human beings (and angels) are the only creatures that are a hypostasization of the divine will. Thus, human beings take on the *personal* character of the Trinity. "God is the creator of his own living images, persons according to his image in its tri-hypostatic character."[33] There have been many suggestions as to the exact nature of the image, such as mans' intellect, his capacity for reproduction, and his free will.[34] In any case, this image is the "common property of all men," and a quality without which man could not be considered human. It is a static term that "signifies a realized state, which, in the present context, constitutes the starting point for the attainment of the 'likeness.'"[35]

Likeness, by contrast, is a dynamic term and points to a potential. This likeness is something that we must acquire ourselves, having been given the possibility of doing so. To become "in the likeness" of God depends upon our will; it is a result of our own activity.

> Likeness to God, while it constitutes the goal of human existence, is not imposed on man, but is left to his own free will. By submitting himself freely to God's will and being constantly guided by his grace, man can cultivate and develop the gift of the "image," making it a possession individual, secure and dynamic, and so coming to resemble God.[36]

This resemblance of God is usually referred to as "deification and is defined as a union or communion with God, which is so complete that it can be said of man that he is like God."[37] Adam was not created perfect

---

[33]Sergei Nikolaevich Bulgakov, *The Bride of the Lamb* (Grand Rapids, MI: W. B. Eerdmans, 2002), 87.

[34]Georgios I. Mantzaridis, *The Deification of Man* (Crestwood, NY: St. Vladimir's Seminary Press, 1984), 21.

[35]Ibid.

[36]Ibid., 21–22.

[37]This idea is captured by Irenaeus when he insists that Christ became the Son of Man

in an absolute sense. But he was created without sin, in communion with
God, and therefore with the potential to achieve that for which he was
created: deification.

However, that potential was squandered in disobedience and rebellion.
Not only did man lose this potential, but his very nature was corrupted.
Generation by generation he drifted further and further away from God,
the source of his life. According to St Athanasius, the human fall consists
precisely in the fact that man limits himself to himself, that man becomes,
as it were, in love with himself. And through this concentration on himself, man separates himself from God and breaks his free contact with
God. It is a kind of delirium, a self-erotic obsession, a spiritual narcissism.
One might call it a progressive de-spiritualization of human existence. All
the rest—death and the decomposition of human structure—comes as a
result.[38] "Indeed 'eternal damnation' is not inflicted by 'the angry God.'
God is not the author of Hell. 'Damnation' is a self-inflicted penalty, the
consequence and the implication of the rebellious opposition to God and
to his will."[39] Because humankind was in need of salvation, Christ came
into the world, becoming incarnate in order to offer what was needed.

i) What Is Being Offered? We normally and correctly associate salvation with the idea of redemption: the ultimate defeat of death and the
forgiveness of sin. Indeed, the death and resurrection of the incarnate
Christ did achieve victory over the curses of sin and death. On the cross
Christ assumed the consequence of our sin, death itself. By doing so he
canceled the "handwriting of requirements [certificate of debt] that was
against us, which was contrary to us. And he has taken it out of the way,
having nailed it to the cross" (Col 2.14). The statement of offense that was

---

"that man also might become the son of God. . . . For all things had entered upon a new
phase, the Word arranging after a new manner the advent in the flesh, that He might win
back to God that human nature (*hominem*) which had departed from God. . . ." Irenaeus,
Against Heresies. Interest in theosis is not limited to the Eastern Church. Cf. Daniel A.
Keating, *Deification and Grace, Introductions to Catholic Doctrine* (Naples, FL: Sapientia
Press, 2007); Roger E. Olson, "Deification in Contemporary Theology," *Theology Today* 64,
no. 2 (2007): 186–200.

[38]Georges Florovsky, *Creation and Redemption*, Collected Works of Georges Florovsky
V 3 (Belmont, MA: Nordland Pub. Co., 1976), I, 85.

[39]Ibid., I, 257.

normally nailed to the cross at the execution of a criminal contained, in the case of Christ, not his sins, but ours. There is obviously a form of expiation[40] (a canceling of sin) involved in what Christ did. But there is so much more at stake, for even death was not able to dissolve the divine-human union in Christ, and as a result this "incorrupt" death[41] "imparted life to death itself."[42] "The resurrection actualizes the triumph over death and opens the ontological possibility of the general resurrection at the end of the ages."[43] The resurrection, then, is concrete evidence that the grip of death has been broken. So the redemption achieved by Christ on the cross "was not just the forgiveness of sins, nor was it man's reconciliation with God."[44] It was the final victory over sin and death, the abolition of the corruption and mortality in human nature.

And yet, the incarnation does not seem to be a divine afterthought, a kind of alternative action occasioned by human fallenness. Apparently God had other good things in store for his creatures even before they rebelled. This implies that the content of salvation must be more than redemption, as important as that is, for we read in the Scriptures that the incarnation was "foreordained before the foundation of the world" (1 Pet 1.20, 1 Cor 2.7, Eph 1.4), before the creation, and before the fall.[45]

---

[40]There is considerable debate as to the exact meaning of the Greek word group (ἱλασμός) to which such terms as expiation and propitiation belong. It has been noted that Greek usage outside the Scriptures involves an averting of wrath. However, some have argued for a specifically biblical (LXX and NT) usage "according to which it denotes expiation (the cancellation of sin), not propitiation (the turning away of the wrath of God)." Leon Morris, "Propitiation," in *Baker's Dictionary of Theology*, ed. Everett F. Harrison (Grand Rapids, MI: Baker Book House, 1960), 425.

[41]"In other words, though separated in death, the soul and the body remained still united through the Divinity of the Word, from which neither was ever estranged. . . . This does not alter the ontological character of death, but changed its meaning. This was an 'incorrupt' death, and therefore corruption and death were overcome in it, and in it begins the resurrection. The very death of the incarnate reveals the resurrection of human nature." Florovsky, *Creation and Redemption*, I, 136.

[42]Bajis, *Common Ground*, 236.

[43]Symeon Rodger, "The Soteriology of Anselm of Canterbury, an Orthodox Perspective," *Greek Orthodox Theological Review* 31.1 (1989): 19–43, 38.

[44]Florovsky, *Creation and Redemption*, I, 225.

[45]Bulgakov, *The Lamb of God*, 168.

These texts make clear that the coming of the Son into the world is not only an act of God's *providential* government of the world, an act proceeding from God's interaction with the world. It is also God's primordial grace, existing before the creation of the world, that is, constituting the very foundation and goal of the world. One can even say that God created the world in order to become incarnate in it, that he created it for the sake of his Incarnation.[46]

Why, then, does God want to enter the world? "In what does the inexorable predeterminedness of the Incarnation consist?"[47] We can give at least two answers. On the one hand, the limitedness of humankind makes it impossible for us to reach fulfillment (God-likeness) on our own; we need divine help.[48] On the other hand, God desires to enter into personal communion with human beings, communicating divine life so that creaturely becoming can find its end in complete communion with God, deification. This means that the incarnation's context and intent are larger than its most obvious and concrete benefit, redemption. The incarnation also includes God's desire to commune personally with humankind in order to move creation's becoming along towards its ultimate end. So we have the tri-hypostatic person of God releasing the world to be on its own, breathing the life of personhood into human beings, and entering the world in order to have direct personal communion with humankind. Christ is truly Emmanuel, God with us. This is the ultimate content of all Christian witness. Establishing and maintaining the divine-human relationship or communion, in spite of sin, is the very essence of becoming, of God moving humanity toward its designated end of deification, that is, salvation. This is what is being offered.

ii) To Whom Is This Offer Being Made? Given God's desire for communion with all his creatures, the scope of his offer is universal. As we have already seen, Jesus commands us to make disciples of all nations. This inclusiveness was reinforced on the day of Pentecost and documented in

[46]Ibid., 169.

[47]Ibid., 171.

[48]See, again, Irenaeus on this topic, as discussed in footnote 37 above. Irenaeus, *Against Heresies*.

the early expansion of the Church. Today it is expressed in the fact that the Church, because of its universal missionary activity, exists in almost every place. Yet still there are many who do not know Christ. For that reason, the missionary intent of the liturgy described above is a constant reminder of God's active, ongoing offer of salvation to the whole world, to every one of its inhabitants. According to Orthodox teaching Christ himself is offered to the whole world. There are no exceptions. This is not to say that all will accept him and be saved,[49] but the divine message is indeed directed to every human being. Each is to be given the chance to follow Christ toward deification.

iii) How Can This Salvation Be Appropriated? The Eastern Church distinguishes between two aspects of salvation. On the one hand there is the healing of human nature. For this no human appropriation is required, since it has already been accomplished by Christ, and since its concretization at the general resurrection will include all mankind. In the words of Florovsky, "Nature is healed and restored with a certain compulsion, by the mighty power of God's omnipotent and invincible grace. The wholeness is in a way forced upon human nature. For in Christ all human nature . . . is fully and completely cured from unwholeness and mortality."[50]

On the other hand, there is the healing of the human will. In this case healing comes only as a result of a genuine turning to God in lifelong repentance, faith, and love.

> The will of man cannot be cured in the same invincible manner; for the whole meaning of the healing of the will is in its free conversion. Only by this spontaneous and free effort does man enter into that new and eternal life which is revealed in Christ Jesus. A spiritual regeneration can be only in perfect freedom, in an obedience of love, by a self-consecration and self-dedication to God.[51]

[49]Orthodoxy does not subscribe to any universalistic teaching. There have been a few theologians, notably Sergius Bulgakov, who have proposed the eventual salvation of all. Nevertheless, mainstream Orthodox teaching makes salvation/deification dependent on individual faith, and even though God desires the salvation of all, not all will accept that offer.

[50]Florovsky, *Creation and Redemption,* I, 147.

[51]Ibid., I, 148.

So we have been saved by the work of Christ, into which we enter by faith and repentance as expressed in baptism and chrismation. We are being saved as we journey through life in repentance and obedience. On this journey the Church aids us through its sacraments, its teaching, and the communion of all the saints. Finally, we will be saved when we are fully united with God and reach the final goal—deification.

b) Missiological Implications of an Orthodox Soteriology

The soteriology outlined above has a twofold effect on the question of the goal of mission. First of all, Orthodox soteriology determines that the goal of mission is not just conversion, but the whole process of discipleship. Secondly, it lends that missionary outreach a certain urgency.

i) Discipleship: The Goal of Mission. The divine offer of salvation is an expression of God's desire to commune personally with humankind. It is God moving humanity toward its designated end—salvation/deification. Entering into that communion and maintaining a lifelong divine-human relationship is the very essence of human destiny. For this reason, inviting individuals to establish this relationship with Christ becomes the primary task of mission. In the context of the soteriology described here, the overall goal of missions can be nothing other than the deification of individual human beings. Deification, however, is a theological category that is neither easily understood nor completed before the end of time—and certainly not something we can readily measure or count. How will we know if we are successfully fulfilling our commission? We need to bring this grand idea down into the practicalities of our world. So without denying that we are, in fact, offering salvation and deification in Christ, we need to define the actual execution of the commission in terms of the phenomenology of our experience.

However, in refining our goal we also need to avoid the dangers of a too-narrow definition. Reducing the goal of mission to individual conversion, as we saw above, represents one such narrowing and illustrates the nature of these dangers. We find this reduction in a statement of the Lausanne Covenant, according to which "evangelism itself is the proclamation of the historical, biblical Christ as Savior and Lord, with a view to persuading people to come to him personally and so be reconciled to God."[52] This view is certainly in keeping with fathers of the evangelical movement such as Theophil Großgebauer, Philipp Jakob Spener, and August Hermann Francke. Although they signaled allegiance to the traditional Protestant theory of justification, they did set a number of new emphases by presenting conversion as a one-time, conscious event in the life of an individual as a result of repentance and faith, and which has an observable effect on the person's behavior. It was probably Zinzendorf who first defined the missionary task "in a way that was determinative for most Protestant missionary efforts that followed."[53] His missionary strategy was encapsulated in two words, "first fruits and individuals." This was a distinct rejection of other models that envisioned a more general christianization or even the conversion of whole nations. He was clearly focused on the individual and individual conversion. This led to his "Method for the Conversion of the Heathen," which was focused on one thing alone: the conversion of individuals. Every other activity was to be avoided by the missionaries, including the political, cultural, and pedagogical. So, beginning with German pietism, this understanding of the missionary task as the conversion of individuals made its way like a golden thread through the formative years of evangelical missions (and it is still with us today). William Carey (1793–1834), Adonirum Judson (1788–1850), and Hudson Taylor (1853–1905), as well as organizations such as the Student Volunteer Movement, all followed this basic goal.[54]

This narrowing of the goal to a single, one-time event opens the missionary up to certain dangers. The concern that an individual enter into a saving relationship with Christ must never be altogether missing from our missiology. But if in practice we limit our efforts to the attainment of this momentary experience, we run a number of risks. The first of these

[52]J. D. Douglas, ed., *Let the Earth Hear His Voice: International Congress on World Evangelization, Lausanne, Switzerland* (Minneapolis, MN: World Wide Publications, 1975), 4.

[53]"Er stellte als Grundsatz auf: Einzelbekehrung!" Th. Bechler, "Einzelbekehrung und Volkskirche nach dem Erfahrung der Brüdermission," in *Einwurzelung des Christentum in der Heidenwelt,* ed. P. Julius Richter (Gütersloh: 1906), 90.

[54]Rommen, *Die Notwendigkeit der Umkehr,* 136–43.

dangers is the possibility of neglecting the role of the Holy Spirit. Reducing our vision to individual conversion seems to presuppose that the individual has to react to God's offer by doing "something," which can lead in
turn to the assumption that the individual is contributing something to
his own salvation. As a result, the missionary is put under great pressure to
bring that "something" about. Strategies of persuasion are developed that
virtually lose sight of Christ and the role of the Holy Spirit. Characteristic
of this orientation are statements by the well-known evangelist Charles
Finney. He was of the opinion that an evangelist had to create the impression in the mind of the listener that religion demanded some human
action.[55] This act might be called a "decision" for Christ or "accepting"
Christ into one's heart. In any case, this emphasis on a human responsibility to decide[56] seems to push the grace of God into the background, leaving the impression that the individual is the source of his own salvation.[57]
Representatives of this approach would surely object to this interpretation
of it, and Finney may not be representative of all contemporary Protestant
missionaries. Nevertheless, in practice an overemphasis on individual
decision-making ability does, indeed, run the risk of a distortion of the
gospel, wherein the listener is put under pressure to do something while

[55]In his lecture "How to Preach the Gospel," Finney offers "professors of religion" practical suggestions for evangelistic preaching: "Sinners ought to be made to feel that they have
something to do, and that is to repent; that is something which no other being can do for
them, neither God nor man, and something which they can do, and do now. Religion is
something to do, not something to wait for. And they must do it now, or they are in danger
of eternal death." Charles G. Finney, *Lectures on Revivals of Religion* (Oberlin, OH: E. J.
Goodrich, 1868).

[56]"The Spirit of God, by the truth, influences the sinner to change, and in this sense is
the efficient cause of the change. But the sinner actually changes and is therefore himself,
in the most proper sense, the author of the change." Ibid., 188.

[57]Finney criticizes a work titled "Regeneration, the Effect of Divine Power." "The very
title to this tract is a stumbling block. It tells the truth, but it does not tell the whole truth.
And a tract might be written upon this proposition, that 'Conversion or regeneration is the
work of man;' which would be just as true, just as scriptural, and just as philosophical, as
the one to which I have alluded. Thus the writer in his zeal to recognize and honor God
as concerned in this Work, by leaving out the fact that a change of heart is the sinner's
own act, has left the sinner strongly intrenched, with his weapons in his rebellious hands,
stoutly resisting the claims of his Maker, and waiting passively for God to make him a new
heart." Ibid.

the speaker is put under an equal pressure to get him or her to do that, all without explicit dependence on the Holy Spirit.

From an Orthodox perspective, it is clear that the individual has a free will and can and must make a choice to follow God. However, that free will, since it has been clouded by sin, is seldom aware of its own failings. For that reason our witness can never be divorced from the work of the Holy Spirit, by which the individual is convicted of his or her own sinfulness. As we have seen above, the Holy Spirit prepares the hearts and minds of individuals (as in the cases of Cornelius and the Ethiopian eunuch in the Book of Acts) who are then enabled to accept the truth of the gospel, that is, to believe. This ministry of the Holy Spirit is indeed about faith and unbelief, bringing the unbeliever to the point of conversion. Consider Augustine's comment on John 16.9:

> When the Lord said of the Holy Spirit, "He shall convict the world of sin," he meant unbelief. For this is what he meant when he said, "Of sin because they believed not on me." And he means the same when he says, "If I had not come and spoken to them, they should not have sin." He was not talking about [a time] before they had no sin. Rather, he wanted to indicate that very lack of faith by which they did not believe him even when he was present to them and speaking to them. These were the people who belonged to "the prince of the power of the air, who now works in the children of unbelief." Therefore those in whom there is no faith are the children of the devil because they have nothing in their inner being that would cause them to be forgiven for whatever is committed either by human infirmity, ignorance or any evil will whatever. But the children of God are those who certainly, if they should "say that they have no sin, deceive themselves, and the truth is not in them," but immediately (as it continues) "when they confess their sins" (which the children of the devil do not do, or do not do according to the faith which is peculiar to the children of God), "he is faithful and just to forgive them their sins and to cleanse them from all unrighteousness."[58]

[58] Augustine, *Against Two Letters of the Pelagians* 3.4.31, ACCS NT 4b:200.

The real encounter with the person of Christ, mediated by the Holy Spirit, is what convinces them, not just the words or persuasion techniques of the missionary. It is the coming together, the synergy of divine and human movements, that leads to the point of conversion.

This point alerts us to a second danger, namely the possibility that we might fail to respect the dignity of the hearer. Sometimes the obsession with individual conversion has led to all manner of abuse. In his book *Betrayal of the West,* French sociologist Jacques Ellul describes a widespread and not completely undeserved opinion of the Christian mission work done during the colonial era. He writes of the colonial powers

> and their missionaries ... everywhere destroying healthy natural morals, and imposing an ideology that was nothing but a front for commerce and death. They rooted out the ancient beliefs that were so well suited to the peoples who had developed them. They destroyed cultures and thus the social groupings, leaving the individual isolated where earlier he had fitted so wonderfully into a balanced society. They imposed a morality and introduced these simple souls to evil and sin. They spread abroad the terror of hell and made men feel for the first time the fear of death. These missionaries with their fixation on the cross committed a worse crime than the soldiers and the merchants: they robbed the peoples of their very soul. Souls were their trade, and the result was total ruin: languages proscribed and replaced by western tongues (German, English, Spanish, French), laws and customs supplanted by those of the invader, who by a single stroke stole honor, dignity, ancestral faith, and the still hidden riches of the earth.[59]

It is obvious that a "trade with souls" is, in fact, a danger inherent in certain types of missionary enthusiasm. We know that many who hear the gospel refuse it because they know nothing of their own eternal fate. While it is natural, then, to try to persuade these individuals, today the techniques of persuasion are so effective that, if used, they actually

---

[59]Jacques Ellul, *The Betrayal of the West,* 2. ‹http://archive.org/stream/BetrayalOfThe West/BetrayalOfTheWestJ.e._djvu.txt›, June 23, 2015.

constitute manipulating the listener. In a book on persuasion, psychologist James McConnell is quoted as making the claim that

> [the] time has come when if you give me any normal human being and a couple of weeks . . . I can change his behavior from what it is to whatever you what it to be, if it's physically possible. I can't make him fly by flapping his wings, but I can turn him from a Christian into a Communist, and vice versa.[60]

Today's techniques are so effective that we can change a person's mind even against his or her will. The sociological insights that are gaining ever more ground in the training of missionaries pose the real danger of manipulation. Such techniques are finding their way into the repertoire of evangelistic methods. Yet it is clear that the very nature of a relationship to Christ rules out any kind of psychological manipulation designed to force a change of belief. If we are motivated by love, then we have no right to violate the listener's independence. Every attempt to force a change of allegiance is misguided.[61]

Another danger of this narrow, conversion-centered focus is the imposition of individual or personal standards of piety. We see this in the way Francke dictated the elements of a "genuine" conversion experience.[62] With the passing of time, this thinking led to the conviction that one may evaluate the spiritual legitimacy of others. An interesting example comes in the form of a Moravian criticism of a Lutheran missionary in Greenland who was declared to be a "naturalistic, unconverted preacher."[63] This

[60]Marvin Karlins and Herbert Irving Abelson, *Persuasion: How Opinions and Attitudes Are Changed,* 2d ed. (New York: Springer Pub. Co., 1970).

[61]On the question "Is Witnessing Brainwashing?" John White suggests that "techniques become immoral when either consciously or unconsciously we use them to tamper with the will, emotions or conscience of another person. They also become immoral when they assume more importance in our thinking than the Spirit of God." John White, *The Race. Discipleship for the Long Run* (Downers Grove, IL: IVP, 1984), 83.

[62]Susi Hausammann, *Busse Als Umkehr und Erneuerung von Mensch und Gesellschaft: Eine theologiegeschichtliche Studie zu einer Theologie der Busse,* Studien zur Dogmengeschichte und Systematischen Theologie 33 (Zurich: Theologischer Verlag, 1975), 289.

[63]Karl Muller, *200 Jahre Brüdermission* (Herrnhut: Missionsbuchhandlung, 1931), I, 124.

narrow critique went so far as to say that only certain experiences, i.e., those matching the missionaries' own, could be considered true conversions. Furthermore, this attitude facilitated the export of culturally bound understandings of what the Christian life was to look like after conversion. Here we need only point to many conservative missionaries' comments on music, theater, and dance.[64] It is true that a genuine conversion to Christ will have an effect on the subsequent behavior of the individual. However, to dictate those consequences based on culturally bound experiences is unacceptable.[65]

In light of our soteriology and the dangers of a too narrowly defined goal, how should the Orthodox Church define the goal of its mission? As we have seen, the task of the missionary is to introduce non-believing or once-believing individuals to the person of Christ. That being the case, mission's primary goal—the outcome of missionary work—is to facilitate the intimate relationship of faith in the Savior, that is, to see individuals follow Christ. In light of the possible dangers of missionary work focused solely on individual conversion, it is reasonable to seek a broader theological understanding of the missionary goal. Further, the idea of discipleship as contained in the Great Commission seems to meet that need.[66]

---

[64]Francke rejected much of what was done in the name of Christian freedom. "Sie glauben / daß sie alles wohl können äußerlich mit machen / Opern und Comoedin besuchen / lustig mit der Welt schmausen / und darnach auffstehen zu spielen / zu tantzen und zu springen / alle neue Moden der Welt zu gefallen mit tragen / und was des eitelen Wesens mehr ist / darinnen sie und die ihrigen fortleben / und doch den Namen behalten wollen / daß es ihnen ein rechter Ernst sey Gott zu dienen / vorgebende / ihr Hertz hängt nicht daran / und man müsse sein Christenthum so führen / daß man nicht für singulair gehalten werde." A. H Francke, *Vom weltüblichen Tanzen*, ed. E. Peschke, Werke in Auswahl (Berlin: Evangelische Verlagsanstalt, 1967), 384. See also A. H. Franke, "Von der Erziehung der Jugend zur Gottseligkeit," in A. H. Francke's *Pädagogische Schriften. Nebst der Darstellung eines Lebens und einer Stiftungen,* ed. G. Kramer (Langensalza: H. Beyer & Söhne, 1885), 38.

[65]A contemporary example of this is the position many North American Christians take toward the use of alcohol. In many cases this opinion, which is the result of American cultural experience, is exported, taken as part of the missionary message, and imposed on others around the world.

[66]It is somewhat puzzling that Evangelicals do not use this idea more often, especially since it is in the Great Commission, which they do emphasize. One notable exception is

This approach is not to be understood as an attempt to create an alternative to conversion, but rather as incorporating into our conception of the missionary "goal" the whole process that is initiated by conversion. We seek to demonstrate that conversion, while necessary, is not the result of human effort, nor is it to be understood as a single, one-time event ending missionary responsibility. Rather, it is a turning point that propels the individual onto the lifelong path of salvation and deification.

The meaning of discipleship is best understood against the backdrop of the rabbinical teacher-student relationship and its theological evolution in the early Church. Since the way in which Jesus approached his public ministry was in keeping with the well-known teachers of the law,[67] he was recognized as a rabbi, that is, as μαθητής (*mathētēs*) or teacher.[68] In keeping with this practice, his group of followers was limited to twelve, at least initially.[69] They were his *talmidim*[70] who had committed themselves to a living community based on trust in him and his teaching of the law. However, after the resurrection Jesus' connection to time and space was transformed. The disciples no longer followed some respected teacher of the past, but the resurrected, ascended Lord.[71] This radically changed the

McGavran, who has transformed the English verb "to disciple" into a *terminus technicus*: "From 1953–1971 in church growth thinking the new technical term 'discipling' meant helping a people (a corporate body of men and women) turn from non-Christian Faith to Christ." Donald McGavran, "How about That New Verb, 'to Disciple'?" *Church Growth Bulletin* 15 (1979), 266. See also C. Peter Wagner, "What Is 'Making Disciples'?" *Evangelical Missions Quarterly* 9 (1973): 285–93.

[67]"Alle Evangelien bezeugen das Auftreten des historischen Jesus wie das eines zeitgenössischen Gesetzeslehrers. Seine Umwelt hat in Jesus von Nazareth einen Thoralehrer gesehen und ihm die gebührende Anrede Rabbi nicht versagt." Anselm Schulz, *Nachfolge und Nachahmen*. (Munich: Kaiser, 1962), 33.

[68]Jn 1.38, 20.16, Mk 9.5, 11.21; Mt 26.49. Cf. K. H. Rengstorf, "Didaskalos," in *Theologische Wörterbuch zum Neuen Testament*, vol. 2 (Stuttgart: Gerhard Friedrich, 1935), 150–162; Rainer Riesner, *Jesus als Lehrer*, 2nd ed., *Wissenschaftliche Untersuchungen zum Neuen Testament* 2.7 (Tübingen: J. C. B. Mohr [Paul Siebeck], 1984), 246.

[69]Schulz, *Nachfolge und Nachahmen*, 46–49.

[70]Mk 2.18, Lk 11.1, Jn 4.1, 9.28. Hermann Leberecht Strack and Paul Billerbeck, *Kommentar Zum Neuen Testament aus Talmud und Midrasch*, 6 vols. (Munich: Beck, 1922), I, 529 and II, 417.

[71]See Hans Dieter Betz, *Nachfolge und Nachahmung Jesu Christi im Neuen Testament* (Tübingen: J. C. B. Mohr, 1967), 33.

concept of discipleship as it developed in the early church. We can summarize these changes by considering the prerequisites of discipleship, the
context of discipleship, and the consequences of discipleship.

The Prerequisites of Discipleship. As it is used in the New Testament, the
teacher-student relationship depends entirely on the "call" of the master.
In contrast to rabbinic practice, where the student chooses the teacher,
this relationship depends on Jesus calling the disciple (Lk 5.1–11). He takes
the initiative and calls them to follow him (Mk 1.17, Lk 9.59–62). Even during the pre-paschal period, we see that the disciples themselves, removing the requirement for personal experience of the incarnate Jesus, could
issue this call. After Pascha, the kerygma of the early eyewitness became
the primary vehicle of this call (Acts 16.1, 8.4, 9.19). In addition to that we
should also consider the witness of the biblical writings (Lk 24.25, Acts
8.35), and in particular the Gospels. From this we can conclude that the
most important element of this process of making disciples is issuing the
call to follow Christ.

The second prerequisite for discipleship was the trust that the student
placed in the teacher (Mk 16.16, Lk 22.32, Mt 18.6, Jn 2.69, 11.44). In that
respect, the twelve set themselves apart from the many unbelieving followers of Christ (Jn 2.11, 6.69). As these ideas were developed theologically, faith itself was eventually equated with discipleship (Jn 8.31, Acts
2.44, 9.26). Since this implies faith in the whole person of Christ as Messiah and Son of God, we see that discipleship presupposes an initial turning to Christ which in turn leads to a lifelong commitment to follow, that
is, to imitate the Master.

In light of this understanding of discipleship, any formulation of the
missionary goal that is limited to individual conversion, as understood in
isolation from the overall process of calling and following, is to be rejected.
This larger process takes time and cannot be circumvented. It is, above all,
Jesus himself who, even if through witnesses, calls people to follow him. In
addition, he is the one who awakens faith. Certainly faith is a response to
the grace and salvific offer of God, but not in the sense of a sovereign decision, as though the disciple stood above the master, as if he had complete
freedom to find his own master. Faith is rather a trust that gradually grows

on the basis of the call of the master and the presence of divine grace. So it is the call itself that leads to faith and enables the act of conversion.

The Context of Discipleship. Three things define the relationship of the disciple to his or her master. First, it must be seen as a reciprocal or interpersonal relationship. In that respect Zinzendorf was right when he stated, "In matters of the heart there are no national discussions."[72] The call to discipleship is issued to individuals, who then acknowledge Jesus as Lord and follow him. A call hurled into the anonymity of the masses dissolves in utter vagueness. Second, certain limitations are set by the word as revealed by Jesus. The disciple is obligated to commit himself or herself to the Master's interpretation of the will of God (Jn 15.8). This comes to us in the form of commandments and teachings, to which the follower submits. The disciple has not become a student in order to one day become a master, but rather to continually be limited by the will of the one he or she is imitating. For that reason it is clear that teaching Christ's commandments is a constitutive aspect of the missionary task. Here we are not dealing with a momentary experience, but rather a continual deepening of understanding and knowledge. Third, we see that the command to baptize presupposes a sacramental and ecclesial context. Discipleship has always been, as can be seen in Acts, closely connected with the eucharistic community. Thus, we see that discipleship can never be a private affair. The disciple is incorporated through baptism into the community to which he or she contributes, and in which the Eucharist sustains him. The disciple is also to be taught everything that Christ commanded. This is obviously a long-term project, and indicates that our missionary responsibility is not over when someone decides to follow Christ. For that reason we conclude that establishing eucharistic communities as a context for issuing the call to discipleship is not only legitimate, but is also a vital aspect of the missionary goal we seek to define.

i) The Consequences of Discipleship. Once this personal relationship to Christ has been established, the disciple receives on the one hand a reward and, on the other hand, a responsibility. The promised reward[73] is,

---

[72]Muller, *200 Jahre Brüdermission,* 229.

[73]"The promised reward (which must not be understood as something deserved, since

of course, forgiveness of sins and renewed communion with God. Those thus ransomed are now on the path to full participation in the divine being, deification. That reward includes the hope of the resurrection and eternal life in the presence of God. This high calling to discipleship is also a call to service, and to suffering. According to the Gospels, the twelve were sent out to perform many different services related to the coming kingdom (Lk 10.1–13). First among those responsibilities was the preaching of Christ's message, with the specific goal of raising up new disciples (Mk 1.17, Lk 5.10). Beyond that they were responsible for bringing peace, healing the sick, and feeding the hungry. So the disciples proclaimed the coming kingdom and, as those already caught up in that coming kingdom, they served as beacons of that which was breaking in on the world. Of course, this service exposed the disciples to the same dangers that Jesus himself suffered (Mk 10.32; Mt 10.24f., 16.24f.): persecution, hatred, and even martyrdom. In other words, the identification of the disciple with his or her master is absolute. It can never be a selective picking and choosing of the more comfortable aspects, or a bracketing of the uncomfortable or even dangerous.

ii) Orthodox Soteriology Gives Mission its Urgency. While our life in Christ compels us to take the Great Commission seriously and to introduce as many as possible to Christ, the eschatological implications of our soteriology lend to the task an added urgency. Christ's death and resurrection has given every human being the hope of eternal life. We will still die. However, death is not the end of individual existence, but merely the separation of the soul from the body. The Scriptures speak of death in terms of the soul being freed from the body (2 Cor 5.1–4, 2 Pet 1.14), after which the immortal soul continues to live unto God (Mt 22.32). Immediately following death the soul is subject to a particular judgment (Heb 9.27) according to his or her deeds, and then conveyed to a state of either blessedness (Lk 23.43) or torment (16.22). At the second coming there will also be a general resurrection of the dead (1 Cor 15.13–15), a universal and

the promise exceeds every kind of merit) is fellowship with God through Jesus and thus a share in Jesus' authority. It is also the new and future life." Collin Brown, *The New International Dictionary of New Testament Theology* (Grand Rapids, MI: Zondervan, 1986), I, 489.

simultaneous resurrection of both the righteous and the unrighteous (Jn 5.28–29, Acts 24.15). This Day of the Lord will also bring with it the Last Judgment. This judgment will be universal, extending to all the living and the dead, the righteous and the unrighteous, and even the fallen angels (2 Pet 2.4, Jude 6). It will be a fearful revelation of God's justice (Rom 2.5). And it will be final and definitive. Those so judged will be divided into two groups and rewarded accordingly. The righteous will go into eternal life in the presence of God. The unrighteous will be sent into eternal punishment. These ideas are captured in the *Epistle of the Eastern Patriarchs on the Orthodox Faith*.

> We believe that the souls of the dead are in a state of blessedness or torment according to their deeds. After being separated from the body they immediately pass over either to joy or into sorrow and grief; however, they do not feel either complete blessedness or complete torment. For complete blessedness or complete torment each one receives after the general resurrection, when the soul is reunited with the body in which it lived in virtue or vice.[74]

According to the Eastern Church, the soul can only exist in one of two states after the judgment, and what determines that unalterable state is the individual's communion with Christ. If we really believed this, we would quite naturally feel compelled to invite people to Christ in order to help them avoid the certainty of eternal separation from God.

These, then, are the eternal, eschatological implications of our understanding of salvation. As we will see in more detail below (chapter 9), the doctrines of heaven and hell[75] have been used by missionaries on the one hand to facilitate conversion, i.e., to convince non-Christians of the benefits and risks associated with a decision for or against following Christ[76]

---

[74]Pomazansky, *Orthodox Dogmatic Theology*, 255.

[75]Green, *Evangelism in the Early Church*, 273–99.

[76]"If we please him in this present world, we shall receive also the future world, according as He has promised to us that He will raise us again from the dead, and that if we live worthily of him, 'we shall also reign together with him,' provided only we believe." Polycarp, *Epistle to the Philippians* V, ‹http://www.ccel.org/ccel/schaff/anf01.iv.ii.v.html›, June 26, 2015.

and, on the other hand, to mobilize Christian involvement in the mission-ary enterprise.[77] While these teachings can be abused, a truly functional belief in the eternal state of our fellow human beings may lead not only to a general desire to share the gospel, but also to a sense of urgency. Perhaps we, like our second century-counterparts, need to develop a "lively aware-ness of the peril of those without Christ."[78] We see some of this at work in St Paul's expressed "obligation" to preach the gospel. Origen comments,

> We must now ask in what sense the apostle is under obligation to Greeks and barbarians, to the wise and to the foolish. What has he received from them that he should be indebted to them? I infer that he is a debtor to the different nations because by the grace of the Holy Spirit he has received the gift of being able to speak in the tongues of all nations, as he himself says: "I speak in tongues more than you all." Given that a man receives the gift of tongues not for himself but for the benefit of those to whom he is called to preach, Paul incurs an obligation to all those whose language he has received as a gift from God. He has incurred an obligation to the wise in that he has received the wisdom hidden in the mystery, which he is to speak to the perfect and to the wise. But how is he indebted to the foolish? In that he has received the grace of patience and longsuffering, for it is the height of patience to be able to endure the furor of the foolish.[79]

---

[77]"But do not forget the future. We who are without fear ourselves are not seeking to frighten you, but we would save all men if possible by warning them not to fight with God." Tertullian, *Ad Scapulam* 3–4.

[78]Green, *Evangelism in the Early Church*, 293.

[79]Origen, *Commentary on the Epistle to the Romans*, ACCS NT 6:27.

8

The Ecclesial Origin of Missionary Outreach

T he biblical, traditional, and theological data we have collected quite clearly leads to the conclusion that the Church is an indispensable component of the missionary enterprise. More than that, we must admit that no mission is even possible without the Church, for it is the point of departure, the means, and the end result of every missionary effort. The Church is simultaneously the agent of that work, the context from which that work is made possible, and the place to which all outreach returns. It is in and through the Church that both the informal and the formal aspects of mission find their actualization. That being the case, we could formulate our missiological axioms by saying that the Great Commission presupposes the presence of the Church because:

1) The Church is the only context from which the Great Commission can be fulfilled, its only point of departure.

2) The Church is the only place in which the sacraments required by the Great Commission can be found and legitimately offered.

3) The Church is the privileged place of Christ's presence on earth today, the place to which we invite individuals to come and meet Christ.

4) The Church is the only place within which the didactic requirements of Christ's command can be accomplished.

5) The Church is the only place where all the other gifts of tradition are available.

6) The Church provides authorization for the formal work of its own extension into the world.

1. Church: The Only Possible Point of Departure

When we look at the Great Commission (Mt 28.19–21, Lk 24.47, Acts 1.9), we notice that the very idea of "going forth" requires the eucharistic community. That is, this "going out" has to be a going out from some already established base of operation, which can only be the Church. As we saw from our review of the Old Testament, Israel was chosen or set aside for the purpose of bearing witness to the light among all nations. Whether we see witness as a centrifugal or centripetal activity, it does mean that it originates or emanates from a very specific place, namely, the context created by the people of God, the law, and their worship of God. They were to be a nation of priests ministering to all the other nations, radiating the light of God out into the whole world. When they did not keep God's commandments, they and their faith became a laughingstock among the nations (Zech 8.13). When they were faithful and spiritually mature, the nations came to seek the Lord of Hosts (Zech 8.21). So witness does not simply develop out of thin air; it presupposes an authority, a sound source, a healthy point of origin, as well as a place in which the message and the willingness to witness is nurtured.

Similarly, the New Testament commission to "go forth," make disciples, baptize, and teach presupposes a place from which that activity originates. St Paul calls us ambassadors (2 Cor 5.20), individuals who have been commissioned by some authority and sent out from some place to represent someone. In this case the ambassador's commissioning authority is Christ himself. But from what place is that emissary to embark? We might answer by saying that it is from that place in which Christ has been given sole authority, that is, his kingdom. Although already inaugurated, the kingdom has not yet been fully implemented. So where, in this interim period before the end of this age, does Christ exercise his reign? The only possible answer is in his own body, the Church, of which he is head and the final authority (Eph 4.15). This place of departure is the context defined by the new people of God, the new nation of priests, that is, the Church. So we go forth from the kingdom, authorized by the king, Christ, representing that kingdom as it is now present on earth in his body, the Church. Absent the Church, there can be no "going forth." One implication of this truth is that going out into mission cannot take place through the agency of para-church organizations. Only those completely embedded in the structures of the Church can, with the blessing of hierarchs, send out missionaries. Only a local Church can send out its own people as witnesses. Every other model (for example, an independent missionary society) violates this fundamental theological principle. The point of origin has to be the Church.

In our examination of the Great Commission, we also noticed that the participle of the verb "to go forth" derives its force from the one actual imperative in the sentence: "make disciples." One might express the lessening of the imperative force of "go forth" by translating it "and when you go forth." The assumption here is that the Christians will, because they are recipients of God's grace, feel compelled to bear witness. So Jesus may have rightly assumed that they would quite naturally be "going forth," with or without a direct command. If that were the case, the impulse to witness must have arisen or been developed within the context of a community of faith, i.e., the eucharistic community. That is where the spiritual formation of the faithful takes place, the context in which Christians learn to live out their faith. That is where they are given the spiritual nourishment needed for the journey. Just as the Old Testament witness of Israel was effective only as long as the people maintained their communion with God, so also does the New Covenant mission depend on the spiritual well-being and maturity of the witnesses. Still, Jesus adds imperative weight to the idea of "going forth." That formalization of the process clearly presupposes some kind of preparation and/or enablement. He tells them to wait in Jerusalem until they are empowered for the missionary task (Lk 24.49), for only in that power will they become his witnesses (Acts 1.9). But if, as we have said, the Church itself is inaugurated by the coming of the Spirit on Pentecost, are they not then also waiting for the establishment of the Church that will serve as their point of embarkation, the place without which mission is impossible?

2. Church: The Only Place of the Sacraments

Taken together, the several expressions of the Great Commission (Mt 28.19–20, Lk 24.47, Mk 16.15) clearly presuppose the active presence of the sacraments and therefore the Church, which is the only context in which they can be offered. Jesus commissioned his disciples to

"preach repentance and forgiveness of sins in his name among all nations." There was certainly a necessary sequence. First, Christ had to shed his blood for the redemption of the world. Then, through his resurrection and ascension, he opened to human beings the gate of the heavenly kingdom. Last, he sent those who would preach to all nations throughout the world the word of life and administer the sacraments of faith. By these sacraments, they could be saved and arrive at the joys of the heavenly fatherland, with the human being Jesus Christ. He is the very mediator between God and human beings working with them. He lives and reigns forever and ever.[1]

Bede's mention of the sacraments is highly significant because it affirms the relationship between mission and sacraments, and by extension the Church. Obviously the Great Commission requires baptism, which is a sacrament. Moreover, in St Luke's version (Lk 24.47), Jesus speaks of repentance and the remission of sins—the primary benefit of the sacraments of baptism, confession, and communion. These are the instruments of forgiveness given to the Church. They channel the saving grace of God, and they are situated within and presuppose the presence of the Church.

[1]Bede, *Homilies on the Gospels* 11.9, ACCS NT 3:391.

First, there is the sacrament of baptism, during which we are cleansed from all previous sin and given new life and the power to become the children of God. After baptism the priest expresses this by praying,

O Thou Who by holy Baptism hast granted forgiveness of sins unto Thy servant, and hast bestowed upon him (*her*) a life of regeneration: Do Thou Thyself, O Master *and* Lord, be pleased that the light of Thy countenance may shine in his (*her*) heart evermore. Keep the shield of his (*her*) faith undefamed by enemies. Preserve for him (*her*) the garment of incorruption, which he (*she*) has put on, pure and [undefiled], preserving unbroken in him (*her*) the spiritual seal by Thy grace. And be merciful unto him (*her*) and unto us, according to the multitude of Thy compassions.[2]

The opportunity for the remission of post-baptismal sin comes during the rite of confession. As time passes and our sins are repeated, our burden increases as the Holy Spirit convicts us of our sin (Jn 16.8). We are then able to take advantage of the sacrament of penance to confess our sins to Christ and be granted absolution. Through the priest a promise of forgiveness is issued, and in that moment God does forgive us. Again, there is no reason to doubt the efficacy of this act. Experience shows that most sinners weighed down by transgressions are greatly relieved by this Spirit-mediated release. Interestingly, absolution is offered with a view toward the sacrament of communion. In one edition of the *Priest's Service Book* we find the following prayer:

May God Who pardoned David through Nathan the Prophet when he confessed his sins, who pardoned Peter who wept bitterly for his denial, the Harlot who wept at his feet, the Publican and the Prodigal, forgive you all things, through me a sinner, both in this world and in the world to come, and set you uncondemned before his terrible Judgment Seat. And I, your unworthy priest, do conjoin you to the unity of the faithful, and the body of Christ's Church and do communicate you

[2]*The Great Book of Needs, Expanded and Supplemented*, Vol. 1: The Holy Mysteries; Translated from Church Slavonic with Notes, by St Tikhon's Monastery (South Canaan, PA: St. Tikhon's Seminary Press, 2000), 47.

with the Divine Mysteries of the Church: In the Name of the Father, and of the Son, and of the Holy Spirit. Amen.[3]

Note the connection between forgiveness, the admonition to rejoin the unity of the Church, and the Church's willingness to offer communion. In this form of the prayer, the penitent is being urged to complete the process of forgiveness by reentering communion with his or her fellow believers and with Christ by receiving the Holy Gifts within the context of the eucharistic community.

The third opportunity for forgiveness comes during the Divine Liturgy. After we once again pray that God will have mercy on us and "pardon our trespasses, voluntary and involuntary, in word, or in deed, in knowledge and in ignorance," we then ask that he make us "worthy to partake of [his] immaculate Mysteries unto forgiveness of sins and unto life eternal." When we receive the Holy Mysteries, God does exactly that.

So in order to fulfill their commission—in order to baptize, preach repentance, and offer remission of sins—the apostles would have had to operate within and go out from an existing Church. As we know from the account in the book of Acts, the eucharistic community had in fact been established on the day of Pentecost. At that point the apostles are finally in a position to fulfill their commission.

> The eucharistic assembly is an assembly of all into one place for one and the same act. This axiom flows out of the very nature of the Eucharist, established by Christ. Christ is inconceivable without the Church just as the Messiah is inconceivable without the messianic people. The People of God are called by God in the Body of Christ, which is the Church. This Divine assembly of the People of God is realized each time in the Eucharist.[4]

[3]David F Abramtsov, *A Priest's Prayer Book*, ‹http://www.stlukeorthodox.com/html/liturgicaltexts/priestsprayerbook.cfm›, June 29, 2015.

[4]Afanasiev and Plekon, *The Church of the Holy Spirit*, 9.

3. Church: The Place of Christ's Special Presence on Earth Today

If the ultimate task of missions is to introduce individuals to the person of Christ, it seems reasonable to ask where and how Christ is present in the world today. Where do we find him present and available for introduction? Of course, Christ is present in all of creation. However, the Scriptures teach that in addition to this general presence, there are specific manifestations of the divine person. For example, in Exodus 3.2–6 we are told that God manifested himself to Moses in the form of a burning bush. Similarly, both the tabernacle and the temple had holy spaces (the holy of holies) where God was said to abide, to meet with the priests (Ex 30.36). Note how often God is referred to as being in the sanctuary (Ps 68.24, 73.17, 77.13, 150.1). Finally, God's presence is most obviously localized in the person of the incarnate Christ, God with us (Mt 1.23). Even after the ascension removed his physical presence from the realm of our experience, we can still speak of his continued presence mediated by the Holy Spirit. The Spirit's descent at Pentecost makes Christ generally available to all, providing each individual with the potential of unmediated contact with him. It also gave birth to the Church, where the particular presence of Christ is made available in the sacraments, particularly the Eucharist. So today the focus of God's special presence is embedded in the sacraments of the Church, which is the body of Christ, the temple of the Spirit. When describing how that presence manifests itself, St Paul teaches us that Christ is truly present in the elements of bread and wine, making us one body when we celebrate the Eucharist. When the people of God gather for the celebration of the Eucharist, they constitute the Church: they are the body of Christ, in the midst of which Christ is present (Lk 24.35).

This presence is particularly manifested in the eucharistic elements of bread and wine. By the operation of the Holy Spirit these elements become the very reality they symbolize. The bread and the wine *are* Christ's body and blood, and these concrete materials are used by God to mediate the present reality of the Savior. So in the consecrated bread and wine we are shown the resurrection of Christ;[5] we see the true light and receive the heavenly Spirit,[6] as well as forgiveness and eternal life.[7] To partake or even to be in the presence of this mystery is to participate in the life of Christ, to actually know him, to be in his presence. Luke reports one of the most remarkable examples of this experience (Lk 24.30–31). Walking with the resurrected Christ, the disciples do not recognize him. But when he breaks bread with them, they immediately know him. "No one should doubt that his being recognized in the breaking of bread is the sacrament," St Augustine assures us.[8]

> Remember, though, dearly beloved, how the Lord Jesus desired to be recognized in the breaking of bread, by those whose eyes had been kept till then from recognizing him. The faithful know what I'm talking about. They know Christ in the breaking of bread. It isn't every loaf of bread, you see, but the one that receives Christ's blessing and becomes the body of Christ. That's where they recognized him. They were overjoyed and went straight to the others. They found whom they already knew. By telling what they had seen, they added to the gospel. It was all said, all done, all written down. And it has reached us.[9]

Without implying that the presence of the Holy Spirit is limited to the canonical boundaries of the Church,[10] we can say that the witness of the Spirit to Christ's continued presence (John 16.14) is clearly located in the Church. What was new at Pentecost was the creation of the Church as the context of Christ's presence and enabled by the gifts of the Spirit to give witness to the whole world. This is "ground zero" for the Christian witness to the world. It is into this place of God's presence, the Church,

[5]Archbishop Dmitri, *The Priest's Service Book. Orthodox Church in America*, trans. Archbishop Dmitri (Dallas: Diocese of the South, 2003), 161.

[6]Ibid., 162.

[7]Ibid., 161.

[8]Augustine, *Letter 149*, ACCS NT 3:382.

[9]Augustine, *Sermon 234* 2 (ibid.).

[10]A favorite prayer in the Eastern Church is addressed to the Holy Spirit, who is said to be everywhere. "O Heavenly King, the Comforter, the Spirit of Truth, who art everywhere present and fills all things, Treasury of Blessings and giver of Life; come and abide in us and cleanse us from every stain and save our souls, O Good One."

to this special place of Christ's manifestation, that we invite nonbelievers to come and see.

4. Church: The Only Context in Which Christ's Didactic Command Can Be Fulfilled

Jesus also commanded his apostles to teach the newly recruited disciples everything that he had taught them. While teaching can take place in any context, Christ's teaching can and should be passed on only within the community of faith. More than anything, this has to do with the fact that his teachings require a foundation of faith, a response of obedience. This commitment has to be in place before the teachings can have their intended impact. For that reason this teaching is not to be carelessly cast into the fields of unbelief. Note what Hippolytus says:

> [Only] see that you do not give these scriptural teachings over to unbelieving and blasphemous tongues, for that is a danger greatly to be avoided. But impart them to pious and faithful men who desire to live in a holy way and righteously with fear. For it is not to no purpose that the blessed apostle exhorts Timothy, and says, "O Timothy, keep that which is committed to your trust, avoiding profane and vain babblings and oppositions of science falsely so called; which some professing have erred concerning the faith." And again, "You therefore, my son, be strong in the grace that is in Christ Jesus. And the things that you have heard from me in many exhortations, the same you should commit to faithful men, who shall be able to teach others also." The blessed apostle delivered these things with a pious caution, aware that they could be easily known and distorted by anyone who does not have faith. How much greater will be our danger, if, rashly and without thought, we commit the revelations of God to profane and unworthy men.[11]

As we saw above, the canonical instructions require us to make primary use of the Scriptures in our efforts to relay Christ's teaching to the faithful. Since the Church is, on the one hand, the source of the Scriptures,

---

[11]Hippolytus, *Treatise on Christ and Antichrist* 1, ACCS NT 9:240.

with the Holy Spirit superintending the writing down of these truths in and for the Church, and on the other the only place in which they can be faithfully interpreted, their proper missiological use obviously presupposes the Church.

Two other aspects of early Church structure emphasize that this teaching is to be done in the Church. First, we note that teaching is one of the ministries given to God's people by the Holy Spirit (Eph 4.11), implying that this kind of teaching requires the special empowerment of the Holy Spirit and can thus only be found and practiced within the Church. Second, we note that teaching is the primary responsibility of bishops and shepherds (1 Tim 3.2). If this is a specific and expected ministry of bishops, then it seems reasonable to conclude that it has to take place within the Church.

An important missiological implication of this conclusion is that our task as missionaries is not completed with the conversion of the nonbeliever. We are required by Christ's commission to continue on to baptism and the other sacraments, and importantly to the continued education of the new believers. Obviously this education can take years, but it must not be neglected. It is truly a shame that many contemporary Orthodox Christians have not been instructed in this way, and thus do not know the Scriptures or teachings of the Church. In all too many cases folk-pietistic, magical ideas are substituted for the actual teaching of the Church. This not only undermines the internal life of the Church, but also makes its witness to the world difficult or even impossible. If we really want to witness, we will need a well "educated" group of faithful, who know the Bible and its teachings.

5. Church: The Only Place Where All the (Other) Gifts of Tradition are Available

As I have argued elsewhere,[12] we Christians need to establish a core invitational context into which we can invite nonbelievers. To help us do this, God in his great mercy has given us a series of what I would like to call

---

[12]Edward Rommen, *Come and See: An Eastern Orthodox Perspective on Contextualization* (Pasadena: William Carey Library, 2013).

"gifts of tradition." These are the things that we can use to establish the framework of the invitational context. Done by specifically commissioned missionaries, this work raises up the local context into which the faithful can invite their non-believing acquaintances. This is where those who "come to see" are offered an opportunity to get to know Christ. It is here that they are engaged by Christ, and it is here that they will negotiate intimacy with Christ, come to love him, to obey his commandments, to commune with him.

As already noted, the Church is established when the faithful come together to celebrate the Eucharist. While this minimalist definition is true and helpful, it does not tell us much about how that gathering is to be constituted: how everything given in Christ passes over into the reality of ecclesial life, and how that life is to be preserved from generation to generation. Fortunately, God in his infinite wisdom has given the Church a number of practical tools that define and limit the Church, thus protecting and preserving this inheritance. These good and perfect gifts come down from the Father of lights (Jas 1.17–18) and include 1) the Holy Scriptures, 2) apostolic succession, 3) liturgical structures, 4) councils (dogma and canons), 5) hagiography, and 6) iconography. Taken together, these constitute the tradition of the Church, authoritatively given by Christ, definitively passed on to the apostles (Eph. 2.20), preserved and developed in stability under the guidance of the Holy Spirit. These gifts of tradition provide a universal yet dynamic reality within which the people of God can live, in which Christ is present, and into which we can invite our friends. They allow us to create the primary missional environment.

6. Church: The Only Source of Authorization for Mission

As we have repeatedly seen, the formal extension of the Church from one location to another requires apostolic authorization. We, as believers, are not free to simply start a new church in an unchurched region without the approval of a hierarch and the assignment of a canonically ordained priest. The contemporary implementation of this principle is rooted in the idea of apostolic succession. This principle is expressed by St Paul in Ephesians 2.20, where he states that the true Church is built on the foundation of the apostles and the prophets with Christ as the chief cornerstone (Heb 3.1). Christ handed down to his apostles everything that the Church is and all that it practices, including his commission to make disciples in the entire world. So the legitimacy of that mission is found in the actual, unbroken chain of individuals who are authorized to execute the mission of the Church. Clearly, this aspect of mission has to do with authority. "It consists in the legitimate transmission of the ministerial power conferred by Christ upon his Apostles. No one can give a power which he does not possess."[13] For that reason only those who have received authority from this unbroken chain of command can legitimately engage in the mission of the Church.

Once again we see that the commission, and in particular the ongoing execution of Christ's command, presupposes ecclesial authority, that is, the Church. It is, after all, the only context in which we find bishops, who in turn pass on the authority and who, by their very presence, define the Church.

> See that ye all follow the bishop, even as Jesus Christ does the Father, and the presbytery as ye would the apostles; and reverence the deacons, as being the institution of God. Let no man do anything connected with the Church without the bishop. Let that be deemed a proper Eucharist, which is [administered] either by the bishop, or by one to whom he has entrusted it. Wherever the bishop shall appear, there let the multitude [of the people] also be; even as, wherever Jesus Christ is, there is the Catholic Church.[14]

---

[13]Thomas C. O'Reilly, "Apostolicity," ‹http://www.newadvent.org/cathen/01648b.htm›, June 29, 2015., 648–649, at 648.

[14]Ignatius, *Letter to the Smyrnaeans* 8, ‹http://www.newadvent.org/fathers/0109.htm›, June 30, 2015.

9

Basic Content of the Gospel and Church Education

The data we have collected indicates that part of our missionary responsibility is to teach the disciples in every nation everything that Christ passed on, and that this teaching be done in the language of the listeners and in keeping with the spirit of our faith. This missionary obligation can be captured in two brief axioms.

1. Teaching all that Christ commanded involves telling the whole grand narrative of the history of God's salvation.

2. This teaching needs to be done in the language of the listener and in keeping with the spirit of our faith.

As I have argued elsewhere,[1] the gospel is not simply information about Christ, but rather the person of Christ himself. Our basic task is to personally introduce him, not simply transfer information about him. However, as the fulfillment of the ancient promise, Jesus was born into and ministered within the flow of a concrete historical context. The evangelist Matthew goes to extraordinary lengths to establish that human context by beginning his account with a detailed genealogy of Jesus; this is certainly information about Jesus. So the historical context established by that information serves as a unified, totalizing backdrop for our encounter with the Person of Christ. Without this overarching narrative, we simply cannot understand Jesus' place or role in the redemptive plan of God.

---

[1] Rommen, *Come and See: An Eastern Orthodox Perspective on Contextualization.*

As we have been gathering data for our theology, we have, in fact, been working with the underlying assumption that all of the diverse stories, authors, events, and sources of this history are best understood as a single grand narrative, an account of God's plan of redemption. This "grand" or "meta" narrative can be understood as a framework that "tries to give a totalizing, comprehensive account to various historical events, experiences, and social, cultural phenomena based upon the appeal to universal truth or universal values."[2] In the case of the tradition of the Church and in particular the Scriptures, the unifying framework is God's specific plan for human salvation. This hermeneutical key enables us to organize and explain various events in history, giving them meaning by relating diverse events and phenomena to an overarching scheme or story. Accordingly, we see everything recorded in the eighty books of the Bible: the thirty-eight of the Old Testament, the fourteen Apocrypha, and the twenty-seven of the New Testament. Written in three major languages, these books span a history of approximately four millennia. Along with everything else continued in the other elements of Tradition (councils, canons, dogma, icons, saints, etc.), they comprise a single story, that of God's salvific dealings with the human race.

There are those, of course, who are quite skeptical about the use of such interpretive frameworks. On the one hand, some believe that with the transition to a postmodern society "meta narratives have lost their power to convince or legitimize various versions of 'the truth.'"[3] In light of this, these scholars suggest that metanarratives should be abandoned in

[2]"Metanarrative," ‹http://www.newworldencyclopedia.org/entry/Metanarrative›, June 30, 2015.

[3]"Simplifying to the extreme, I define postmodern as incredulity toward meta narratives. This incredulity is undoubtedly a product of progress in the sciences: but that progress in turn presupposes it. To the obsolescence of the meta narrative apparatus of legitimation corresponds, most notably, the crisis of metaphysical philosophy and of the university institution which in the past relied on it. The narrative function is losing its functors, its great hero, its great dangers, its great voyages, its great goal. It is being dispersed in clouds of narrative language elements—narrative, but also denotative, prescriptive, descriptive, and so on [. . .] Where, after the meta narratives, can legitimacy reside?" Jean-François Lyotard, *The Postmodern Condition: A Report on Knowledge*, Theory and History of Literature (Minneapolis: University of Minnesota Press, 1984), xxiv.

favor of more modest and "localized" narratives[4] offering a multitude of possible interpretations or "truths."[5] Of course, this supposedly universal skepticism of a totalizing story could itself be considered a metanarrative. "If one is skeptical of universal narratives such as 'truth,' 'knowledge,' 'right,' or 'wrong,' then there is no basis for believing the 'truth' that metanarratives are being undermined."[6] More importantly, this contemporary abandonment of grand narratives leads to a level of fragmentation that makes it extremely difficult to maintain a grasp on any "big picture." Without the grand narrative, on what basis could we insist that Christ is the fulfillment of a divine promise made to the Old Testament saints? Without that framework, the stories of Abraham, Isaac, and Jacob lose all meaning outside of their immediate historical and social contexts, even though they are clearly connected to Christ as co-bearers of the seed promised to Abraham. This is a heavy price to pay. For when we do try to see the "big picture," as we eventually will want to do, when we try to reassemble the fragments in our minds, to list and organize all the pieces, we will fail. It is like trying to reassemble the fragments of a broken mirror that deny us a true reflection and cause us to misinterpret the "local" narratives.[7]

On the other hand, some scholars are concerned that the use of metanarratives gives the interpreter too much control over the text, an ability to impose on it an agenda not in keeping with the text. We need to ask to what extent the framework itself skews, distorts, or predetermines the perceived meaning. We may see this at work when more contemporary frameworks such as feminism, revolution, psychology, multi-cultural perspectives, or modern marketing principles are applied. The outcomes of such work, while occasionally providing some new ideas, are often quite surprising in the sense that we would never have expected the text to yield those particular insights.

---

[4]"Metanarrative."

[5]Ibid.

[6]Ibid.

[7]"The task is futile—similar to trying to reassemble the fragments of a broken mirror to see a true reflection. Thus, after a while we give up trying to see the whole altogether." Peter Senge, *The Fifth Discipline* (New York: Doubleday, 1990), 3.

For example, a number of years ago Korean theologians generated considerable interest in what they called "minjung" theology. The word is a combination of two Korean characters, *min* and *jung*, that mean "people" and "masses," respectively. These theologians define the term as "the poor, oppressed and deprived people as opposed to the rich and powerful."[8] Using this socio-political concept as a framework for interpretation, they proceeded to describe the exodus as "a socio-economic event [which is given] the status of an archetype or paradigm for God's intervention in history," and claim that "such intervention takes place in the socio-economic arena today as well."[9] Turning to the Gospel of Mark, they say that the term ὄχλος (*ochlos*) [=*minjung*, or crowd] is actually a technical theological term that refers to the poor, the oppressed, the despised, the sick, and so on, including tax collectors, harlots, and sinners. According to Ahn, "Jesus did not love all equally, but rather showed a partisan love for the ὄχλος (=*minjung*), accepting them unconditionally and protecting them without evaluating them in any way."[10] This reasoning leads to an understanding of Jesus' crucifixion as a political event, resulting from political motivation. So these theologians call the death of Jesus a political murder, and the resurrection a protest and a resolution. That opens the way to a new and unusual interpretation of the general resurrection, which according to them will exclude all who have died naturally. The resurrection will only be for those who were killed, as Jesus was. Thus, the minjung framework transforms the resurrection into a "socio-political concept" and the life of Christ into messianic politics aimed at a new society.[11]

Obviously, the use of this interpretive framework yields some rather unexpected and even disturbing results that are simply not sustained by the text (Jesus clearly teaches that he is not setting up a new earthly society or kingdom, and that his message is not political) or by the teachings of the Church (a limited resurrection at the end of time has never been

[8]Eunsoo Kim, "Minjung Theology in Korea: A Critique from a Reformed Theological Perspective," *Japan Christian Review* 64 (1998): 53–65, 54.

[9]Ibid., 56.

[10]Ibid.

[11]Ibid., 57.

taught). So, while we do need to preserve a diversity of interpretive starting points, we also have to insist on some limits. The question here is not whether we can legitimately use a framework or not; we actually have to do so. We have to start somewhere. The question is whether or not a particular framework distorts the text or does justice to it.[12] For this reason we need to begin with "a careful application of grammatico-historical tools in seeking to determine as far as is possible their authors' and editors' intended meaning in the contexts they were spoken or written."[13] The next step, which is just as important, is to determine how the passage has been used or applied within the context of the Church. Taken together, this exegetical work and the mind of the Church give us the range of meanings that a particular passage can bear, and some idea of what to expect even before we apply a framework. The framework, then, acts something like a map that brings together and makes overall sense of the disparate parts or elements of the story. This is what Wright and others call hermeneutic coherence, with the framework providing a sense of coherence and commonality to the whole story.[14] "If all hermeneutical frameworks are like maps of the territory of Scripture, then the only test of a map is how faithfully it interprets the territory for the traveler in terms of what he or she wants or needs to know to make sense of the journey."[15]

With this in mind, we could legitimately make use of a number of frameworks, such as the two covenants, the incarnation, the Gospels, and the kingdom of God. Each one provides some insight. However, in light of the data we have collected, the best roadmap would appear to be the history of God's efforts to bring salvation to fallen humanity. The major elements of this storyline are creation and fall; the promise to Abraham; the exodus; Israel the bearer of the promise; fulfillment of the promise in the life, work, passion, resurrection, and ascension of Christ; the institution

---

[12]Christopher J. H. Wright, *The Mission of God: Unlocking the Bible's Grand Narrative* (Downers Grove, IL: IVP Academic, 2006), 25-26.

[13]Ibid., 40.

[14]James V. Brownson, "Speaking the Truth in Love: Elements of a Missional Hermeneutic," in *The Church between Gospel and Culture*, ed. George R. Hunsberger, Craig Van Gelder (Grand Rapids, MI: Eerdmans, 1996), 257–58.

[15]Wright, *The Mission of God*, 26.

of the Church; divine authorization for the continuation of Christ's work; and the inauguration of the kingdom at the second coming.

What follows is an expanded outline of this story, but not in full detail. Further elaboration can be found in the numerous catechetical and theological books of the Church.[16] Here, we are more concerned with establishing a missiological checklist of the topics to be covered with new (and not so new) disciples, if we are to fulfill the requirements of our commission to "teach everything" that Christ commanded. I provide some indication of how the material is to be incorporated into the overall pattern of the metanarrative, without repeating what we have already looked at above. The end of the chapter presents a more extensive treatment of just one topic, in order to show how this kind of teaching might be structured and presented in the missionary setting.

1. The Grand Narrative of Redemption

1. Creation (Genesis 1.1)

Here we seek to communicate the concept of a divine *creatio ex nihilo*. The theological content of this general understanding can be summarized in terms of three basic affirmations: 1) God is the source of all that there is; 2) creatures are dependent, yet real and good; and 3) God creates in freedom and with purpose.[17] We could organize our teaching under the following headings:

> 1.1. *"In the Beginning."* As in John 1.1 and Isaiah 46.10, this refers to a moment before which there is no reckoning of moments. It is a beginning before which there was nothing, not even time.

---

[16]M. Oliver Clement, *The Living God: A Catechism for the Christian Faith* (Crestwood, NY: St Vladimir's Seminary Press, 1989).

[17]Langdon Gilkey, *Maker of Heaven and Earth: A Study of the Christian Doctrine of Creation*, 1st ed., Christian Faith Series (Garden City, NY: Doubleday, 1959), 41.

1.2. *"God Created."* According to Delitzsch, the Hebrew term *bara* "always means *to create*, and is only applied to a divine creation, the production of that which had no existence before."[18]

1.3. *"The Heavens and Earth."* A summary statement that includes everything that exists outside of God.

1.4. *The Creation of Humankind*

    1.4.1. "Image of God" is that which reflects God's nature in man.

    1.4.2. "Likeness of God" is a dynamic term that points to the potential of developing the gift of the image so as to make it a possession—individual, secure, and dynamic—and thus coming to resemble God.

    1.4.3. Deification is a process by which, through God's grace, it is possible for mankind to advance towards God-likeness.

2. *The Fall (Gen 2–3)*

2.1. *Basic Meaning of Sin.* To miss or miss a mark, as in violating a command.

2.2. *New Testament Meaning of Sin.* That which is contrary to God, and used to describe human offenses against God. Here it should be emphasized that sin is not simply breaking some rule, but breaking a relationship.

2.3. *Consequences of Sin.* In Adam, human nature was corrupted and became subject to death.

2.4. *Unmitigated Disaster.* Something wholly unintended and undesired by God. Nevertheless, it is the natural consequence of turning away from God.

2.5. *The Promised Descendant.* God's initial offer of salvation (Gen 3.15).

2.6. *Initial Reactions to Human Sinfulness.* Noah, the flood, and Babel (Gen 6–11).

---

[18]Keil and Delitzsch, *The Penteteuch*, 47.

3. The Promise to Abraham

3.1. *The Call of Abram and the Promise.* Election of one man and his family, chosen for the purpose of bringing blessing to others (Gen 12).

3.2. *Failures of Nerve and Hope*

3.2.1. Constant challenges to Abram's faith: Sarai is barren, famine in the land.

3.2.2. Abram in Egypt (Gen 1.10–20), with an emphasis on the effect on the promised land and people.

3.2.3. Abram and Melchizedek (Gen 1.18–24).

3.2.4. Hagar and Ishmael (Gen 1.1–16). Abraham takes things into his own hands and tries to secure an heir (helping God?).

3.2.5. Abraham deceives Abimelech (Gen 2.1–18). Repeat of the same mistake.

3.3. *Renewal of Faith and Hope*

3.3.1. God repeatedly renews the promise and strengthens faith (Gen 15, 17).

3.3.2. The Three Visitors reaffirm the promise (Gen 18).

3.3.3. Isaac (Gen 21–26). The son God promised is born. When Abraham is asked to sacrifice that son, his trust is weighed in the balance against common sense, human affection, and hope (the promised seed).

3.3.4. Jacob (Gen 25–36). His life can be summarized by Hosea 1.3.

4. The Exodus

4.1. *Joseph* (Gen 37–50). The story of Joseph leads Israel into captivity in Egypt, a train of events set in motion by rivalry, jealousy, and differing attitudes towards God's message.

4.2. *Moses*

4.2.1. The Call of Moses (Ex 1–2). The burning bush.

4.2.2. Let My People Go: The Plagues (Ex 4–12).

4.2.3. The Passover (Ex 11–13). "I will take you as my people, and I will be your God. Then you shall know that I *am* the LORD your God. . . ." (Ex 6.7).

4.2.4. Crossing the Red Sea (Ex 14–15). Salvation in the literal sense of saving life and avoiding defeat. This event has a lasting effect on both the Old and New Testaments. Repeated in the psalms, it is later interpreted as a type of salvation in general and baptism in particular.

4.2.5. The Law (Ex 19–23). Ten commandments stated in the negative (no conditions, no room for argument), given to keep the chosen people on course toward the fulfillment of the promise.

4.2.6. Rebellion (the Golden Calf) and Atonement (Ex 32–34). The tablets of the law are destroyed and then rewritten; the promise is renewed (Ex 3.10).

4.2.7. The Wilderness Wanderings. Discouraged in spite of God's provision of manna (Ex 16), quail (Num 11), water (Ex 17), protection, and victory over enemies (Num 21), they rebel again. The consequence is a plague of poisonous serpents. Salvation: a brass serpent put up on a pole, a clear type of the coming crucifixion of Christ.

5. Entering and Occupying the Promised Land

5.1. *Rahab* (Josh 1–2). Prefiguring faith: "Was not Rahab the harlot also justified by works when she received the messengers and sent them out another way?" (Jas 2.25).

5.2. *Jericho* (Josh 6). A promise of victory through obedience and divine intervention.

5.3. *Judges* (Judg 1–2). Cycle of crisis and deliverance through the Judges.

5.4. *Samson* (Judg 13–16). Question of God's will and human freedom.

5.5. *Ruth* (Ruth 1–4). Inclusion of a non-Jewish person in the benefits of the covenant, anticipating the incorporation of all peoples into God's kingdom. Inclusion of Ruth in the genealogy of Christ.

5.6. *Samuel* (1 Sam 1–3). Promise and fulfillment in the life of Samuel.

5.7. *We Want a King* (1 Sam 8).

    5.7.1. Saul. Samuel anoints Saul king. As a symbol of the Holy Spirit (like priests), the monarchy is inaugurated as a divine institution, the medium of all the blessings of the Lord, consecrated and set aside for this purpose.[19]

    5.7.2. David (2 Sam 12–13). A story of sin, repentance, and forgiveness.

    5.7.3. Solomon (1 Kg 1–29). Known for his great wealth, remarkable wisdom, and literary achievement (Proverbs, Ecclesiastes, the Song of Solomon, the Wisdom of Solomon). Completed the temple and opened it to non-Jewish worshipers.

    5.7.4. Solomon sinned against the Lord, and the Lord determined that the kingdom should be divided (1 Kg 11–12).

6. The Divided Kingdom

6.1. *Isaiah.* During the divided kingdom and the time of exile, God provided prophets to deliver his word, to call the people back to himself, and to announce the coming of the Messiah.

6.2. *The Suffering Servant* (Is 53). The prophet, as if present during the Messiah's ministry on earth, is deeply moved to see how few believed on him (Is 4.4; Mk 6, 9.19; Acts 1.15). Two reasons are given why all ought to have believed: the "report" of the "ancient prophets," and "the arm of Jehovah" exhibited in the Messiah while on earth.

---

[19]Carl Friedrich Keil and Franz Delitzsch, *Biblical Commentary on the Books of Samuel*, trans. James Martin (Edinburgh: T & T Clark, 1866), 95.

7. Exile and Restoration

7.1. *The Assyrians.* Exiled the Israelites of the northern kingdom (Samaria). There were two phases, first under Tiglath-Pileser III (2 Kg 15.29), and then under Shalmaneser and his successor, Sargon II, when the city of Samaria was destroyed and the northern kingdom ceased to exist (2 Kg 17.5–6).

7.2. *The Babylonians.* Destroyed the southern kingdom (Judah) and the city of Jerusalem. This occurred under the Babylonian king Nebuchadnezzar II (Jer 52.28–30). This was when Solomon's temple was destroyed and the dynasty of David came to an end.

    7.2.4. Daniel (Dan 1–6). Stories of faithful witness in a hostile environment.

    7.2.5. A renewed vision of the future of salvation (Dan 7–9).

    7.2.6. Jeremiah (Jer 31). The promise of a new covenant.

    7.2.7. Restoration of Israel (Ezra, Nehemiah). Repentance unto salvation.

8. The Fulfillment of the Promise

8.1. *When the Time Had Come* (Gal 4.4). God sends his Son, the promised Seed. This was the same promise made to Abraham, and is now considered the gospel (Gal 3).

8.2. *The Annunciation to Mary* (Lk 1.26–38). "The Holy Spirit will come upon you, and the power of the Highest will overshadow you; therefore, also, that Holy One who is to be born will be called the Son of God" (Lk 1.35), that is, the promised Seed.

8.3. *The Forerunner* (Jn 1.1–9, Mk 1.1–8). Prepares the way for the beloved Son of God.

8.4. *The Incarnation*

    8.4.1. Birth of Jesus (Mt 1). Tied into the long history of Israel (the seed carrier), and addressed to all peoples (Lk 2.10–14, 2.31, 3.6).

    8.4.2. The life and work of the Savior (Lk 4.18). Empowered by the Holy Spirit, he preaches the gospel to the poor, heals the brokenhearted, and announces the coming kingdom to all peoples.

    8.4.2.1. His teaching shows that the approaching end times involve a universal eschatological salvation that will envelop all peoples (Mt 5.14, 8.11, 25.32, Jn 10.16).

    8.4.2.2. His inclusive treatment of the people he encountered includes the Samaritan woman (Jn 4.1–42), the centurion from Capernaum (Mt 8.5–13), the Syrophoenician woman (Mt 15.21–28), the Gadarene demoniac (Mk 5.1–20), and the deaf man in the Decapolis (Mk 7.31–37).

    8.4.2.3. To the Jews first? (Mt 10.5ff., 15.24); the Syrophoenician woman (Mk 7.27).

8.5. *The Death and Resurrection of Christ* (Heb 9.12, 10.10–18). The twin curses of sin and death are overcome.

8.6. *The Great Commission* (Mt 25.16–20, Lk 24.46–49, Acts 1.8). Anticipating the Church; an authorization to do its work by extending salvation to all peoples.

8.7. *The Ascension of Christ* (Jn 16.5–15, Lk 24.50–53, Acts 1.9–10). Making way for the coming of the Holy Spirit, and thus the continuation of Christ's presence and ministry among us.

8.8. *Pentecost* (Act 2). The inauguration of the eucharistic community.

    8.8.1. The nature of the Church as body of Christ (1 Cor 10.16–17, 11.29, 12.12ff., Eph 2.16) and a creation of the Holy Spirit (1 Cor 3.16–17, Eph 2.17–22, 1 Pet 2.4–7).

    8.8.2. The sacraments, the sanctification by the Holy Spirit of some earthly or creaturely substance (water, wine, bread) for the revelation of divine personhood (Mt 3.16, Jn 3.5, Tit 3.5).

9. *The New Covenant*

9.1. *A New Relationship to God.* Salvation through faith (Acts 4.12, 1 Jn 3.23), recapitulation (Rom 5.1, Eph 1.10–14, Col 1.18), deification, and sanctification (2 Pet 1.3–4).

9.2. *A New People of God.* The priesthood of all believers (1 Peter 2.5, 9–10).

    9.2.1. The new work of the Holy Spirit, empowering believers for the work of the Church including its missionary outreach (Acts 2.4, 4.8, 4.31, 13.9, 13.52; Gal 5.16–26).

    9.2.2. The new structure. The charismatic structure of ministries, according to which each member has a Spirit-given ministry in the body (1 Cor 12, Eph 4.4–6, Heb 2.4).

    9.2.3. New life in the Spirit (Eph 5.18, Gal 5.16–26).

9.3. *A New Responsibility.* The twofold responsibility of informal witness (Acts 8.4, Eph 5.1–14, Phil 2.4, 1 Pet 2.11) and formal mission (Acts 13.1–3).

10. *The Coming Kingdom*

10.1. *Death.* Every human being will die, but death is not the end of individual existence, merely the separation of the soul from the body. The immortal soul is freed from the body (2 Cor 5.1–4, 2 Pet 1.14), after which the soul continues to live unto God (Mt 22.32). After death the soul is subjected to a particular judgment (Heb 9.27) according to its deeds, and then conveyed to a state of blessedness (Lk 23.43) or torment (Lk 16.22).

10.2. *The Second Coming* (Mt 16.27, 24, Mk 8.38, Lk 12.40, 17.24, John 14.3). Also referred to by the angels (Acts 1.11) and various apostles (Jude 14–15, 1 Jn 2.28, 1 Pet 4.13, 1 Cor 4.5). It will come suddenly and visibly (Mt 24:27), with power and glory (Mt 24:30, 25:31, Mk 8:38), and in judgment of the world (Acts 17:31, Mt 16:27).

10.3. *The General Resurrection* (1 Cor. 15.13–15). A universal and simultaneous resurrection of both the righteous and the unrighteous (Jn 5.28–29, Acts 24.15).

10.4. *The Final Judgment* (Mt 16.27, 24.30, 25.31–46; Acts 17:31, Jude 14–15, 2 Cor 5.10, 2 Thess 1.6–10, Rev 20.11–15). This judgment will be universal, extending to all the living and the dead, the righteous and the unrighteous, and even the fallen angels (2 Pet 2.4, Jude 6). A public affair in the presence of Christ and his angels, it will be a fearful revelation of God's justice (Rom 2.5), final and definitive.

10.5. *Eternity, Heaven and Hell.* The judged will be divided into two groups and rewarded accordingly: righteous will go into eternal life in the presence of God (Rev 3.12, 21.1–27), the unrighteous into eternal punishment in a place of separation from God, fire, and torment, called gehenna (Mt 25.41–46).

2. Teaching in the Language of the Listener and in Keeping with the Spirit of Our Faith

As indicated in the didactic outline above, the end of our metanarrative culminates either in the agony of eternal separation from God or the bliss of being eternally in his presence. In what follows we will consider how these doctrines of heaven and hell should be used and taught in the missionary setting of the Church. Here, we must consider not only how we might teach those who have not yet chosen to follow Christ, but also those who are already part of the eucharistic assembly. Historically, the doctrines of heaven and hell have been used in Christian missions within a context limited by the twin categories of punishment and reward. On the one hand, these doctrines have been used in an attempt to facilitate conversion, i.e., to convince non-Christians of the benefits and risks associated with a decision for or against following Christ. On the other hand, the prospects of heaven and hell have been used to mobilize Christian involvement in the missionary enterprise, either by pointing out the desperate plight of the hell-bound nonbelievers or the heavenly rewards of missionary service. Using the same basic appeals to reward and punishment, individuals have been encouraged first to join the Church, and then to join its mission.

Today, of course, we have to contend with a steady decrease in this argument's effectiveness. Increasingly, nonbelievers reject the concept of a place of punishment. Avoiding eternal punishment by trading it off against the equally incredible promise of an unending heavenly abode hardly sounds like "good news." To many skeptics, it sounds more like substituting one myth ("pie in the sky") for another at the cost of one's personal freedom. In the case of many contemporary believers, a self-centered attachment to this world renders largely ineffective any appeal to the plight of others. Perhaps Christians themselves have been so affected by the prevailing worldview that they, too, are now questioning the reality of hell. One wonders if this questioning also applies to heaven.

In order to prepare to meet the challenge of teaching this material in a missions setting, either before or after the eucharistic community has been established, let us ask several questions. First, how have these doctrines been used in relation to the missionary outreach of the Church? Second, how adequate have those traditional uses of these doctrines been? Third, how should they be applied to mission and discipleship in the modern world? This is not a lesson in didactic technique, but rather an attempt to apply missions-theological principles to a part of our missionary responsibility. This model can then serve to structure the teaching of the other topics in the didactic checklist.

a) Traditional Uses of the Doctrines Within the Context of Mission

For purposes limited to illustration, the various uses of these dogmas can be grouped according to addressee (believer or nonbeliever) and motivational intent (reward or punishment). What follows is obviously not exhaustive, nor is it intended to imply a chronological sequence of development. Rather, it is simply an attempt to illustrate, with examples from a number of epochs, four different ways in which these doctrines have been used in the service of the mission of the Church.

i) Heaven as the Ultimate Reward for Belief. This use of the doctrine of heaven is obviously addressed to the nonbeliever. A good example of this approach is evident in the message that Augustine of Canterbury delivered to the English king. Commissioned by Pope Gregory, Augustine set out on a long and at times dangerous journey to reach an island on the southern coast of England. There, his mission stalled because the local king refused to grant him entrance. So Augustine responded by sending a translator to King Ethelbert to tell him that he had come from Rome to bring good news, namely, an everlasting reward for believing. This was a "joyful message, which most undoubtedly assured to all that hearkened to it everlasting joys in heaven, and a kingdom that would never end, with the living and true God."[20]

ii) Heaven as Reward for Christian Service. In this case, the message is addressed to believers. According to Michael Green, Christian participation in the missionary enterprise was initially associated with the Christian's sense of responsibility or duty, i.e., a responsibility before God to live a life consistent with one's profession.[21] To justify that orientation, we need only point to Jesus' command to carry the gospel to all nations. However, during the second century "the emphasis on rewards and punishments grows, and there is a strong tendency to see Christian obedience in terms of merit. Desire for eternal life, escape from eternal judgment led to a willingness (desire?) to do missions."[22]

Green traces this tendency through the writings of the early apostolic fathers. Justin, for example, writes:

> We would not live by telling a lie. For impelled by the desire of the eternal and pure life, we seek the abode that is with God. . . . In contrast to punishment at the hand of Christ upon the wicked in the same bodies united again to their spirits, which are now to undergo everlasting punishment.[23]

Similarly, Barnabas in his *Two Ways* admonishes believers to

> remember the day of judgment night and day. And thou shalt seek each day the society of the saints either laboring by speech, and going out to exhort, and striving to save souls by the Word, or else working

---

[20]Bede, *Ecclesiastical History of England* 1.25, ‹http://www.ccel.org/ccel/bede/history.v.html›, July 1, 2015.

[21]Green, *Evangelism in the Early Church*, 246.

[22]Ibid., 287.

[23]Ibid., from Justin Martyr, *First Apology* 8.

with thine hands for the ransom of thy sins . . . taught of God, seeking out what the Lord asks from you: and do it that you may be safe in the day of judgment.[24]

Polycarp expresses the same idea in his letter to the Ephesians.

If we please him in this present world we shall receive also the future world, according as he has promised to us that he will raise us up again from the dead, and that if we live worthily of him, we shall also reign with him provided only we believe. . . . Persuaded that we shall give an account of everything in the present life to God, who made us and the world, we adopt a temperate and benevolent and generally despised manner of life, believing that we shall suffer no such great evil here, even should our lives be taken from us, compared with what we shall there receive from the great Judge.[25]

This motivation was not limited to the early believers. The same tendency can be seen in some of the most influential missions of the Middle Ages. Constantine of Constantinople, when asked by his emperor to answer the Muslim challenge to the doctrine of the Trinity, accepted the dangerous assignment with the words, "With joy I go forth to defend the Christian religion. For what could be sweeter to me in the whole world, than to die and continue to live [in heaven] for the Holy Trinity?"[26]

Similarly, early Irish missionaries such as Columban and Killian, who were instrumental in spreading Christianity throughout the British Isles and on to the continent, appear to have been motivated by a longing to travel (*peregrinus*), which

was a combination of purely human *Wanderlust* with a jealous desire to extend the limits of asceticism to the point of renouncing not only family life and worldly possessions but even fatherland and the comforting companionship of their monastic community.[27]

[24]Ibid., 287–88. Barnabas, *Two Ways* 19.

[25]Ibid., 288. Polycarp, *Epistle to the Ephesians* 1.2.

[26]Grivec, *Konstantin und Method.*

[27]James Thayer Addison, *The Medieval Missionary* (Philadelphia: Porcupine Press, 1976), 6–7.

The aim was to depart into unknown wilds, forsaking all. Whether those wilds were in a country that might be described as Christian or in one known still to be pagan was a matter of accident or indifference, for in a sense not ignoble the *peregrinus* was much more concerned to save his own soul than to save the souls of others.[28]

The early Pietists and Puritans, as well as many modern missionaries, have also been motivated by an emphasis on obedience, which was seen as necessary to avoid judgment (hell) and to earn a reward (heaven). Often, heaven has been seen as compensation for the very real sacrifice and suffering incurred in the course of missionary work. For example, contemplating the high importance of missions, Cotton Mather exclaims:

> What a magnificent thing! What a high and heavenly work! O how blessed are those who are found servants of God in this work! They are to be counted fortunate even if they are tired by work, watching, and sorrows without end; even more than fortunate if they consider how well off they are. This duty, of course, is a burden, which is likely to make even the shoulders of angels bow and flinch. But it is indeed such a work that angels' wings would also like to be used in it with all their speed and joy. It is even such a work that those servants, who carry out God's pleasure and commands and are endeavoring to bring about God's universal kingdom, not only imitate those angels, but are also helped and accompanied in their undertakings by them.[29]

iii) Hell as Something Believers Should Fear More Than Persecution. As we have seen, part of the traditional motivation for witness is the reward promised for that service. The flip side of that argument is how the fear of hell enables believers to persevere under the severe persecution associated with declaring allegiance to Christ. In his second epistle, Clement writes:

> What, then, if the wolves shall tear in pieces the lambs? Jesus said unto Peter, "The lambs have no cause after they are dead to fear the wolves;

---

[28]Ibid., 7.

[29]Ernst Benz, "The Pietist and Puritan Sources of Early Protestant World Missions (Cotton Mather and A. H. Francke)," *Church History* 20.2 (1951): 28–55, 42–43.

and in like manner, fear not ye them that kill you, and can do nothing more unto you; but fear him who, after you are dead, has power over both soul and body to cast them into hell-fire." And consider, brethren, that the sojourning in the flesh in this world is but brief and transient, but the promise of Christ is great and wonderful, even the rest of the kingdom to come, and of life everlasting. By what course of conduct, then, shall we attain these things, but by leading a holy and righteous life, and by deeming these worldly things as not belonging to us, and not fixing our desires upon them? For if we desire to possess them, we fall away from the path of righteousness.[30]

In his work on martyrdom, Polycarp describes the motivation of the martyrs who gave witness to Christ by claiming that

they despised all the torments of this world, redeeming themselves from eternal punishment by [the suffering of] a single hour. For this reason the fire of their savage executioners appeared cool to them. For they kept before their view escape from that fire which is eternal and never shall be quenched, and looked forward with the eyes of their heart to those good things which are laid up for such as endure.[31]

iv) The Plight of the Unsaved (Hell) as a Focal Point of Missionary Fervor. The most powerful motivational use of these doctrines seems to be the consistent emphasis on hell as the place of future punishment reserved for all unbelievers. Based on Jesus' affirmation that he came to seek and to save the lost, this idea has been present in every age. Tertullian uses this line of argument when he explains to Scapula, the proconsul of Carthage responsible for persecuting the Christians, why he has written to him.

We have sent, therefore, this tract to you in no alarm about ourselves, but in much concern for you and for all our enemies, to say nothing of our friends. For our religion commands us to love even our enemies,

---

[30]Clement, *Second Epistle* V, ⟨http://www.newadvent.org/fathers/1011.htm⟩, July 1, 2015.

[31]Polycarp, *The Martyrdom of Polycarp* II, ⟨http://www.ccel.org/ccel/schaff/anf01.iv.iv. ii.html⟩, July 1, 2015.

and to pray for those who persecute us, aiming at a perfection all its own, and seeking in its disciples something of a higher type than the commonplace goodness of the world. For all love those who love them; it is peculiar to Christians alone to love those that hate them. Therefore mourning over your ignorance, and compassionating human error, and looking on to that future of which every day shows threatening signs, necessity is laid on us to come forth in this way also, that we may set before you the truths you will not listen to openly.[32]

He goes on to tell Scapula that he is "not seeking to frighten [him], but we would save all men if possible by warning them not to fight with God."[33] He reminds him "that no state shall bear unpunished the guilt of shedding Christian blood."[34] While he does list examples of immediate punishment, the references to being saved or punished carry the weight of a future that is "in its universal and final form."[35]

During the height of medieval missions, the fate of unbelievers was often contrasted with that of the Christians. Consider, for example, Boniface's (c. 738) commentary on a fellow monk's vision of the plight of the nonbeliever.

Inside this tunnel he sinks further down into the deepest abyss, that is the lowest hell, and hears the ghastly, fearful, and difficult to describe sighing and crying of whining souls. And the angel said to him, "The moaning and crying that you hear in the depths comes from the souls to whom the kind mercy of God will never come, but rather the inextinguishable fire will torment them to the end."[36]

Of course, something quite different awaits those who believe.

He sees a wonderful place where a shining group of the finest people gave off an amazing joy and invited him to come to their joy if he was

[32]Tertullian, *Ad Scapulam* 1.
[33]Ibid. 4 (*ANF* 3:106).
[34]Ibid. 3 (*ANF* 3:106).
[35]Tertullian, *Ad Scapulam* 3–4.
[36]Reinhold Rau, *Briefe des Bonifatius: Willibalds, Leben des Bonifatius* (Darmstadt: Wissenschaftliche Buchgesellschaft, 1968), 36.

allowed and to rejoice with them and from that place there came an odor wonderfully sweet, which was the very breath of the rejoicing spirits. This place was, as the angels assured him, the famous paradise of God.[37]

In light of this contrast, Boniface calls on all Anglo-Saxon believers to pray

that God and our Lord Jesus Christ, who desires all men to be saved and to come to the knowledge of the truth, may convert the hearts of the pagan Saxons to the faith, may make them repent of the devilish errors in which they are entangled and unite them to the children of Mother Church. Have pity on them, because their repeated cry is: "We are of one and the same blood and bone." Remember that we go the way of all flesh, and in hell no man praises the Lord nor can death honor him.[38]

A more recent example of this line of thought is Finney's approach to the task of evangelistic preaching. In his ninth lecture on revivals in religions, "Means to be Used with Sinners," he discusses the responsibility of the evangelist to warn "sinners of their awful conditions, and exhort them to flee the wrath to come, and lay hold on everlasting life. . . . Go to a sinner, and talk with him about his guilt and danger; and if in your manner you make an impression that does not correspond, you in effect bear testimony the other way, and tell him that he is in no danger of hell."[39]

Almost every Western missionary pioneer has pursued the same goal, from William Carey (1793–1834), Adonirum Judson (1788–1850),[40] and

[37]Ibid.

[38]C. H Talbot, *The Anglo-Saxon Missionaries in Germany, Being the Lives of Ss. Willibrord, Boniface, Leoba and Lebuin Together with the Hodoepericon of St. Willibald and a Selection from the Correspondence of St. Boniface* (London and New York: Sheed and Ward, 1954), 97.

[39]Finney, *Lectures on Revivals of Religion*, Lecture IX.

[40]Judson's joy over the first conversion in Burma is a clear reflection of his missiological orientation. "I begin to think that the Grace of God has reached his heart. He expresses sentiments of repentance for his sins, and faith in the Saviour. The substance of his profession is, that from the darknesses, and uncleannesses, and sins of his whole life, he has found no other

Hudson Taylor (1853–1905),[41] to mission organizations such as the Student Volunteer Movement for Foreign Missions. Through their work, reports, and publications, they confronted the Christians of the West with the fate of the lost, thereby motivating many to missionary action. The belief that those without Christ are lost is still an important aspect of Western missionary motivation today.

> Any poll of missionaries who have gone to the ends of the earth with the gospel in this generation will reveal that many, if not most of them were motivated by the knowledge that men are lost without Jesus Christ.[42]

Understandably, the urgency of the missionary task grows out of a soteriological orientation that views the proclamation of the gospel as the only path of salvation open to the lost. Without the missionary activity of the Church, thousands would die without Christ every day. Such a perspective deeply distressed the pioneers mentioned above and became not only the motive for their own willingness to sacrifice, but also the foundation of their successful efforts to recruit additional coworkers.

Hudson Taylor, founder of the China Inland Mission, in 1895 wrote a small booklet entitled "China's Spiritual Needs and Claims." In order to give his readers an impression of that nation's terrible spiritual need, he compared the population figures of several regions with the number of missionaries working there. "Manchuria, Mongolia and the territories in the Northwest with Tibet make up an area of 3,951,130 square miles.

Saviour but Jesus Christ; nowhere else can he look for salvation; and therefore he proposes to adhere to Christ, and worship him all his life long." Quoted by Courtney Anderson, *To the Golden Shore: The Life of Adoniram Judson* (Valley Forge, PA: Judson Press, 1987), 222.

[41] Hudson Taylor's statements about the situation in China leave no doubt about his understanding of the primary goal of missions. "Do you believe that each unit of these millions has a precious soul? . . . Do you believe that He (Jesus) alone is 'the door of the sheepfold . . .'? If so, think of the state of these unsaved ones; and solemnly examine yourself in the sight of God, to see whether you are doing your utmost to make him known to them." Ralph D. Winter, Steven C. Hawthorne, *Perspectives on the World Christian Movement* (Pasadena: William Carey Press, 1981), 256.

[42] Harold Lindsell, "Missionary Imperatives: A Conservative Exposition," in *Protestant Crosscurrents in Mission*, ed. Norman A Horner (Nashville, TN: Abingdon Press, 1968), 69.

There are a million people in this area but with the exception of New-chwang there are no missionaries. They die left to their own fate." The vision of "a dying China" completely captivated Taylor and many of his contemporaries.[43]

Often, this sense of urgency caused people to break off their studies or abandon prospects for a successful career. At the first international con-ference of the Student Volunteer Movement (SVM) in 1891, participants were told about the advantages of immediate departure. Mission work was likened to the distribution of food among the starving. "If people are in need, they need immediate help."[44]

Others actually suffered under the perceived burden. It was been reported that "the burden of a Christ-less world" caused severe depression in A. B. Simpson, the founder of the Christian and Missionary Alliance.[45] His unusual sensitivity to the fate of the lost led to his determination to develop an organizational basis for world evangelization, i.e., to establish a denomination that would dedicate itself completely to the task of world mission.

Those who recognized the plight of peoples not yet reached with the gospel felt an obligation to do something toward others' salvation. Thus, human lostness became a significant motivation to missions. If Christians were to believe that people without Christ were not lost (universalism), or

[43]"Shall not the low wail of helpless, hopeless misery, arising from one-half of the hea-then world, pierce our sluggish ear, and rouse us, spirit, soul, and body, to one mighty, continued, unconquerable effort for China's Salvation?" Winter, *Perspectives on the World Christian Movement*, 292–93.

[44]"Going to the foreign field is bringing bread to starving men and light to the man who is stumbling and liable to fall into the ditch. If these people need help at all they need it immediately. . . . Don't stay in this country theorizing, when a hundred thousand heathens a day are dying without hope because we are not there teaching the Gospel to them. Go to them as soon as you can, dear friends." William H. Cossum, "Student Mission Power," (paper presented at the First International Convention of the Student Volunteer Movement for Foreign Missions, Cleveland, Ohio, U.S.A, 1891), 42–45.

[45]This is clearly stated on the text of one of his hymns: "A hundred thousand souls a day, are passing one by one away, in Christless guilt and gloom. Without one ray or hope or light, with future dark as endless night, they're passing to their doom." Ruth Tucker, *From Jerusalem to Irian Jaya : A Biographical History of Christian Missions* (Grand Rapids, MI: Zondervan, 1983), 292–93.

might find other paths to salvation (syncretism), there would be no reason to engage in missionary proclamation.

It is interesting to note how statistics have been used in this context. Over and over, the number of those facing death without faith in Christ has been compared with the missionary presence in order to underscore the urgency of the task and to press Christians into missionary service. Typical of this emphasis is the recent debate over the "two billion," that large number of unevangelized intended to serve as a standard for measuring various aspects of the missionary enterprise. Shortly before the fourth general assembly of the World Council of Churches, McGavran criticized the ecumenical understanding of the missionary task by asking, "Will Uppsala betray the two billion?" In doing so, he expressed his concern that the conference had assumed a missions-strategic stance that, because it was overwhelmed with a full program of social tasks, could contribute nothing to the salvation of the lost. Four years later, McGavran came to the conclusion that, yes, Uppsala "betrayed" the two billion, because the conference had called for a rejection of the goals implicit in the Great Commission.[46]

To summarize, we see that the rewards of heaven and punishment of hell are directed at nonbelievers in order to facilitate conversion.[47] Jesus came to seek and to save the lost, so concern for the state of the unevangelized has been one of the great driving forces behind Christian preaching of the gospel.[48]

b) Adequacy of These Uses

So what are we to make of this use of the doctrines of heaven and hell? From an Orthodox perspective, the effectiveness and legitimacy of such use can certainly be challenged because it is clearly mitigated by possible—

---

[46]"By 'betray' I mean planning courses of action whose sure outcome will be that the two billion will remain in their sins and in their darkness, chained by false and inadequate ideas of God and man." Donald McGavran, "Will Uppsala Betray the Two Billion?," *Church Growth Bulletin* IV (1968): 1–6, 1.

[47]Green, *Evangelism in the Early Church*, 248.

[48]Ibid., 249.

and actual—dangers, as well as the secular, modern, postmodern mindset or worldview. The appeal to these doctrines has certainly proven effective in recruitment and conversion. But in spite of this apparent effectiveness, or perhaps because of it, a number of potential dangers and/or theological problems emerge. On the one hand, this emphasis on heaven and hell can lead to a one-sidedness that ignores other New Testament motives. On the other hand, we run the risk of a sterile, manipulative, fear-based, and thus distorted presentation of the gospel. Such a view is characterized by fanciful speculation about the nature of hell's torments and heaven's pleasures, all of which threatens the dignity of the listener, undermines the seriousness of the message, violates the conditions of true missionary work, and undermines the believer's understanding of these important teachings. So how should these teachings be used in the missionary setting of the Church?

c) Conditions for the Proper Missionary Use of These Doctrines

Since just reward and punishment are so clearly contained in the teaching of Christ and the apostles, we cannot simply remain silent and withhold teaching on these doctrines. But while these doctrines have been part of the Church's teaching from the very beginning, and while some Orthodox Fathers were indeed motivated to missionary action by them, we need to find a more appropriate way of using them in the contemporary setting and preserving the dignity of both the message and the listener. One such way is to underscore understanding rather than fear, and to emphasize the personal nature of the heavenly rewards promised by Christ.

i) Hell: Facilitating Understanding Rather Than Inciting Fear. First of all, both the nonbeliever and the believer must be led to an understanding of the true reasons for our present and future suffering. Basically, this comes down to our having knowingly and repeatedly cut ourselves off from the only source of life available to us, God himself. We have constantly rejected the commandments that he has given us in order to regulate our relationship with him, others, and the world, and refused to believe in the promised One sent for our salvation. Because we have been created in the image of God and been made personal beings by the inbreathing of his Spirit, we possess the ability to freely actualize our relationships by loving God and others. If we do that—that is, stay in communion with God—we are able to live life to its God-intended fullest. Unfortunately, we instead have chosen to live as if we were independent agents, as if we did not need God or his commandments. These choices have had two devastating consequences: death and the propensity to sin. In this context we speak of sin as missing the mark (failing to keep the divine standards) and death as voiding our relationship with God. While death is not a punishment imposed by God, but rather the inevitable and natural consequence of separation from a life-giving relationship with God, we nevertheless will be held accountable for our self-loving sinfulness and subjected to the wrath of God.

The Church has little choice but to openly proclaim these truths. As difficult as it may be to accept, this is the clear teaching of both the Old and the New Testaments. In Genesis 6.5, we learn that God's punitive action in the flood was prompted by his observation that man's wickedness had become so great that "every intent of the thoughts of his heart was only evil continually." First Kings 8.46 asserts "there is no one who does not sin." Psalm 130.3 asks "who could stand" if God kept a record of sins. The implied answer is a categorical "no one!" In Romans 3, Paul picks up the Old Testament theme and claims that all are under sin (9), and all have gone astray (10–12) because all have sinned (23). We find the same idea in Ephesians 2.3 and Galatians 3.22. Although many more passages could be cited, these texts adequately establish the universality of sin.

Scripture is equally clear in its insistence that sin will draw a divine response (Lev 26.18, Ps 89.32, Is 13.11, Mt 25.46, Rom 13.4). But as we saw in Genesis 6.5, this is certainly not what God intended. This is a "wrath" tempered by sorrow. As Sylvan the Presbyter puts it,

> Let us consider how both the solicitude and severity of the Lord are shown equally in all these words. First, he said, "And God saw that the wickedness of man was great." Second, he said, "He was touched inwardly with sorrow of heart." Third, "I will destroy man whom I

have created." In the first statement, wherein it is said that God sees all things, his providential care is shown. In the statement that he has sorrow is shown his solicitude amid the dread of his wrath. The statement about his punishment shows his severity as a judge. Holy Scripture says, "God repented that he had made man on earth." This does not mean that God is affected by emotion or is subject to any passion. Rather, the Divine Word, to impart more fully to us a true understanding of the Scriptures, speaks "as if" in terms of human emotions. By using the term "repentant God," it shows the force of God's rejection. God's anger is simply the punishment of the sinner.[49]

Nevertheless, in the case of the unrepentant, this punishment will be fearful and everlasting (Mt 18.8, 25.41, 46; 2 Thess 1.9). Jesus communicates something of the horror of that prospect when he says, "It is better for you to enter into life maimed, rather than having two hands, to go to hell, into the fire that shall never be quenched" (Mk 9.43). He refers to hell as a place where "their worm does not die, and the fire is not quenched" (Mk 9.48). Some of his statements indicate the irreversibility of the verdict. He speaks of being "cast into outer darkness" (Mt 8.12, Lk 13.28) and of an impassable chasm (Lk 16.26). At issue here is an eternal separation from God, resulting in that horrible, everlasting, irreversible torment spoken of by our Lord (Rev 2.11, 20.6, 14, 21.18). All of this is the natural result of our choosing to separate ourselves from the only source of life; it is self-inflicted.

So rather than scaring people with the prospect of punishment, we should be trying to get them to understand their own responsibility (and the fact that in Christ repentance unto salvation has been given to us).

But to the others he says, "Depart from me, you cursed." He does not say they are cursed by the Father, for the Father had not laid a curse upon them, but only their own works. He does not say that the eternal fire is prepared only for you but "for the devil and his angels." For concerning the kingdom indeed, when he had said, "Come, inherit the kingdom," he added, "prepared for you before the foundation of the

[49]Sylvan, *Governance of God* 1.7, ACCS OT 1:127.

world." But concerning the fire, he does not say this but "prepared for the devil." I prepared the kingdom for you, he says, but the fire I did not prepare for you but "for the devil and his angels." But you have cast yourselves in it. You have imputed it to yourselves.[50]

Is this not something we should fear? We often pray that we not anger God by falling into sin, and strive for a holy fear of not offending him.[51] Are we not admonished to "always remember death, for this displaces all cares and vanities, allowing us to guard our intellect and giving us unceasing prayer, detachment from our body and hatred of sin"?[52] There are, however, two basic forms of this fear. One is the fear of his punishments, the other is a fear of being without his blessings.[53] The first fear is born of faith; it is a fear of sin and the impending judgment of God. This kind of fear is characteristic of beginners in the spiritual life. Some of the Fathers indeed recommend the thought of death as a means for the purification from the passions. But since the true Orthodox believer is not afraid of death, this fear has to be focused on the judgment that follows death. The other fear, born of a love for God, is the fear of a broken relationship, disrupted communion, and the associated blessings of God. This serves as a powerful deterrent in the life of the mature believer, who immediately senses the break caused by sin and the passions. The fear of God leads to the consciousness of sin and the need for *repentance*.

So when we Orthodox think of hell and the Last Judgment, as we do on the Sunday of the Last Judgment shortly before the start of Great Lent, our attitude is expressed in the following hymn.

When Thou comest, O God, upon the earth with glory, the whole world will tremble. The river of fire will bring men before Thy judgement-seat, the books will be opened and the secrets disclosed. Then

---

[50]John Chrysostom, *Homilies on the Gospel of Matthew* 79.2, ACCS NT 1b:234.

[51]Anthony M. Coniaris, *My Daily Orthodox Prayer Book: Classic Orthodox Prayers for Every Need* (Minneapolis, MN: Light & Life Publishing, 2001).

[52]Hesychius the Priest, *On Watchfulness and Holiness* 155, *Philokalia* 1:189–90.

[53]Maximus the Confessor, *First Century on Love* 81, *Philokalia* 2:62.

deliver me from the unquenchable fire, and count me worthy to stand on Thy right hand, Judge most righteous.[54]

ii) Heaven: Emphasizing the Relational Aspect of a Future Reward. Those we work with must also be led to a full understanding of the eternal benefits of the life in Christ. Even at the risk of offering a "pie-in-the sky" message, the prospect of eternal life with God, proleptically initiated now, must be communicated with reference to its present concrete benefits (hope). Here, we should not overlook the fact that, notwithstanding his unyielding demand for accountability, God does love the world. That love is expressed in God's desire for an alternative to death. It is a love that searches for a way to satisfy the demands of justice and, at the same time, provide escape for the condemned. This boundless love is willing to bear any cost to achieve that end. Surely, this is how God so loved the world (Jn 3.16). The word "so" is not so much an indication of the degree to which God loved, but rather the way in which that love was expressed. He demonstrated his love for the world by sending his Son. In other words, the direct consequence of that love was Jesus' mission to provide life. But what a costly undertaking! Christ died. God gave up that which was dearest to him in order to intervene in our human situation. Divine love achieved its end, the possibility of life. Life eternal was established.

It would, however, be a mistake to view this act of love as soft, sentimental abandonment of the requirements of justice. We are not speaking of some kind of general amnesty or random pardon. What was accomplished in the death of Christ actually satisfied the demands of justice. Jesus carried the sins of the world (Jn 1.29). He bore the punishment deserved by each of us (1 Pet 2.24). As a result, an objective basis for forgiveness has been established. The unfathomably selfless love of God sent Christ into the world in order to satisfy the demands of justice himself. Chrysostom speaks of two advents, one of pardon, one of judgment.

---

[54]Kontakion of the Sunday of the Last Judgment. *The Lenten Triodion,* translated from the original Greek by Mother Mary and Archimandrite Kallistos Ware (South Caanan: Saint Tikhon's Seminary Press, 2002), 159.

But let us remember that there are two advents of Christ, one past, the other to come. The first was not to judge but to pardon us. The second will be not to pardon but to judge us. It is of the first that he says, "I have not come to judge the world but to save the world." But of the second he says, "When the Son shall come in the glory of his Father, he will set the sheep on his right hand and the goats on his left." And the sheep will go into life and the goats into eternal punishment. . . . But because he is merciful, for a time he pardons instead of judging. For if he had judged immediately, everyone would have been rushed into perdition, for "all have sinned and fallen short of the glory of God." Don't you see the unspeakable surplus of his loving kindness?[55]

That being the case, we understand why John maintains that Jesus did not come into the world in order to judge or condemn the world, but rather to save it from death (3.17). The verdict had already been spoken. The world had been found guilty and justly condemned. It would hardly have been necessary for Christ to come only to condemn. However, in other passages we learn that Christ has the authority to judge (9.39), and that he did in fact judge. John tells us that he judges men (8.16, 12.48), the world (12.31), and even Satan (16.11). His judgments are just (5.30) and true (8.16). Yet on the other hand the whole point of the incarnation is salvation, not judgment (Mt 27.42, Mk 8.35, Lk 19.9).

How might this apparent contradiction be resolved? Perhaps it would be best to view salvation and judgment as two sides of the same concept. If salvation is being offered to all who believe, then the obvious implication is that it leads to condemnation for those who do not believe. The very act of love turns into judgment (Job 37.13) for some who refuse the offer and remain in their initial state of death. The role that Christ's sacrifice assumes depends on an individual's faith. "Whoever believes in him is not condemned" (Jn 3.18), that is, he is given life. Those who do not believe are already judged and, in keeping with the demands of God's justice, are condemned to eternal death.

---

[55]John Chrysostom, *Homilies on the Gospel of John* 28.1, ACCS NT 4a:127.

Therefore the Lord declared, "He who believes in me is not condemned," that is, he is not separated from God, for he is united to God through faith. On the other hand, he says, "He who believes not is condemned already, because he has not believed in the name of the only begotten Son of God," that is, he has separated himself from God by his own doing.[56]

The way this works is spelled out in John 3.19–21. The world is in darkness. The light of God's love has been revealed. When confronted with the light of God's offer, some whose deeds are evil retreat into the darkness, fearing exposure to the light. The result is self-condemnation. Outside of faith in Christ, there is no salvation (Acts 4.12). But it is precisely the saving love of God that is expressed in the gift of his Son. The whole point of Christ's coming was so that he himself might offer the possibility of life, even in the context of death. So the joyous prospect of eternal life cannot be separated from the person of Christ. It is Christ, and our eternal personal relationship with him, that allows heaven to be seen as a reward— not as some commodity or treasure, but as communion, as a relationship. So what are we being given? Streets of gold? Unending worship? Eternal safety? Perhaps, but in essence we are being given Christ himself. This idea is captured in one of St Basil's prayers:

> And grant us to pass through the night of the whole present life with watchful heart and sober thought, ever expecting the coming of the bright and appointed day of Thine Only-begotten Son, of our Lord and God and Savior, Jesus Christ, whereon the Judge of all shall come with glory to reward each according to his deeds. May we not be found fallen and idle, but watching, and upright in activity, ready to accompany Him into the joy and the divine palace of His glory where there is the ceaseless sound of those that keep festival, and the unspeakable delight of those that behold the ineffable beauty of Thy countenance.[57]

---

[56]Irenaeus, *Against Heresies* 5.27.2 (*ANF* 1).
[57]*Prayer Book*, 4th ed. (Jordanville, NY: Holy Trinity Monastery, 2011), 18–19.

It is for this reason that on the Sunday of the Last Judgment we sing, "Unworthy though I be, may I also hear Thy voice, so greatly desired, that calls Thy saints to joy, and may I attain the ineffable blessings of the Kingdom of Heaven."[58]

c) Conclusion

Will a merciful God condemn anyone to hell? Mercy has reached as far as it can. As with the Israelites, whom we referred to earlier, death is inevitable. God intervened by sending Christ, and an escape has been provided. It remains for individuals to look at the uplifted symbol of God's mercy, for in its absence they will surely die. So it is to the blessedness of heaven that we must look.

> To what other blessedness could this blessedness be compared? To be blessed of the Father! Why were they counted worthy of such a great honor? "I was hungry and you gave me food, I was thirsty and you gave me drink." What honor! What blessedness! He did not say "take" but "inherit" as one's own, as your Father's, as yours, as due to you from the first. "For before you were," he says, "these things had been prepared and made ready for you, because I knew you would be such as you are."[59]

---

[58]Sunday of the Last Judgement, Matins Ode One. *The Lenten Triodion*, 153.
[59]John Chrysostom, *Homilies on the Gospel of Matthew* 79.2, ACCS NT 3:232.

10

Guidelines for
the Implementation of Mission

A s a final step in this theological exercise, we need to ask if there are any specific instructions for the practical implementation of the missionary task(s) contained in or implied by the data we have collected so far. Our first conviction is that even the very practical aspects of missionary work must be guided by our theology, and not by the secular models and principles offered by the social sciences and modern business. Unfortunately, these influences have all but halted theological reflection on mission in some places.[1] That may well be happening because pragmatism has been elevated to the status of a missiological norm. Ever since the beginning of the Christian mission, there has been an understandable interest in the practical execution of the Great Commission. This interest has been expressed in the strategies developed and advanced by missionaries of almost every confession, and in almost every epoch of Christian history. But recently this pragmatic dimension of missiology has taken on an added intensity, particularly in the form of what Donald McGavran refers to as "fierce pragmatism."[2] This direction is, of course, the result of a fundamental methodological decision, according to which missionary work is evaluated on the basis of its "success." But how does one determine how success is to be measured? Some concentrate on membership statistics, while others focus on the number of baptisms, conversions, schools, hospitals, or clinics. So, just what constitutes success in the Church?

---

[1] Edward Rommen, "On the Detheologization of Missiology," *Trinity World Forum* 19 (Fall 1993).

[2] See C. Peter Wagner, "Fierce Pragmatism in Missions: Carnal or Consecrated?" *Christianity Today* 17.5 (1972): 13–18.

1. On Success in the Church and its Mission

It seems that there are at least two things that determine our perception of what success is in any given situation. One thing is the *nature* and the *goal* of the activity being evaluated, that is, the given activity, taken as a whole. For example, in the game of soccer, success is measured in terms of the number of goals scored. These are easily counted, and success means, quite simply, having more of them than your opponent. In the banking world, success is measured in terms of a financial return on an investment. This too is easily counted in terms of profit and loss. Now, obviously, we cannot apply the banking model of success to the game of soccer. Perhaps, if we broke the sport down into its component parts, we might say that any soccer club will have financial interests (tickets sold, players' salaries, etc.) and think in terms of a financial return on an investment. However, if we are to take the game as a whole, the banking model does not help us determine success. One team may have made millions of dollars but lost the championship, in which case they cannot be and are not considered a success. Another team may have less money, but still win the championship. Since that is the whole point of the game, they are considered a success. So each unique activity generates its own model of success, according to its own nature.

When considering the Church as a whole, what model of success should we apply? What would successful growth look like or mean? Well, we can start with St Paul's statement that he wants us to come "to the unity of the faith and of the knowledge of the Son of God, to a perfect man, to the measure of the stature of the fullness of Christ" (Eph 4.13). So a successful Church, taken as a whole, is one that has achieved "the fullness of Christ-likeness," that is, it has "grow[n] up in all things into him who is the head—Christ" (4.15). That might be our starting point. But since the Church has to interact with the world around it, we might be tempted to isolate certain aspects of its work and apply other standards. We could, for example, measure its financial state using the banking model of gain and loss. Or, we might adopt a broader marketing model[3] to imply that

[3] As examples of this thinking see Richard Reising, *Churchmarketing 101: Preparing Your*

the Church is a for-profit business with something to sell (Jesus?). But this model seems to suggest that the Church is in some sense a business seeking to gain a monetary return on investment. Although Jesus does use financial imagery (the talents, forgiveness of debt, etc.), he never teaches us that any gain other than a spiritual one is the goal of the Church. So, the banking model does not work, nor the marketing model, because of the nature of the Church. It is not a business, but rather a living, dynamic, growing, and spiritual entity. It has nothing to sell. It is not about making a profit. For that reason the application of techniques and standards of success not in keeping with its nature can only harm and eventually destroy it.[4] However, Ephesians 4 does work as a model of success, since it fits the nature of the Church and can be applied to all facets of its work. Ecclesial finance, for example, might be evaluated not on the basis of profit and loss, but rather in terms of the degree to which these transactions are carried out in a way that honors Christ and contributes to the spiritual maturity of the believers.

We might also be tempted to isolate the Church's witness to the world by arguing that success can be measured in terms of the number of converts we make. That might be, some suggest, the only tangible way to measure our compliance with the Great Commission. Indeed, McGavran and other Church Growth proponents have defended the legitimacy of quantitative growth as a goal and ultimate measure of the Church's mission.[5] In their view, everything can be measured in terms of a group's ability to bring new converts into the church. The problem with all of this is that, as

Church for Greater Growth (Grand Rapids, MI: Baker Books, 2006); Peter Metz, *Marketing Your Church to the Community*, Abingdon Press & the Church of the Resurrection Ministry Guides (Nashville, TN: Abingdon Press, 2007); George Barna, *A Step-by-Step Guide to Church Marketing: Breaking Ground for the Harvest* (Ventura, CA: Regal Books, 1992); Yvon Prehn, *Ministry Marketing Made Easy: A Practical Guide to Marketing Your Church Message* (Nashville, TN: Abingdon Press, 2004).

[4]Note the warnings and critique of Philip D. Kenneson and James L. Street, *Selling out the Church: The Dangers of Church Marketing* (Nashville, TN: Abingdon Press, 1997); Douglas D. Webster, *Selling Jesus: What's Wrong with Marketing the Church* (Downers Grove, IL: InterVarsity Press, 1992); Os Guinness, *Dining with the Devil : The Megachurch Movement Flirts with Modernity* (Grand Rapids, MI: Baker Book House, 1993).

[5]Donald A McGavran, "How to Evaluate Missions," *HIS* 27 (1967): 22-27.

we have seen, making disciples is not a simple, one-time, and momentary event. It is a lifelong process. The actual command of Christ is to make disciples, not converts, and to do so by baptizing and teaching them. In other words, the goal of our outreach is not simply a decision, but rather a life of discipleship. Since that word means imitating or following Christ, the Ephesians 4 model of success fits nicely. Conversion is simply the first step in an ongoing process of becoming like Christ, which can take years. Conversion is not the end, but rather the beginning of the Church's responsibility to its members. So if we simply count conversions or new members, we are addressing only one element of the overall process. No matter how many converts we win, we can never claim to have fulfilled our responsibility to the Great Commission until those converts have been baptized and thoroughly instructed. In other words, the number of converts does not by itself indicate "success" or "failure." If discipleship is the actual goal of outreach, then counting conversions on the assumption that more is better is simply answering the wrong question.

The second thing that tends to determine our perception of success is its meaning in the prevailing culture. In modern post-enlightenment society, most people seem to be convinced that as knowledge becomes both broader and more unified, we will experience continued progress—not only technological progress, but also social, political, and moral progress. This expectation of relentless progress is reflected in a certain restlessness or dissatisfaction with the way things are. Having grown accustomed to the constant evolution of technology, the modern post-enlightenment tends to generalize and project this movement onto almost every area of life. Accordingly, the economy, our material and financial holdings, our schools and clubs, and yes, even our churches have to grow. The underlying assumption here is that bigger or more is always better.

So what happens when we apply this progress-oriented model of success to the Church? If we accept these presuppositions, then having more members is inherently better. Two hundred members is better than one hundred, more converts better than just a few, etc. However, Jesus and the apostles clearly caution us against this simplistic equation. Jesus specifically tells us that we are not to expect large numbers of people responding positively to our invitation. In Matthew 7.13–14, he says, "Enter by the narrow gate; for wide is the gate and broad is the way that leads to destruction, and there are many who go in by it. Because narrow is the gate and difficult is the way which leads to life, and there are *few* who find it." This perspective does not fit in well with our contemporary notion of success. In Luke 15.10, Christ says, "There is joy in the presence of the angels of God over *one* sinner who repents." Will there then be more joy over ten than over one hundred? Of course not! But because some are applying the wrong model of success, asking the wrong questions, they might be tempted to think that that is the case. St Paul tells us that "we preach Christ crucified, to the Jews a stumbling block and to the Greeks foolishness" (1 Cor 1:23). Again, here is no recipe for "success" in the modern sense, where we consider making the gospel as palatable and attractive as possible the key to successfully "selling" the message. Likewise, if we were to use the banking and business models, we would get a rather dismal picture of failure, having invested a lot and received little but resistance, persecution, and martyrdom in return. However, when we apply Ephesians 4 we see that what we can measure is not numbers and returns, but our faithfulness to Christ: our willingness to keep his commandments and give witness to what we ourselves have seen. As counterintuitive as it might sound to the modern ear, this means that if the Church remains faithful to Christ and his teaching, it can be considered a success even during times of persecution and decline. In any case, the Ephesians 4 model works because it fits the nature of the Church.

It is sometimes argued that because we have been sent out into all the world (Mt 28.16–20, Mk 16.15–16, Lk 24.47–48, Acts 1.8) to preach the gospel to every person in the world, we are under a certain pressure or urgency to achieve as many conversions as possible. Indeed, we have been sent to all, and God does desire the salvation of all (1 Tim 2.4). However, what we need here is some sense of balance between our desire for effective witness and the biblical warnings against "thinking big," as mentioned above. This balance is clearly expressed by St Paul in 2 Corinthians 4.8–9: "We are hard-pressed on every side, yet not crushed; we are perplexed, but not in despair; persecuted, but not forsaken; struck down, but not

258 INTO ALL THE WORLD

destroyed. . . ." The measure of mission is a balance between faithfulness to Christ and our utter dependence on his ability to achieve the desired results. In other words, we should concentrate on our faithfulness to Christ, our reflection of his character and love, and not be distracted by questions driven by a "more is better" mentality.

As we have already seen, another downside of the modern preoccupation with numbers is that the insistence on certain types of outcomes sanctions the use of manipulative techniques of persuasion that are clearly not Christ-like. This is particularly true in the case of the missiological use of the social sciences. Most missionaries today are convinced that effective communication of the gospel depends, at least in part, on their ability to thoroughly understand the receptor's culture. This has led to deliberate and intense involvement in several social sciences including communication science, and in particular ethnology. In the early twentieth century, European missionaries actually gained recognition for their knowledge of non-Christian religions, languages, and cultures. They came to view the social sciences not only as a necessary part of the practical implementation of missions, but also as an area of study to which they could make significant contributions. They were well aware of the potential dangers, e.g., unintentionally accepting the presuppositions of secular anthropologists. Nevertheless, the prospect of a "friendly pact" between missions and science seemed to outweigh any risk involved. Nor was it viewed as a one-sided exchange, but rather a *propagatio fidei per scientias*.

But after just a few decades of such enthusiastic fraternization, the early proponents of missionary anthropology were embroiled in controversy. The missionary movement was accused of having replaced the proclamation of the gospel with various forms of propaganda, i.e., a deliberate attempt to impose European civilization and church structures on other peoples with the aid of social science.[6] Perhaps the missionaries had developed too lofty a view of their own cultures and their scientific abilities. More likely, they were so blinded by their desire for success that they were willing to overlook the dangers of using these secular techniques.

---

[6]One example of this approach can be seen in Emory A. Griffin, *The Mind Changers: The Art of Christian Persuasion* (Wheaton, IL: Tyndale House, 1976).

Of course, some did recognize the dangers. As enthusiasm for a scientific approach began to wane significantly, there were intense discussions among missiologists on how to find a balanced approach. There were also deliberate attempts to put missions back on a more biblical footing and to define the conditions under which the social sciences could be rightly used.[7] Typical of this debate and the desire for balance is the following statement:

> Missiology may make use of social science to facilitate/complement its understanding of shared objects of study. Scripture does not insist on specific research tools and/or methods. It does not recommend specific models of communication. Many of the social sciences have developed techniques which are not at odds with the teaching of the Bible and do provide practical means of gathering information important for understanding the human situation. However, it is precisely in the area of shared concerns that missiology must be most vigilant against uncritical acceptance of presuppositions at variance with Scripture. This is not to say that missiology must reject all data gathered by a social scientist with differing presuppositions. For example, an interpretation of religious phenomena that is completely functional, i.e., that rejects the supernatural, may not provide missiology with acceptable explanations, but may still prove to be an important source of data.[8]

In any case, the experience of these missiologists provides valuable insights and warnings to contemporary enthusiasts. There is, of course, an understandable desire to make use of any legitimate tools that will help us fulfill our mission. And there is certainly nothing inherently wrong with a missionary application of social science. However, we may run the risk of accepting uncritically—and perhaps unknowingly—certain presuppositions that are at odds with our ultimate purpose. Moreover, a fascination with the wrong model of success, one driven by numbers, will

[7] Edward Rommen and Gary Corwin, *Missiology and the Social Sciences: Contributions, Cautions, and Conclusions*, Evangelical Missiological Society Series (Pasadena, CA: William Carey Library, 1996).

[8] Ibid., 222.

only intensify the temptation to make uncritical use of these questionable methods.

So how, then, should we do missions? What methods can be legitimately used? Do the materials we have gathered from Scripture and tradition, that is, our theological data, give us any guidance on the practical implementation of this work? In what follows, those precepts are systematically presented in the form of missiological axioms organized around the six basic missiological tasks outlined in the third chapter. Attached to each activity is a set of principles that define the range of expected and acceptable modes of implementation. The six multilayered activities may be summarized as follows. Taken together with their respective axioms, they represent a manifesto of missionary action. These steps are to be pursued in logical (rather than chronological) sequence.

1) *Sending authorized delegates* in order to proclaim the gospel to all nations and ethnic groupings that have not yet heard it.

2) *Making disciples*, which includes bringing men and women to the point of conversion, teaching them all that Christ has commanded, and baptizing them.

3) *Establishing eucharistic/liturgical communities* to serve as bases of ongoing missionary operation.

4) *Teaching the fundamentals of the faith,* which would include all educational ministries of the Church.

5) Addressing social and humanitarian needs, which takes up the ancient practice of almsgiving.

6) *Re-evangelizing* peoples and areas that were once Christian.

2. Guidelines for Mission

1. Mission begins with the sending of authorized delegates in order to proclaim, that is, personally introduce Christ to everyone who does not yet know or no longer knows him.

    1.1. *On the Act of Sending*

        1.1.1. This move must originate within the Church, not with some extra- or para-ecclesial entity such as an independent missions society.

            1.1.1.1. The informal sending (in the case of home missions) takes place at the end of the liturgy. It results in the general witness of the faithful to what they have seen during the liturgy (the resurrection, the true light, the one faith) or in other words, to Christ himself. This is what we have called the liturgy after the liturgy.

            1.1.1.2. The formal sending (for foreign or cross-cultural missions) is intended to extend the Church, that is, to establish eucharistic communities in areas in which they do not yet exist.

        1.1.2. The entire process, both formal and informal, remains the primary responsibility of the presiding bishop, and secondarily of the local clergy.

        1.1.3. The formal sending will need to be done in accordance with the canons of the Church that prevent one bishop from working in another's area of jurisdiction.

    1.2. *Authorizing Delegates*

        1.2.1. The actual authorization or commissioning of these delegates remains the prerogative of the bishop, who will also provide specific instruction for the work. The bishop and not the academy is the primary source of missiological instruction and thought in the Church.

1.2.1.1. In the case of the informal mission of the faithful, authorization comes at the hand of a local priest as delegated by a bishop.

1.2.1.2. In the case of the formal extension of the Church, only the bishop can authorize.

1.2.2. There thus can be no legitimate sending, either formal or informal, through so-called para-church agencies. Because these are not eucharistic communities, they cannot send the faithful to give witness to what they have not seen (in the liturgy), nor can they be tasked with extending the Church. However, some such groups may be needed to accomplish specific sub-tasks (translation, social services, medical services, and specialized training) while serving under the authority of a bishop.

1.2.3. Choosing the delegates sent out

1.2.3.1. The informal sending presupposes a certain level of spiritual maturity, knowledge of the Scriptures, and personal holiness. This is to be taught and fostered by the local priest in each parish. It is primarily a spiritual state and not a particular set of apologetic skills, publications, or techniques. While it is assumed that all the faithful will participate, we need to be sensitive to the gifting by the Holy Spirit for specific ministries. We allow the exercise of these gifts to be distributed along the whole range of the charismatic structure of the Church, for not all are teachers, etc.

1.2.3.2. Selecting delegates for a formal sending is also done in accordance with the leading of the Holy Spirit and the gifting of the Spirit, rather than on the basis of contemporary hiring practices (education, resumes, recommendations, psychological evaluations), which have little place in the spiritual/charismatic structure of the Church.

1.3. *Proclaiming the Gospel*

   1.3.1. The primary focus of the sending must be centered on the effort to introduce the person of Christ.

      1.3.1.1. This introduction involves witness, not proselytizing. It is a dialogue with others, an intense and completely kenotic engagement.

      1.3.1.2. In addition to the personal introduction, information about God's redemptive plan in Christ has to be communicated in the language and culture of the recipient. While this will certainly require translation and cross-cultural sensitivity, nevertheless it must remain a personal witness, a true engagement and not a mechanistic technique. It is an offer, an invitation, not the imposition of information.

      1.3.1.3. This proclamation is to be done with deliberate reliance on the empowering and validating work of the Holy Spirit and not depend upon our own persuasive techniques, marketing abilities, or communication skills.

      1.3.1.4. All other activities, however good in their own right, should be considered secondary to the primary mission, or perhaps not even a part of the Church's task.

   1.3.2. A secondary focus of this sending will be, preliminarily, the telling of the Grand Narrative of Redemptive History.

1.4. *To All Nations*

   1.4.1. No people or demographic group or place may be excluded from the list of recipient populations. This means that Christ is to be introduced, without exception or reservation, to all peoples, even those of other social, cultural, secular, or non-Christian religious persuasions.[9] This principle may mean

---

[9]While it is beyond the scope of this study, our missions theological work would also have to include a basic Orthodox approach to the non-Christian religions. Some indication of how this might be developed can be seen in the following: Edward Rommen, "An Eastern Orthodox Perspective" in "Wheaton and the Controversy over Whether Muslims and Christians Worship the Same God," 27, ‹https://www.emsweb.org/images/occasional-bulletin/special-editions/OB_SpecialEdition_2016.pdf›; Edward Rommen, "Synthesis," in Edward Rommen, *Christianity and the Religions: A Biblical Theology of World Religions*,

bearing witness under opposition and a willingness to suffer, or even be martyred.

1.4.2. Identifying these populations is the work of the whole Church, aided by the Holy Spirit, and never the function of a census or a statistical and cultural analysis. It is rather the direct result of being led to our listeners by the dynamic work of the Holy Spirit.

1.4.3. The content of the proclamation must always be delivered in the local language, and in keeping with the social structures (tribal, familial, lines of authority) present in the local culture. This involves sociological and anthropological expertise on the part of the missionaries, and will require timely translation of the Scriptures, service books, and catechisms by expert linguists.

1.5. *For All of Time (Unto the End of the Age)* These activities are fixed aspects of the Church's activities that are to be continually performed until the great day of Christ's coming again. Until then we must never voluntarily suspend our witness.

2. The next phase of missions involves making disciples, which includes bringing men, women, and children to the point of conversion, baptizing them, and then teaching them all that Christ has commanded.

2.1. *Making Disciples.* The overall goal is to bring individuals into a personal relationship with Christ so that they are willing to follow him and all that he teaches. This involves issuing the call of Christ and helping individuals to trust and have faith in him, to follow and imitate him, to submit to the authority of his word, and to negotiate their ongoing (transformative) relationship with him in the context of the eucharistic community.

Evangelical Missiological Society Series (Pasadena, CA: William Carey Library, 1995), 241–53; "Dialogue with Islam from an Orthodox Point of View" in Archbishop Anastasios, *Facing the World: Orthodox Christian Essays on Global Concerns* (Crestwood, NY: St Vladimir's Seminary Press, 2003), 103–26; "A Theological Approach to Understanding Other Religions," in ibid., 127–54.

2.2. *Conversion*

2.2.1. The first step toward becoming a disciple involves a definite act of turning around, away from a life of sin. It is a conscious decision to follow Christ, to make Christ and his message one's own.

2.2.2. This conversion cannot be reached by means of coercion. It is not something that involves argument or human persuasion, but rather results from the convicting power of the Holy Spirit validating the words of witness and mediating the personal presence of Christ.

2.2.3. Conversion represents only the first step of a lifelong journey. It cannot be seen as a one-time, once-for-all experience that settles all accounts forever. It is rather an induction into the process of salvation, transformation, and deification.

2.3. *Baptism*

2.3.1. The modus of baptism is to be in accordance with the instructions of tradition, that is, triple immersion in the name of the Holy Trinity.

2.3.2. This initial sacramental act cannot under any circumstances be neglected. There can be no life in Christ, nor life in the Church, without baptism.

2.3.3. This sacrament generally presupposes the authorization of a bishop, usually in the form of a properly delegated and ordained priest.

2.3.4. Given the proliferation of Christian sects, the question of whether to re-baptize or not may have to be determined by the bishop.

2.3.5. Baptism is to be followed by chrismation, the sealing of the candidate with the Holy Spirit. If re-baptism is not necessary, then the candidate will be brought into the Church by chrismation.

3. Next the missionary needs to establish the eucharistic-liturgical community, which will serve as the setting for the sacraments, the context of life in Christ, and the basis for an ongoing missionary operation. This task need not be done in strict chronological sequence after the previous phase, but may well happen conterminously. This is true because

3.1. *All Mission Work Presupposes the Church*

3.1.1. As we have seen, the Great Commission requires baptism and anticipates communion. Without the Church, these things cannot take place.

3.1.2. As a result, we conclude that the Church is a necessary component of mission. Even in the pioneer stage of the work, it is already present in the missionary situation in the person of the bishop or his delegate.

3.1.3. Because of the Church's indispensability, one of the primary tasks of the pioneering missionary is to make use of all the gifts of tradition in order to establish a local expression of the Church (initially a mission outpost) that can grow into a full-fledged parish.

3.2. *First and Foremost the Eucharist*

3.2.1. Given the immediacy of the presence of Christ in the Eucharist, missionary proclamation is unthinkable without the Eucharist.

3.2.2. The celebration of the Eucharist presupposes the presence of a duly ordained representative of the bishop and his authorization.

3.2.3. The initial celebrations of the sacraments in a new area represent a foothold or beachhead among that particular population.

3.3. *Fully Liturgical Communities*

3.3.1. The gathering of the newly won disciples to celebrate the Eucharist constitutes the Church.

3.3.2. A regular and full cycle of liturgical services should be established as soon as possible.

3.3.3. In keeping with the notion of the priesthood of all believers and the missionary intent of the Church's liturgical cycle, these communities become the local point of departure for missionary witness.

3.4. *The Ongoing Missionary Activity of the Newly Established Eucharistic Community.*

3.4.1. Once established, these local communities become the permanent point of embarkation for the witness of the faithful into the surrounding region. They serve as the place to which nonbelievers are ultimately invited and as the context for ministry to them.

3.4.2. These communities also constitute the potential platform from which the Church can be formally extended into additional non-ecclesial regions.

4. *The next phase of the work involves teaching the fundamentals of the faith, including all that Christ taught and everything he passed down to his apostles; it should involve all the educational ministries (opportunities) of the Church.*

4.1. *Fundamentals of the Faith.* The Church is responsible for teaching everything that Christ passed on to his disciples. In essence, this teaching contains the whole grand narrative of the history of God's redemptive efforts on behalf of humankind.

4.2. This activity has to be pursued using every educational ministry possible in the Church, including homilies, discipleship classes, church school, and the ecclesially supported teaching of children by parents in the homes of the faithful.

4.3. This teaching will take place according to the requirements laid down in the canons of the Church, and be gentle, nonviolent, and complete.

4.4. As new disciples are brought into the Church, this pattern repeats itself indefinitely.

5. Another aspect of mission involves addressing social and humanitarian needs by taking up the ancient practice of almsgiving.

5.1. *Social Needs*

5.1.1. While the ordinary social needs of the faithful are to be taken seriously, it is not the purpose of the local eucharistic assembly to meet those needs. For that reason the Church is not to be distracted from its main task by unrelated activities such as exercise classes, sports programs, and the like.

5.1.2. However, the assembly can and should act as a family of faith, with all of the intimacy and trust implied by the term fellowship.

5.1.3. This fellowship involves providing any and all support and aid needed by the members of the community, i.e., the faithful taking care of their own.

5.1.4. It also involves the family of faith forming a fellowship of service to meet the needs of those outside the community.

5.2. *Humanitarian Needs*

5.2.1. One of the signs of Christian love for others must be the local Christian concern for humanitarian needs (hunger, education, justice, housing) of the populations that surround it.

5.2.2. While these concerns are not the initial focus of formal missionary outreach, they become necessary expressions of our love for others once the eucharistic assemblies have been established.

5.2.3. While the Church cannot replace the work of secular institutions (hospitals, aid agencies, governments), the local parish should actively support their work and never use the presence of these entities as an excuse for inaction.

5.2.4. *Almsgiving.* The specific nature of this ministry is captured in the multi-faceted and ancient practice of almsgiving.

6. A final aspect of mission is re-evangelizing peoples and areas that were once Christian. Given the modern threats and challenges to the Christian faith, there are now many individuals who have been lured away from the Church, either converting to other religions, reverting to their former ways, or espousing no belief system at all. In some areas this is so widespread that we can now speak of whole regions as "formerly" Christian.

6.1. *Focusing on Peoples.* We can analyze populations by their demographic characteristics to identify those that have abandoned the faith. In many cases these groups remain within the jurisdiction of an authorizing hierarch, and can thus be re-addressed by the informal witness of the local Church.

6.2. *Focusing on Areas.* Clearly identifiable non-Christian geographic regions can become the object of a renewed formal missionary effort. Obviously such efforts will take great sensitivity and an understanding of why people have turned from the faith, and maybe even a humble acknowledgement of the Church's own failings.

Conclusions

W e began this journey by gathering as much theological information as we could, from every available source, in order to craft
a coherent statement of a theology of the Church's mission in the world.
As we have seen, there is no lack of data. The challenge has been to bring
the data together in a way that practically informs our practice of mission. While we cannot specify every detail of missiological eventualities,
we have in some small fashion succeeded in our task. We have identified
the Church as the recipient of the ancient promise made to Abraham. We
have affirmed that the new people of God, the new nation of priests, has
been authorized to go into this world bearing witness to what we have
experienced in Christ and, where necessary, establishing new eucharistic communities, making disciples, and baptizing and teaching them. We
have learned that these activities are to be done in the power of the Spirit,
not through the efficiency of modern persuasive techniques. As these
communities mature, they are to actively minister to the needs of those
who surround them and to continue to teach the faithful all that Christ
commanded until he returns. These tasks are summed up in the aposticha
verse sung during Great and Holy Tuesday Matins, a fitting end to our
journey.

> Come, O faithful,
> let us work zealously for the Master,
> for He distributes wealth to His servants.
> Let each of us, according to his ability,
> increase his talent of grace:
> let one be adorned in wisdom through good works;
> let another celebrate a service in splendor!

The one distributes his wealth to the poor;
the other communicates the Word to those untaught.
Thus we shall increase what has been entrusted to us,
and, as faithful stewards of grace,
we shall be accounted worthy of the Master's joy.
Make us worthy of this, O Christ our God,
in Thy love for mankind.[1]

---

[1]Great and Holy Tuesday, Vespers, Lord I Call verses. Text from *The Liturgy of the Pre-sanctified Gifts*, ed. David Drillock and John H. Erickson (Crestwood, NY: St. Vladimir's Seminary Press), 245.

Bibliography

Patristic Sources

The quotations from the Fathers in the text are derived from the following sources.

Ancient Christian Commentary on Scripture: New Testament. Edited by Thomas C. Oden. 12 vols. (vol. 1 in 2 parts). Downers Grove, IL: IVP Academic, 2000–2007.

Ancient Christian Commentary on Scripture: Old Testament. Edited by Thomas C. Oden. 15 vols. Downers Grove, IL: IVP Academic, 2001–2010.

Anselm of Canterbury. *Prosologium*, in *Prosologium; Monologium; An Appendix in Behalf of the Fool by Gaunilon; and Cur Deus Homo.* Translated by Sidney Norton Deane. Chicago, IL: Open Court, 1926.

The Ante-Nicene Fathers. Edited by Alexander Roberts and James Donaldson. 10 vols. Buffalo, 1885–1896. Reprint, Peabody, MA: Hendrickson, 1994.

Bede. *Bede's Ecclesiastical History of England: A Revised Translation.* Translated by J. A. Giles and edited by A. M. Sellar. London: George Bell and Sons, 1907.

John Chrysostom. *Homilies on Genesis 18–45.* Translated by Robert C. Hill. The Fathers of the Church: A New Translation 82. Washington, DC, Catholic University of America Press: 1990.

The Nicene and Post-Nicene Fathers, Series 1. Edited by Philip Schaff. New York, 1886–1889. 14 vols. Reprint, Peabody, MA: Hendrickson, 1994.

Nicene and Post-Nicene Fathers, Series 2. Edited by Philip Schaff and Henry Wace. New York, 1890. 14 vols. Reprint, Peabody, MA: Hendrickson, 1994.

Origen. *Prayer, Exhortation to Martyrdom.* Translated by John J. O'Meara. Ancient Christian Writers 19. New York, NY: Newman Press, 1954.

The Philokalia: The Complete Text. Translated and edited by G.E.H. Palmer, Philip Sherrard, and Kallistos Ware. 4 vols. London: Faber and Faber, 1979–1995.

Rimbert. *Anskar, The Apostle of the North, 801–865.* Translated by Charles H. Robinson. London: The Society for the Propagation of the Gospel in Foreign Parts, 1921.

Patrologia Graeca [= Patrologiae cursus completes: Series graeca]. Edited by J.-P. Migne. 162 vols. Paris, 1857–1866.

Pseudo-Dionysius: The Complete Works. Translated by Colm Luibheid. Classics of Western Spirituality Series. New York, NY: Paulist Press, 1987.

Other Sources

Abramtsov, David F., and Daniel Swires, eds. *A Priest's Prayer Book.* St Luke the Evangelist Orthodox Church. Accessed June 29, 2015. http://www.stlukeorthodox.com/html/liturgicaltexts/priestsprayerbook.cfm.

Addison, James Thayer. *The Medieval Missionary.* Philadelphia, PA: Porcupine Press, 1976.

Afanasiev, Nicholas, and Michael Plekon. *The Church of the Holy Spirit.* Notre Dame, IN: University of Notre Dame Press, 2007.

Agourides, Savas. "Salvation According to the Orthodox Tradition." *Ecumenical Review* 21.3 (July 1969), 190.

Allen, Roland. *The Spontaneous Expansion of the Church and the Causes Which Hinder It.* 1st American ed. Grand Rapids, MI: Wm. B. Eerdmans, 1962.

Anastasios (Yannoulatos). "Dialogue with Islam from an Orthodox Point of View." In *Facing the World: Orthodox Christian Essays on Global Concerns,* 103–26. Crestwood, NY: St Vladimir's Seminary Press, 2003.

_____. "Monks and Mission in the Eastern Church During the Fourth Century." *IRM* 58 (1969): 208–26.

_____. "Orthodox Spirituality and External Mission." *IRM* 52 (1963): 300–02.

_____. "Purpose and Motive of Mission." *IRM* 54 (1965): 281–97.

_____. "A Theological Approach to Understanding Other Religions." In *Facing the World: Orthodox Christian Essays on Global Concerns,* 127–54. Crestwood, NY: St Vladimir's Seminary Press, 2003.

Anderson, Courtney. *To the Golden Shore: The Life of Adoniram Judson.* Valley Forge, PA: Judson Press, 1987.

"Annunciation of Our Most Holy Lady, the Theotokos and Ever-Virgin Mary: Troparion and Kontakion." Orthodox Church in America. Accessed June 16, 2015. http://oca.org/saints/troparia/2014/03/25/100884-the-annunciation-of-our-most-holy-lady-the-theotokos-and-ever-vi.

Athenagoras (Kokkinakis). "Tradition and Traditions." *St Vladimir's Seminary Quarterly* 7.3 (1963): 102–14.

Bajis, Jordan. *Common Ground: An Introduction to Eastern Christianity for the American Christian.* Minneapolis, MN: Light and Life, 1996.

Barna, George. *A Step-by-Step Guide to Church Marketing: Breaking Ground for the Harvest.* Ventura, CA: Regal Books, 1992.

Bebis, George S. *The Mind of the Fathers.* Brookline, MA: Holy Cross Orthodox Press, 1994.

Bechler, Th. "Einzelbekehrung und Volkskirche nach dem Erfahrung der Brüdermission." In *Einwurzelung des Christentum in der Heidenwelt,* edited by P. Julius Richter, 87–144. Gütersloh, 1906.

Beeby, H. D. *Canon and Mission.* Christian Mission and Modern Culture. Harrisburg, PA: Trinity Press International, 1999.

Benz, Ernst. "The Pietist and Puritan Sources of Early Protestant World Missions (Cotton Mather and A.H. Francke)." *Church History* 20.2 (1951): 28–55.

Betz, Hans Dieter. *Nachfolge und Nachahmung Jesu Christi im Neuen Testament.* Tübingen: J. C. B. Mohr, 1967.

Billington, James H. *The Icon and the Axe: An Interpretive History of Russian Culture.* New York, NY: Vintage Books, 1966.

Blauw, Johannes. *Gottes Werk in dieser Welt: Grundzüge einer biblischen Theologie der Mission.* Munich: Kaiser, 1961.

Boer, Harry R. *Pentecost and Missions.* Grand Rapids, MI: Wm. B. Eerdmans, 1961.

Bolshakoff, Serge. *The Foreign Missions of the Russian Orthodox Church.* London: Society for Promoting Christian Knowledge, 1943.

Bosch, David. *Die Heidenmission in der Zukunftsschau Jesu: Eine Untersuchung zur Eschatologie der synoptischen Evangelien.* Zurich: Zwingli Verlag, 1959.

Bria, Ion. *Go Forth in Peace: Orthodox Perspectives on Mission.* WCC Mission Series. Geneva: World Council of Churches, 1986.

_____. *The Liturgy after the Liturgy: Mission and Witness from an Orthodox Perspective.* Geneva: World Council of Churches, 1996.

_____. *Martyria/Mission: The Witness of the Orthodox Churches Today.* Geneva: Commission on World Mission and Evangelism, World Council of Churches, 1980.

Bromiley, Geoffrey William, and Gerhard Friedrich. *Theological Dictionary of the New Testament.* 10 vols. Grand Rapids, MI: Wm. B. Eerdmans, 1964.

Brown, Colin, ed. *The New International Dictionary of New Testament Theology.* Vol. 1. Grand Rapids, MI: Zondervan, 1986.

Brownson, James V. "Speaking the Truth in Love: Elements of a Missional Hermeneutic." In *The Church Between Gospel and Culture,* edited by George R. Hunsberger and Craig Van Gelder, 228–59. Grand Rapids, MI: Wm. B. Eerdmans, 1996.

Bulgakov, Sergius. *The Bride of the Lamb.* Translated by Boris Jakim. Grand Rapids, MI: Wm. B. Eerdmans, 2002.

_____. *The Lamb of God.* Translated by Boris Jakim. Grand Rapids, MI: Wm. B. Eerdmans, 2008.

Calian, C. Samuel. "Eastern Orthodoxy's Renewed Concern for Mission." *IRM* 52 (1963): 33–37.

Carey, William. *An Enquiry into the Obligations of Christians to Use Means for the Conversion of the Heathens.* Leicester, 1792.

"CEEAMS–Central and Eastern European Association for Mission Studies." Central and Eastern European Association for Mission Studies. Accessed May 25, 2015. http://www.ceeams.org.

Clement, M. Olivier. *Living God: A Catechism for the Christian Faith.* Crestwood, NY: St Vladimir's Seminary Press, 1989.

Coniaris, Anthony M. *My Daily Orthodox Prayer Book: Classic Orthodox Prayers for Every Need.* Minneapolis, MN: Light & Life Publishing, 2001.

"Cosmas of Aetolia, Equal to the Apostles." Greek Orthodox Archdiocese of America. Accessed June 17, 2015. http://www.goarch.org/chapel/saints_view?contentid=581&type=saints.

Cossum, William H. "Immediate Sailing: Its Advantages, and How Secured." In *Report of the First International Convention of the Student Volunteer Movement for Foreign Missions held at Cleveland, Ohio, U. S. A., February*

26, 27, 28, and March 1, 1891, 42–45. Boston, MA: Press of T. O. Metcalf & Co., 1891.

Deissmann, Adolf. *Licht vom Osten. Das Neue Testament und die neuentdeckten Texte der hellenistisch-römischen Welt.* 4th ed. Tübingen: J. C. B. Mohr, 1923.

Dix, Gregory. *The Shape of the Liturgy.* Westminster [London]: Dacre Press, 1945.

Douglas, J. D., ed. *Let the Earth Hear His Voice: International Congress on World Evangelization, Lausanne, Switzerland.* Minneapolis, MN: World Wide Publications, 1975.

Dragas, George D. "Orthodox Ecclesiology in Outline." *Greek Orthodox Theological Review* 26.3 (1981): 185–92.

Dupont, Jacques. "The Conversion of Paul, and Its Influence on his Understanding of Salvation by Faith." In *Apostolic History and the Gospel: Biblical and Historical Essays Presented to F. F. Bruce on his 60th Birthday,* edited by W. Ward Gasque and Ralph P. Martin, 176–94. Grand Rapids, MI: Wm. B. Eerdmans, 1970.

Ehrenfeuchter, Friedrich A. E. *Die praktische Theologie.* Abt. 1. Göttingen: Dieterich, 1859.

Ellul, Jacques. *The Betrayal of the West.* Translated by Matthew J. O'Connell. New York, NY: Seabury Press, 1978.

"Entry of the Most Holy Mother of God into the Temple: Troparion and Kontakion." Orthodox Church in America. Accessed June 16, 2015. http://oca.org/saints/troparia/2014/11/21/103357-the-entry-of-the-most-holy-mother-of-god-into-the-temple.

"Equal of the Apostles Great Prince Vladimir, in Holy Baptism Basil, the Enlightener of the Russian Land." Orthodox Church in America. Accessed May 23, 2015. http://oca.org/saints/lives/2013/07/15/102031-equal-of-the-apostles-great-prince-vladimir-in-holy-baptism-basi.

Finney, Charles G. *Lectures on Revivals of Religion.* Oberlin, OH: E. J. Goodrich, 1868.

Fitzgerald, Thomas E. *The Orthodox Church.* Westport, CT: Greenwood Publishing Group, 1998.

Florovsky, Georges. *The Collected Works of Georges Florovsky.* Vol. 3, *Creation and Redemption.* Belmont, MA: Nordland Pub. Co., 1976.

Francke, August Hermann. "Von der Erziehung der Jugend zur Gottselig-keit." In *Pädagogische Schriften. Nebst der Darstellung eines Lebens und einer Stiftungen*, edited by D. G. Kramer, 17–47. Langensalza: H. Beyer & Söhne, 1885.

_____. "Was vom weltüblichen Tanzen zu halten sei." In *Werke in Auswahl*, edited by Erhard Peschke. Berlin: Evangelische Verlagsanstalt, 1967.

Gavrilyuk, Paul L. "The Orthodox Renaissance." *First Things* 228 (December 2012): 33–37.

Geraci, Robert P., and Michael Khodarkovsky. *Of Religion and Empire: Missions, Conversion, and Tolerance in Tsarist Russia*. Ithaca, NY: Cornell University Press, 2001.

Gerhard, Johann. *Loci Theologici*. Vol. 6. Leipzig: J. C. Hinrichs, 1885.

Gilkey, Langdon. *Maker of Heaven and Earth: A Study of the Christian Doctrine of Creation*. 1st ed. Christian Faith Series. Garden City, NY: Doubleday, 1959.

Gillet, Lev. "Dialogue with Trypho." *IRM* 31 (1942): 172–179.

Gilliland, Dean S. *Pauline Theology & Mission Practice*. Grand Rapids, MI: Baker Book House, 1983.

Glazik, Josef. *Die Islammission der russisch-orthodoxen Kirche: eine missionsgeschichtliche Untersuchung nach russischen Quellen und Darstellung*. Münster: Aschendorff, 1959.

_____. "The Meaning and the Place of Missiology Today." *IRM* 57 (1968): 393–492.

_____. *Die russisch-orthodoxe Heidenmission seit Peter dem Grossen: ein missionsgeschichtlicher Versuch nach russischen Quellen und Darstellungen*. Missionswissenschaftliche Abhandlungen und Texte. Münster: Aschendorff, 1954.

Glover, Robert Hall. *The Bible Basis of Mission*. Chicago, IL: Moody Press, 1946.

The Great Book of Needs: Expanded and Supplemented. Translated and edited by St. Tikhon's Monastery. Vol. 1, *The Holy Mysteries*. South Canaan, PA: St. Tikhon's Seminary Press, 2000.

Green, Edward Michael Bankes. *The Meaning of Salvation*. Philadelphia, PA: Westminster Press, 1965.

Green, Michael. *Evangelism in the Early Church*. London: Hodder & Stoughton, 1970.

Griffin, Emory A. *The Mind Changers: The Art of Christian Persuasion.* Wheaton, IL: Tyndale House, 1976.

Grivec, Frantisek. *Konstantin und Method: Lehrer der Slaven.* Wiesbaden: O. Harrassowitz, 1960.

Guinness, Os. *Dining with the Devil: The Megachurch Movement Flirts with Modernity.* Grand Rapids, MI: Baker Book House, 1993.

Hahn, Ferdinand. *Mission in the New Testament.* Studies in Biblical Theology 47. Naperville, IL: A. R. Allenson, 1965.

_____. "Zu 2. Kor 5,14–6,2." *Evangelische Theologie* 3 (1973): 244.

von Harnack, Adolf. *Die Mission und Ausbreitung des Christentums in den ersten drei Jahrhunderten.* 2 vols. Leipzig: J. C. Hinrichs'sche Buchhandlung, 1924.

Hatfield, Chad. "Missiology: A New Academic Discipline." St Vladimir's Orthodox Theological Seminary. February 9, 2011. Accessed May 25, 2015. http://www.svots.edu/voices/on_our_minds/missiology-new-academic-discipline.

Hausammann, Susi. *Busse als Umkehr und Erneuerung von Mensch und Gesellschaft: Eine theologiegeschichtliche Studie zu einer Theologie der Busse.* Studien zur Dogmengeschichte und systematischen Theologie 33. Zurich: Theologischer Verlag, 1975.

Healy, John. *The Life and Writings of St. Patrick with Appendices, etc.* Dublin: M. H. Gill & Son / Sealy, Bryers & Walker, 1905.

Hedlund, Roger E. *The Mission of the Church in the World: A Biblical Theology.* Grand Rapids, MI: Baker Book House, 1991.

Hegel, Georg Wilhelm Friedrich. *On Christianity: Early Theological Writings.* Translated by T. M. Knox. Chicago, IL: University of Chicago Press, 1948.

Hesselgrave, David J., and Earl J. Blomberg. *Planting Churches Cross-Culturally: A Guide for Home and Foreign Missions.* Grand Rapids, MI: Baker Book House, 1980.

Ioann (Popov). "Missionary Congresses and the Prospects of the Orthodox Mission in the 21st Century." Synodal Department of Missions of the Moscow Patriarchate. November 1999. Accessed June 3, 2015. http://www.portal-missia.ru/node/17.

Irvin, Joseph. *St Innocent's Missionary Instructions: An Inquirer's Guide to Orthodox Christianity.* Raleigh, NC: Lulu, 2013.

Jamieson, Robert, A. R. Fausset, and David Brown. *A Commentary: Critical, Practical, and Explanatory, on the Old and New Testaments.* Vol. 1, *Genesis–Psalms.* Toledo, OH and Hillsdale, MI: J. B. Names, 1882.

Jeremias, Joachim. *Jesu Verheissung für die Völker.* Stuttgart: Kohlhammer, 1956.

Kaiser, Walter C. *Mission in the Old Testament: Israel as a Light to the Nations.* 2nd ed. Grand Rapids, MI: Baker Academic, 2012.

Kaiser, Walter C., and Lyman Rand Tucker. *Toward Rediscovering the Old Testament.* Grand Rapids, MI: Zondervan, 1987.

Kallistos (Ware). "Theological Education in Scripture and the Fathers." Unpublished paper presented at the 5th Consultation of Orthodox Theological Schools, Halki, Turkey, August 13–20, 1994.

Karlins, Marvin, and Herbert Irving Abelson. *Persuasion: How Opinions and Attitudes Are Changed.* 2nd ed. New York, NY: Springer Pub. Co., 1970.

Keating, Daniel A. *Deification and Grace.* Introductions to Catholic Doctrine. Naples, FL: Sapientia Press, 2007.

Keil, Carl Friedrich, and Franz Delitzsch. *Biblical Commentary on the Old Testament.* Translated by James Martin. Vol. 1, *The Pentateuch.* Edinburgh: T & T Clark, 1872.

_____. *Biblical Commentary on the Books of Samuel.* Translated by James Martin. Edinburgh: T & T Clark, 1866.

Kelly, J. N. D. *Early Christian Doctrines.* 4th ed. London: Black, 1968.

Kenneson, Philip D., and James L. Street. *Selling out the Church: The Dangers of Church Marketing.* Nashville, TN: Abingdon Press, 1997.

Kharlampovych, Konstantin. *Archimandrite Makarii Glukharev: Founder of the Altai Mission.* Translated by James Lawton Haney. Studies in Russian History. Lewiston, NY: E. Mellen Press, 2001.

Kim, Eunsoo. "Minjung Theology in Korea: A Critique from a Reformed Theological Perspective." *Japan Christian Review* 64 (1998): 53–65.

Korsun, Sergei, and Lydia Black. *Herman: A Wilderness Saint: From Sarov, Russia to Kodiak, Alaska.* Translated by Daniel Marshall. Jordanville, NY: Holy Trinity Monastery, 2012.

Kozhuharov, Valentin. "Christian Mission as Teaching and Liturgical Life: An Orthodox Perspective." *Baptistic Theologies* 2.2 (Autumn 2010): 1–45.

_____. "Christian Mission in Eastern Europe." *International Bulletin of Missionary Research* 37.2 (April 2013): 73–8.

_____. "Developments in the Mission of the Russian Orthodox Church."
Acta Missiologiae 2 (2009): 7–26.

Kruse, Heinz. "Exodus 19:5 and the Mission of Israel." *Northeast Asia Journal of Theology* 24–25 (1980): 129–35.

Latourette, Kenneth Scott. *A History of the Expansion of Christianity*. Vol. 4, *The Great Century in Europe and the United States of America: A.D. 1800– A.D. 1914*. Contemporary Evangelical Perspectives Series. Grand Rapids, MI: Zondervan Pub. House, 1970.

The Lenten Triodion. Translated by Mother Mary and Kallistos (Ware). South Caanan, PA: St Tikhon's Seminary Press, 2002.

Lindsell, Harold. "Missionary Imperatives: A Conservative Exposition." In *Protestant Crosscurrents in Mission*, edited by Norman A. Horner. Nashville, TN: Abingdon Press, 1968.

The Liturgy of the Presanctified Gifts. Edited by David Drillock and John H. Erickson. Crestwood, NY: St. Vladimir's Seminary Press, 1990.

Lossky, Vladimir. *In the Image and Likeness of God*. London: Mowbrays, 1975.

_____. *The Mystical Theology of the Eastern Church*. Crestwood, NY: St Vladimir's Seminary Press, 1976.

_____. *Orthodox Theology: An Introduction*. Crestwood, NY: St Vladimir's Seminary Press, 1978.

Lyotard, Jean-François. *The Postmodern Condition: A Report on Knowledge*. Theory and History of Literature. Minneapolis, MN: University of Minnesota Press, 1984.

Mantzaridis, Georgios I. *The Deification of Man*. Crestwood, NY: St Vladimir's Seminary Press, 1984.

Martin-Achard, Robert. *A Light Unto the Nations: A Study of the Old Testament Conception of Israel's Mission to the World*. Edinburgh: Oliver and Boyd, 1962.

McComiskey, Thomas Edward. *The Covenants of Promise: A Theology of the Old Testament Covenants*. Grand Rapids, MI: Baker Book House, 1985.

McGavran, Donald A. "How About that New Verb 'to Disciple'?" *Church Growth Bulletin* 15 (1979): 266.

_____. "How to Evaluate Missions." *HIS* 27 (1967): 22–27.

_____. "Will Uppsala Betray the Two Billion?" *Church Growth Bulletin* 4 (1968): 1–6.

McGavran, Donald A., and C. Peter Wagner. *Understanding Church Growth.* 3rd ed. Grand Rapids, MI: Wm. B. Eerdmans, 1990.

Meletios (Webber). *Bread and Water, Wine and Oil: An Orthodox Christian Experience of God.* Chesterton, IN: Conciliar, 2007.

The Menaia. Holy Trinity Mission. Accessed Jan 31, 2017. http://www.holy-trinitymission.org/books/english/menaia.htm.

Mershman, Francis. "St Boniface." In *The Catholic Encyclopedia*, 2:656–8. New York: Robert Appleton, 1907.

"Metanarrative." *New World Encyclopedia.* Accessed June 30, 2015. http://www.newworldencyclopedia.org/p/index.php?title=Metanarrative&oldid=984936.

Metz, Peter. *Marketing Your Church to the Community.* Abingdon Press & the Church of the Resurrection Ministry Guides. Nashville, TN: Abingdon Press, 2007.

"The Mission of God: The First Consultation of the Lausanne-Orthodox Initiative." Lausanne-Orthodox Initiative. September 6, 2013. Accessed May 25, 2015. http://www.loimission.net/st-vlash-consultation/communique/.

"Mission, Vision, & Values." Orthodox Christian Mission Center. Accessed June 18, 2015. http://www.ocmc.org/about/index.aspx.

"Missions Institute of Orthodox Christianity at Hellenic College Holy Cross." Hellenic College Holy Cross. Accessed May 25, 2015. http://www.hchc.edu/missions.

Moore, Raphael. "In Memory of the 50 Million Victims of the Orthodox Christian Holocaust." Edited by Nektarios Serfes. Last modified October 1999. http://www.serfes.org/orthodox/memoryof.htm.

Morris, Leon. "Propitiation." In *Baker's Dictionary of Theology*, edited by Everett F. Harrison, 425. Grand Rapids, MI: Baker Book House, 1960.

Müller, Josef. *Wozu noch Mission?: eine bibeltheologische Überlegung.* Biblisches Forum 4. Stuttgart: Katholisches Bibelwerk, 1969.

Müller, Karl. *200 Jahre Brüdermission.* Vol. 1. Herrnhut: Missionsbuchhandlung, 1931.

Myklebust, Olav Guttorm. *The Study of Missions in Theological Education.* Oslo: Egede Institut, 1955.

Nicodemus the Hagiorite and Agapius the Monk. *The Rudder (Pedalion) of the Metaphorical Ship of the One Holy Catholic and Apostolic Church of Orthodox Christians or, All the Sacred and Divine Canons . . . As Embodied in the Original Greek Text*. Translated by Denver Cummings. Chicago, IL: Orthodox Christian Educational Society, 1957.

Nikolai (Velimirović). *The Prologue of Ohrid: Lives of Saints, Hymns, Reflections and Homilies for Every Day of the Year*. Translated by T. Timothy Tepsić and edited by Janko Trbović. 2nd ed. Vol. 1, *January to June*. Alhambra, CA: Sebastian Press, 2008.

Nissiotis, Nikos A. "The Unity of Scripture and Tradition." *Greek Orthodox Theological Review* 11.2 (Winter 1965–1966): 183–208.

O'Reilly, Thomas C. "Apostolicity." In *The Catholic Encyclopedia*, 1:648–9. New York, NY: Encyclopedia Press, 1913.

Oepke, K. "K. Grauls Bedeutung für die deutsche Missionswissenschaft und das deutsche Missionsleben." *Allgemeine Missions-Zeitschrift* 44 (1917): 314–23.

Oktoichos. Holy Trinity Mission. Accessed Feb 3, 2017. http://www.holytrinitymission.org/books/english/oktoichos_english.htm.

Oleksa, Michael, ed. *Alaskan Missionary Spirituality*. 2nd ed. Crestwood, NY: St Vladimir's Seminary Press, 2010.

Olson, Roger E. "Deification in Contemporary Theology." *Theology Today* 64 (2007): 186–200.

"Orthodox Christian Mission Center (OCMC) – Make Disciples of All Nations." Orthodox Christian Mission Center. Accessed May 25, 2015. http://www.ocmc.org.

Pannenberg, Wolfhart. *Theology and the Philosophy of Science*. Philadelphia, PA: Westminster Press, 1976.

Panteleimon (Berdnikov). "Reviews of the [Missiology] Textbook." Synodal Department of Missions of the Moscow Patriarchate. Accessed June 2, 2015. http://www.portal-missia.ru/sites/default/files/Отзывы на учебник.doc.

Papathanasiou, Athanasios N. "Tradition as Impulse for Renewal and Witness: Introducing Orthodox Missiology in the IRM." *IRM* 100.2 (2011): 203–15.

The Pentecostarion (Brookline, MA: Holy Transfiguration Monastery, 1990).

Pickett, Jarrell Waskom, and Donald A. McGavran. *Church Growth and Group Conversion*. Pasadena, CA: William Carey Library, 1973.

Pomazansky, Michael. *Orthodox Dogmatic Theology*. Platina, CA: St Herman of Alaska Brotherhood, 1994.

Prehn, Yvon. *Ministry Marketing Made Easy: A Practical Guide to Marketing Your Church Message.* Nashville, TN: Abingdon Press, 2004.

The Priest's Service Book. Translated by Dmitri (Royster). 2nd ed. Dallas, TX: Orthodox Church in America, Diocese of the South, 2003.

Proceedings and Debates of the General Assembly of the Free Church of Scotland Held at Edinburgh, May 1867. London and Edinburgh, 1867.

von Rad, Gerhard. *Theologie des Alten Testaments.* 2 vols. Einführung in die evangelische Theologie. Munich: C. Kaiser, 1960.

Rau, Reinhold. *Briefe des Bonifatius: Willibalds, Leben des Bonifatius.* Darmstadt: Wissenschaftliche Buchgesellschaft, 1968.

Ray, T. B., ed. *The Highway of Mission Thought: Eight of the Greatest Discourses on Missions.* Nashville, TN: Sunday School Board, 1907.

Reising, Richard. *Church Marketing 101: Preparing Your Church for Greater Growth.* Grand Rapids, MI: Baker Books, 2006.

Rengstorf, K. H. "*Didaskalos.*" In *Theologische Wörterbuch zum Neuen Testament,* 2:150–162. Stuttgart: Gerhard Friedrich, 1935.

Rétif, André, and P. Lamarche. *The Salvation of the Gentiles and the Prophets.* Baltimore, MD: Helicon, 1966.

Riesner, Rainer. *Jesus als Lehrer.* 2nd ed. Wissenschaftliche Untersuchungen zum Neuen Testament 2.7. Tübingen: J. C. B. Mohr [Paul Siebeck], 1984.

Rodger, Symeon. "The Soteriology of Anselm of Canterbury, an Orthodox Perspective." *Greek Orthodox Theological Review* 34 (1989): 9–43.

Rommen, Edward. *Come and See: An Eastern Orthodox Perspective on Contextualization.* Pasadena, CA: William Carey Library, 2013.

_____. "The De-Theologizing of Missiology." *Trinity World Forum* 19.1 (Fall 1993): 1–4.

_____. "An Eastern Orthodox Perspective." In *Occasional Bulletin: Special Edition 2016.* Evangelical Missiological Society. Accessed Feb 6, 2017. https://www.emsweb.org/images/occasional-bulletin/special-editions/OB_SpecialEdition_2016.pdf

_____. *Get Real: On Evangelism in the Late Modern World.* Pasadena, CA: William Carey Library, 2009.

_____. "God Spoke: On Divine Thought in Human Language." *Pro Ecclesia* 15.4 (2006): 387–402.

_____. "Missiology's Place in the Academy." *Trinity World Forum* 17.3 (1991): 1–4.

_____. *Die Notwendigkeit der Umkehr: Missionsstrategie und Gemein-deaufbau in der Sicht evangelikaler Missionswissenschaftler Nordamerikas.* Giessen: Brunnen Verlag, 1987.

_____. *Die Notwendigkeit der Umkehr: Missionsstrategie und Gemein-deaufbau in der Sicht evangelikaler Missionswissenschaftler Nordamerikas.* 2nd ed. Giessen: Brunnen Verlag, 1994.

_____. "Synthesis." In *Christianity and the Religions: A Biblical Theology of World Religions,* edited by Edward Rommen and Harold Netland, 241–53. Evangelical Missiological Society Series. Pasadena, CA: William Carey Library, 1995.

Rommen, Edward, and Gary Corwin. *Missiology and the Social Sciences: Con-tributions, Cautions, and Conclusions.* Evangelical Missiological Society Series. Pasadena, CA: William Carey Library, 1996.

Rosenkranz, Gerhard. *Die christliche Mission: Geschichte und Theologie.* Munich: Kaiser, 1977.

Schmemann, Alexander. *For the Life of the World: Sacraments and Orthodoxy.* 2nd ed. Crestwood, NY: St Vladimir's Seminary Press, 1973.

Schnackenburg, Rudolf. *God's Rule and Kingdom.* Translated by John Murray. 2nd ed. New York, NY: Herder and Herder, 1968.

Scholz, Heinrich. *Schleiermachers Kurze Darstellung des theologischen Studi-ums.* Leipzig: A. Deichert'sche Verlagsbuchhandlung, 1935.

Schulz, Anselm. *Nachfolge und Nachahmen.* Munich: Kaiser, 1962.

Schütz, Joseph. *Die Lehrer der Slawen Kyrill und Method.* St Otilien: EOS Ver-lag, 1985.

Senge, Peter. *The Fifth Discipline.* New York, NY: Doubleday, 1990.

Senior, Donald and Carroll Stuhlmueller. *The Biblical Foundations for Mis-sion.* Maryknoll, NY: Orbis Books, 1983.

The Services of Christmas: The Nativity of Our Lord Jesus Christ. Crestwood, NY: St Vladimir's Seminary Press, n.d.

Skarsaune, Oskar. *The Proof from Prophecy: A Study in Justin Martyr's Proof-Text Tradition: Text-Type, Provenance, Theological Profile.* Leiden: Brill, 1987.

"St Nicholas, Equal of the Apostles and Archbishop of Japan." Ortho-dox Church in America. Accessed June 17, 2015. http://oca.org/saints/lives/2015/02/16/100419-st-nicholas-equal-of-the-apostles-and-arch-bishop-of-japan.

"St Nicholas, Equal of the Apostles and Archbishop of Japan: Troparion." Orthodox Church in America. Accessed June 17, 2015. https://oca.org/ saints/troparia/2015/02/16/100419-st-nicholas-equal-of-the-apostles- and-archbishop-of-japan.

"St Nino (Nina), Equal of the Apostles and Enlightener of Georgia." Ortho- dox Church in America. Accessed Jan 31, 2017. https://oca.org/saints/ lives/2017/01/14/100191-st-nino-nina-equal-of-the-apostles-and-enlight- ener-of-georgia.

"St Patrick the Bishop of Armagh and Enlightener of Ireland." Orthodox Church in America. Accessed June 17, 2015. http://oca.org/saints/tropar ia/2014/03/17/100821-st-patrick-the-bishop-of-armagh-and-enlightener- of-ireland.

Stampe, L. "Collegium de cursu Evangelii promovendo." *Dansk Teologisk Tidsskrift* (1946): 65–88.

Staniloae, Dumitru. *The Experience of God*. Translated and edited by Ioan Ionita and Robert Barringer. Brookline, MA: Holy Cross Orthodox Press, 1994.

Stokes, Whitley, ed. *Three Middle-Irish Homilies on the Lives of Saints Patrick, Brigit and Columba*. Calcutta: 1877.

Stokoe, Mark, and Leonid Kishkovsky. *Orthodox Christians in North Amer- ica (1794–1994)*. Brooklyn, OH: Orthodox Christian Publication Center, 1995.

Strack, Hermann Leberecht, and Paul Billerbeck. *Kommentar zum Neuen Tes- tament aus Talmud und Midrasch*. 6 vols. Munich: Beck, 1922.

Struve, Nikita. "Macaire Goukharev, a Prophet of Orthodox Mission." *IRM* 54 (1965): 308–314.

Stuhlmacher, Peter. "Mt. 28:16–20 and the Course of Mission in the Apos- tolic and Postapostolic Age." In *The Mission of the Early Church to Jews and Gentiles*, edited by Jostein Adna and Hans Kvalbein, 17–43. Tübingen: J. C. B. Mohr, 2000.

"Sunday of Meatfare of the Last Judgment—Troparion & Kontakion." Ortho- dox Church in America. Accessed Feb 6, 2017. https://oca.org/saints/ troparia/2012/02/19/5-sunday-of-meatfare-of-the-last-judgment.

Talbot, C. H. *The Anglo-Saxon Missionaries in Germany, Being the Lives of Ss Willibrord, Boniface, Leoba and Lebuin Together with the Hodoepericon of*

St Willibald and a Selection from the Correspondence of St Boniface. London and New York: Sheed and Ward, 1954.

Thomas Aquinas. *Catena aurea: Commentary on the Four Gospels*. Vol. 1, *St. Matthew*. Oxford: J.H. Parker, 1841.

Tucker, Ruth. *From Jerusalem to Irian Jaya: A Biographical History of Christian Missions*. Grand Rapids, MI: Zondervan, 1983.

Vassiliadis, Petros. *Eucharist and Witness: Orthodox Perspectives on the Unity and Mission of the Church*. Brookline, MA: Holy Cross Orthodox Press, 1998.

Vicedom, Georg F. *The Mission of God: An Introduction to a Theology of Mission*. Translated by G. A. Thiele and D. Hilgendorf. St Louis, MO: Concordia, 1965.

Voulgarakis, Elias. "Mission and Unity from the Theological Point of View." *IRM* 54 (1965): 298–307.

Wagner, C. Peter. "What Is 'Making Disciples'?" *Evangelical Missions Quarterly* 9 (1973): 285–93.

Wagner, Falk. *Über die Legitimität der Mission*. Theologische Existenz heute 154. Munich: C. Kaiser, 1968.

Warneck, Gustav. "Das Studium der Mission: Wie ist es am praktischsten einzurichten?" *Allgemeine Missions-Zeitschrift* 34 (1907): 493–509.

Weber, Otto. *Grundlagen der Dogmatik*. Vol. 2. Neukirchen: Neukirchener Verlag, 1987.

Webster, Douglas D. *Selling Jesus: What's Wrong with Marketing the Church*. Downers Grove, IL: InterVarsity Press, 1992.

White, John. *The Race: Discipleship for the Long Run*. Downers Grove, IL: InterVarsity Press, 1984.

White, Newport J. D. *St. Patrick: His Writings and Life*. Translations of Christian Literature Series V: Lives of the Celtic Saints. London: Society for Promoting Christian Knowledge, 1920.

Winter, Ralph D., and Steven C. Hawthorne. *Perspectives on the World Christian Movement*. Pasadena, CA: William Carey Press, 1981.

Wright, Christopher J. H. *The Mission of God: Unlocking the Bible's Grand Narrative*. Downers Grove, IL: IVP Academic, 2006.

Yannaras, Christos. "Theology in Present-Day Greece." *St Vladimir's Theological Quarterly* 16.4 (1972): 195–214.

Zernov, Nicolas. "The Christian Church of the East." *IRM* 23 (1934): 539–46.

_____. "Christianity in India and the Eastern Orthodox Church." *IRM* 43 (1954): 390–96.

Zizioulas, John. *Communion and Otherness: Further Studies in Personhood and the Church.* Edited by Paul McPartlan. London: T&T Clark, 2006.

Znamenski, Andrei A. *Shamanism and Christianity: Native Encounters with Russian Orthodox Missions in Siberia and Alaska, 1820–1917.* Contributions to the Study of World History. Westport, CT: Greenwood Press, 1999.